C-MOAT FO...

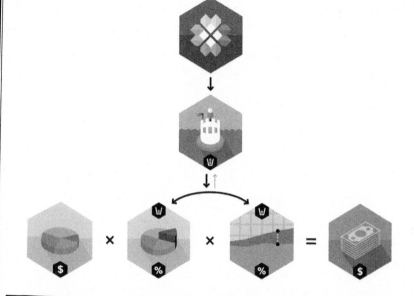

---

8 MOAT BUILDERS

CUSTOMER MOAT

TOTAL MARKET SIZE

MARKET SHARE

PROFIT MARGIN

PROFIT

8 MOAT BUILDERS

LOW COST (O): The Low Cost moat builder uses the three internal resources of a business (i.e., people, processes, and physical assets) to reduce the cost of serving customers.

HIGH SATISFACTION (O): The High Satisfaction moat builder uses the three internal resources of a business (i.e., people, processes, and physical assets) to enhance the customer experience.

ECONOMY OF SCALE (S): The Economy of Scale moat builder leverages customers to provide a low-cost benefit to other customers.

NETWORK EFFECT (S): The Network Effect moat builder leverages customers to improve the experiences of other customers.

LOCATION (P): The Location moat builder uses physical position to increase the likelihood that customers choose a business.

BRANDING (P): The Branding moat builder creates mental associations with customers to increase the likelihood that they choose a business.

SUPPLY (I): The Supply moat builder reduces the competitive intensity of an industry by limiting the alternatives available to customers.

DISTRIBUTION (I): The Distribution moat builder creates pathways to customers that rivals cannot access.

O - Operations   S - Scale   P - Positioning   I - Industry Control

CUSTOMER MOAT
HOW LOYALTY DRIVES PROFIT

◆

EDDIE SUNG

Library of Congress Control Number:
ISBN-13: 978-0-9969190-5-0
ISBN-10: 0-9969190-5-8
0 9 8 7 6 5 4 3 2 1

CONTENTS

PART II: THE EIGHT MOAT BUILDER TOOLS

PART III: THE ORIGIN OF PROFITS

INTRO

A JOURNEY BEGINS

———— ◆ ————

*"Give me a lever long enough and a place
to stand, and I will move the world."*

ARCHIMEDES

ANSWERING THE CALL

I t was on a cool Saturday morning in October 2004 that I finished packing the last of my possessions into a rented Ford Windstar van. I was leaving behind a life that I established in Chicago. After finishing my undergraduate degree, I landed a job as an operations consultant. Everything had been going well, but now I suddenly found myself heading far away from the towering skyscrapers of the Windy City.

My destination was Lake Charles, Louisiana—a small city that sits at the southwestern heel of the state, near where the warm waters of the Gulf of Mexico butt against the Texas-Louisiana border. This region has long been shrouded in a cloud of industry. Its landscape is dominated by oil refineries and chemical plants, with a river that cuts through that both divides the land and serves as its economic lifeblood. By far the most important attribute of Lake Charles was that it was the place my parents called home.

My parents immigrated to the United States from Taiwan in the 1970s. In their search for opportunity, they discovered a life of hard work and long hours. Even though they encountered numerous setbacks, they believed in the promise of the American dream: those who worked hard would be rewarded.

In 1980, they decided to pursue their ambition by becoming entrepreneurs. They purchased a small grocery store on the northern outskirts of town in a relatively underserved neighborhood. As is often the case with small family businesses, their store quickly took over their lives. My sister and I grew up knowing the store as our perpetually demanding third sibling.

Over the years, I watched as my parents worked tirelessly. The grocery store was open seven days a week, from seven in the morning to nine thirty at night, 365 days a year. On holidays, the entire family pitched in to keep the doors open when most other stores were closed. These were some of our busiest times.

Survival sat first and foremost on my parents' minds. Always looming in the background were national giants like Wal-Mart and Kroger. To combat their presence, my parents adopted a strategy of pushing for greater sales through the use of heavy promotions and large discounts. Over the years, this appeared to work, as revenue soared thirtyfold, and at its peak, the store employed twenty-five workers.

Success, however, cannot be measured by size alone. My parents achieved substantial sales growth, but they accomplished little in the way of financial success. Profits remained elusive, and what seemed a prosperous, thriving business was a growing internal disaster. In a vicious cycle, the more the store grew, the more capital investment it took: purchasing coolers, fixing freezers, repairing roofs, repaving parking lots. The business was a bottomless money pit. With each passing year, my parents had to run faster just to stay in place.

In 2002, after two decades of struggle, they threw in the towel and sold the store. They realized that their situation was unsustainable. Luckily, a bright spot remained that allowed my parents to hold onto their entrepreneurial dreams. Over the years, a small side business inside the grocery store had been growing and prospering—a booth dedicated to cashing checks and paying utility bills. Upon selling the grocery business, my parents opened a small storefront across the street, dedicated to those limited financial offerings.

As my parents embarked on this new venture, they were not wealthier people, but their years of hard work had paid off in less tangible ways. My sister and I had the fortunate opportunity to attend the University of Chicago. Thanks to my parents' strong encouragement, college was not a place for teaching me a specific skill set but a fleeting time and space where I could learn anything that my heart desired. It was a rare gift for which I am still grateful.

I majored in public policy, but my curriculum was largely liberal arts based. My curiosity drove me to explore all facets of the world. From behavioral economics to probability to immunology, any subject that piqued my interest was fair game. My deep underlying fascination was in discovering the nature of systems—whether they happen to be economic, mathematical, or biological.

Out of all subjects, I was most drawn to business. While my college did not offer a degree in the field, I devoted innumerous hours devouring everything I could find on the subject matter: its strategies, theories, and practices. The forces and behaviors that drove and doomed companies captivated me. In front of me was an incredibly complex game that was not only poorly understood but held such vast implications for the health of our society.

After graduating, I continued to explore my business fascination through various job roles in consulting and finance. I was learning a great deal and had built a comfortable life far away from the troubles of Louisiana.

And then the phone rang.

Over the telephone, my parents explained to me that their new venture, which was supposed to make life simpler, was instead on the verge of collapse. They asked me to drop everything to help them. I knew that my parents carried enormous pride and that involving their children in their problems would be a last resort. Their situation had become dire.

As the autumn leaves began changing colors, I got into the van and embarked on a thousand-mile journey southward to Louisiana.

Upon arriving in Lake Charles, I quickly took inventory of the situation. My investigation revealed two deeply painful facts: first our business was bleeding money, and second we owed far more than we were worth. On paper, we were already bankrupt. The outlook was so grim that our first order of business was to decide whether the store was worth saving. I secretly placed its odds of survival at 1 percent.

Despite the immense challenges, two factors led us to say "yes" in trying to save the business. First, my parents believed in paying their debts. Since their word was their bond, no matter what happened to the business, they felt personally responsible for keeping all their promises. If we were going to repay our debts regardless of the situation, there was little benefit to declaring bankruptcy.

The second reason was that, as bad as things appeared, I realized that we held an invaluable "hidden" asset. While the particular benefit was hard to quantify at the time, I realized that my parents' standing with the local community was priceless. Our store acted as a financial hub for hardworking and typically underserved people—construction workers, port workers, temporary workers—and, surprisingly, people who held bank accounts but preferred dealing with us. For more than twenty years, we worked hard to improve the lives of the people in our community, and in return they trusted us implicitly.

Our customers were far more than just random faces. We knew their stories: the woman who worked night shifts at Wal-Mart, the UPS delivery man who came once a week to pay some bills, the grandfather who sent his daughter a few dollars every month to help out, and the young man who played music for churches around town. These were the people of our community and we served them on a daily basis. We were as important to them as they were to us.

It took us eighteen months of grueling work and drastic, agonizing changes to get our house in order, but our finances finally stabilized. During this period, we still almost went bankrupt twice and also dealt with two of Louisiana's worst hurricanes on record, but in the end, we managed to save ourselves.

There was no magic bullet. Instead, we made a conscious decision to persistently push for small improvements; my personal goal was to make one positive change per day. We overhauled our bookkeeping system, reduced high-risk areas, and increased efficiency three- to fourfold. Where it once took four workers to process three hundred transactions, we streamlined the work so that it could be done by a single individual. What never changed, however, was our commitment to providing customers with the best possible experience.

Saving the business was a huge personal victory. We were not only financially sounder, but we became more effective at serving people. This played an important role during the 2009 Great Recession when we fared relatively well compared to our competitors. While our sales were not immune, we estimated that our decline was roughly half of what our rivals experienced.

As the outlook continued to improve, I began reflecting on my experience. I wondered, "How did our business manage to survive against such overwhelming odds? What decisions were critical to our success? And now that we survived and were no longer in emergency mode, what should our game plan be for the future?" What I really longed to know was how our actions led us to be successful and, just as importantly, why.

These questions could not be answered overnight. If I wanted to decipher the inner workings of business strategy, my quest needed to broaden beyond our store. As I set out in search of answers, I transitioned from overseeing our store's operations to being its strategic adviser. I began intensively researching the subject. In doing so, a central question emerged to guide my quest: "What is the origin of profits?" Specifically, how do a business's actions relate to its profits?

Along my journey, I came across many great minds. I retraced the footsteps of Bruce Henderson, a pioneer of strategy consulting and founder of the Boston Consulting Group, a man who had studied everything from military history to evolution in an effort to forge his own theories of business competition. I absorbed the wisdom of Peter Drucker, whose insights revealed businesses for what they truly are—collections of workers bound by systems moving towards an ultimate purpose of creating customers. And I peered from the vantage point of Warren Buffett, who, as the world's greatest investor, saw beyond a business's financial statements to discover its true intrinsic value.

These great thinkers, along with others, provided many valuable clues. But in the end, I was left without a clear answer. I realized that if I wanted to solve the riddle of the origin of profits, I had to forge my own path.

From the vast pool of information that I accumulated, I began synthesizing a new model of how the business world works. Eventually, I not only came up with a model that explains the origin of profits, but I developed a powerful set of tools for helping businesses apply these discoveries. This model is the Customer Moat Formula and its tools are the eight moat builders.

● ● ●

This book is the story of the Customer Moat Formula (CMF), a framework for explaining how businesses use and defend customer loyalty to make money.

At its heart, the CMF is based on the concept of the *customer moat*, or c-moat. Loosely defined, a c-moat is a business's ability to maintain the loyalty of its customers and prevent them from choosing alternatives.

Importantly, c-moats are the precursors to two important outcomes: market share and profit margin. Both play key roles in determining how much businesses earn.

As we will discuss later on, c-moats, market share, and profit margin form the core of the CMF framework. From this core, we will be able to build out a complete model for understanding which actions lead to greater profits.

The CMF was originally developed as a model for describing the ecosystem of business competition, as such, its tools are applicable to all businesses regardless of industry or size. Whether you run a convenience store, own a chain of restaurants, or manage a multi-national electronics manufacturer, the CMF provides a road map for showing you where your profits originate and what steps can be taken to grow them.

•   •   •

It is important to point out that during my research the term "competitive advantage" presented a bit of an obstacle. As I tried to build a strategy around this phrase, my logic kept running in circles. For months, I got nowhere.

Eventually I realized that the fatal flaw with the term "competitive advantage" is that there is no standard agreed-upon definition. The phrase encompasses more than eight competing definitions, many of which fail to overlap in meaning.[1]

Michael Porter, a Harvard Business School professor, wrote, "Competitive advantage grows fundamentally out of value a firm is able to create for its buyers that exceeds the firm's cost of creating it." Margaret

Peteraf, a management professor at Dartmouth, described it as "sustained above normal returns." And Jay Barney, a teacher of strategic management at The University of Utah, suggested, "A firm experiences competitive advantage when its actions in an industry or market create economic value when few competing firms are engaging in similar actions."

The *Cambridge Business English Dictionary* takes a giant step back by loosely defining competitive advantage as "the conditions that make a business more successful than the businesses it is competing with, or a particular thing that makes it more successful."[2]

It dawned on me that if I built a strategy around a weakly defined principle, I would end up with a weakly defined strategy. If I wanted to create a better strategy, a more precise vocabulary was needed.

The term "c-moat" overcomes competitive advantage's ambiguity problem. It provides a specific and useful definition and in most cases can replace our usage of "competitive advantage." There are, however, a few subtle differences between the two terms that we will discover later on. With this newer and more nuanced vocabulary in hand, we can paint a far more accurate picture for understanding how a business's actions ultimately lead to greater profits.

PART I

CUSTOMER MOAT FORMULA

◆

*"You don't get better by getting bigger;
you get bigger by getting better."*

JOHN G. STUMPF

CHAPTER ONE

SOURCES OF WEALTH

long the eastern shore of the Mediterranean, a peninsula juts out awkwardly and seemingly at random into the sea. The protrusion is so geologically out of place that one pictures a divine force had pinched the land outward as if it were a soft dough. This strange formation, however, was not the creation of some divine power, but the deliberate work of man—in particular, one man.

In 332 BC, Alexander the Great came to what today is the modern coast of Lebanon. Upon arriving, he did not find a peninsula; instead, he gazed at an island sitting half a mile offshore. The island was a thriving metropolis of the ancient world, the independent city of Tyre.[1]

For six hundred years, Tyre dominated as the main corridor of trade between the Mediterranean countries and eastern lands of Phoenicia. The city's port served as its economic hub, and the island defended itself with both natural and man-made barriers. The sea protected it to the west, and a half-mile channel to the east acted as a wide moat buffering the island from the mainland. The island's perimeter was further fortified by an immense stone wall towering 150 feet high.

Tyre became the envy of the world by protecting its sources of income—its port and citizens. The city reduced its rivals' ability to challenge or attack it through its vast moat and strong defenses. An invading force would have to cross the massive waterway and then scale the equivalent of a twelve-story building before getting a chance to inflict any damage. Importantly, the island's formidable defenses not only guarded the city against attacks but deterred them as well. Tyre gained a reputation for being impenetrable. To bolster this status, the city adopted none other than Hercules as its patron protector.

When Alexander gazed upon Tyre, he saw both its strength and its threat. As a stronghold, the island could be a staging ground for his enemies and become an Achilles' heel to his growing empire. To ensure his future, Alexander needed to conquer the island.

Even as Alexander gathered a naval force by enlisting hundreds of warships from neighboring kingdoms, he realized that Tyre could withstand a naval assault. In a previous war, the city island had staved off a thirteen-year siege. With a seaborne attack deemed impossible to win, Alexander began laying out a plan that even his own officers considered outlandish. If he could not conquer it by sea, he would conquer it by land: Alexander would physically bring the mainland to the island.

For six months, Alexander's army toiled in building a causeway towards the city. Stones, earth, and whole trees served as the bedrock of a makeshift bridge spanning two hundred feet in width, equivalent to a modern fourteen-lane highway. As construction progressed, two 150-foot towers rolled along the bridge's edge to protect its builders from Tyre's defensive response, an onslaught of arrows. Little by little, day by day, the continent inched closer towards the island. Tyre's moat whittled away.

In the end, Tyre fell to Alexander's forces, but conquering the island carried an enormous price. The undertaking absorbed the efforts of tens of thousands of troops, more than 250 ships, and six months of precious time. Five percent of Alexander's military career was spent capturing the 250-acre island, a plot of land approximately one-third the size of New York City's Central Park. In a final tally of Alexander's conquests, the island would represent less than one-thousandth of 1 percent of his total empire.

We begin with the tale of Tyre and Alexander because it is one of prosperity, competition, and failure. For half a millennium, Tyre enjoyed the prosperity associated with the success of its heavily guarded port. When Alexander breached that defense, the city fell and its fortunes were lost.

In business strategy, the lesson is that we want to be like Tyre in building moats to defend our sources of income. In protecting these assets, we must never forget about the larger ecosystem of competitors—the Alexanders of the world—that are working to chip away at our defense.

The ultimate purpose of a business is to defend its source of prosperity: its customers. By building and ensuring a strong customer moat, businesses can prosper in the long run.

A DEFINING MOMENT
What Is a Customer Moat?

The concept of customer moats, or c-moats, was originally inspired by Warren Buffett's idea of *economic moats*. Buffett described competition as the ultimate destroyer of profits, and in his eyes, if a business could widen its economic moat and insulate itself from competition, then it could earn above-average profit margins. As an example, the Coca-Cola Company enjoys a wide economic moat–thanks in part to its strong branding and distribution capability which few rivals can challenge–thus earning it higher profits.

While Buffett's idea was intriguing, it pointed me to a larger question: "How exactly do businesses protect themselves from competition?"

I realized that a key ingredient was missing from Buffett's term: the customer. From an economic moat perspective, companies build defenses around themselves to protect themselves from competition. A more accurate perspective is that a company builds defenses around their *customers* to protect their *customers* from going to competitors. Companies are not fighting against each other as much as they are fighting to maintain the loyalty of their customer base.

Importantly, the customer moat concept shifts customers toward the center of the universe where they belong. In doing so, it provides two strategic benefits.

First, strategies can be built around the actual sources of profitability and survival. Sales and profits originate from customers. Sam Walton, the founder of Wal-Mart, said it best: "There is only one boss—the customer. And he can fire everybody in the company from the chairman on down, simply by spending his money somewhere else."[2]

Second, businesses are less likely to get tunnel vision with their specific products. For companies to stay focused on serving their customers and their needs, they need to avoid getting fixated on particular products. We have to ask, "Are companies in the market of selling cupcakes, MP3 players, and DVDs? Or are they selling ways for people to treat themselves, enjoy quality and convenient listening experiences, and have a fun temporary escape from the confines of everyday life?" Products come and go, but customers will always have needs; there is only one durable business model: to identify and serve customer needs.

●　●　●

Building a c-moat involves a bit more than just defending customers; it requires defending the *likelihood* that customers will choose a business over competing alternatives. A wide c-moat will maximize this probability while minimizing the ability of competitors to lure customers away. It is through the act of increasing this loyalty that companies become stronger competitors.

Thinking in terms of probabilities is important. In modern competitive markets, customers choose probabilistically from sets of choices. While people may have their favorites, they will rarely stick to that one option alone and will continue shopping at other venues. If a person likes Target, Lowe's, or a local burger shop, does that mean they only buy household goods, DIY products, and burgers from them? It is unlikely. People will still shop elsewhere.

One problem that some businesses face is getting caught up on trying to close on a specific sale. Will this customer decide to purchase or not purchase from us today? While a customer's choice might seem binary, the truth is that their decision is probabilistic. Customers only have a percentage chance of choosing a business. The big question is whether they choose the business 30 percent of the time or 60 percent. We want to know, what steps can we take to increase this probability over the long run?

A useful perspective is to picture customers as voters who cast ballots using their wallets. Each purchasing decision is like a new election cycle. While one vote probably won't make much of a difference, overall voting patterns make enormous differences. The long-term goal is to stack the statistical odds towards winning the most elections.

In concrete terms, it does not help Starbucks to know whether a particular person bought coffee from them this morning. What is worth knowing, however, is if that person is choosing Starbucks 40 percent of the time. If so, the question becomes, "How can Starbucks move the needle to 45 percent?"

C-moat strength will naturally vary from business to business. A sole restaurant in an airport will enjoy a wide c-moat because it holds a fairly captive audience. In contrast, a gas station sharing a street corner with three rivals stations will hold a narrower c-moat. In this case, drivers are able to easily switch between different choices, and customer loyalty is most likely minimal. (If you own a gas station, don't fret. We will discover some steps that you can take to widen your c-moat.)

With c-moats being so vastly important, the next question to ask is, "What factors go into determining the strength of a c-moat?" What accounts for the likelihood that customers will choose a business?

C-moats themselves are created by many factors working together simultaneously. To stick with the Starbucks example, what drives a customer to visit its cafés? Is it the ambiance or a particularly tasty drink? Is it the fast service or a convenient location? Each reason contributes to the overall probability of how often a customer chooses to frequent Starbucks' stores. The c-moat represents all these different factors combined. In later chapters, we will discover how the eight moat builders are the building blocks that create this overall probability.

● ● ●

This brings us to the more precise definition of c-moat: it is the *intrinsic probability* that a customer will choose a business over competing alternatives. (This is also known as the business's *intrinsic loyalty*.) The key is that "intrinsic probability" includes *all actions* that a business takes to affect the outcome of a customer's decision with the *exception* of the influence of price.

Price is excluded from the c-moat definition because it doesn't alter intrinsic loyalty. While price is a powerful lever for affecting customer purchases, it does so as a unique tradeoff. The tradeoff is that profit margin can be sacrificed for market share, and vice versa. Importantly, making this tradeoff does not lead a company to be superior to another. Whether a company decides to charge 10 cents or $1 million for a product or service, in neither case has its pricing decision fundamentally altered its competitiveness.

In the introduction, I asserted that the phrase "competitive advantage" had become convoluted and needed replacement. In most situations, we can substitute our daily use of the term with "customer moat." In doing so, we should be aware of three key differences. C-moats, unlike competitive advantage, are fundamentally mathematical probabilities; c-moats revolve around customers and not businesses; and c-moats isolate the variable of price from the rest of the equation.

● ● ●

With the c-moat concept now in hand, we have taken a big step towards understanding how businesses make money, how enterprises succeed or fail, and how we can improve the profitability of our own businesses.

Chapters 1 through 4 (Part I) piece together the Customer Moat Formula (CMF) as a model for explaining how intrinsic loyalty leads to two important outcomes: market share and profit margin. It lays the groundwork for answering, "What is a c-moat? How are c-moats the precursors to market share and profit margin? And how do we use price to manage the relationship between c-moats, market share, and profit margin?" And last but not least, "What are the eight actionable tools available for widening our c-moats?"

Chapters 5 through 12 (Part II) take a closer look at each of the eight moat builder tools. Emphasis is placed on how to use each tool to drive greater intrinsic loyalty within our customer base and how to create a wider c-moat for our businesses.

Chapter 13 (Part III) introduces the variable of market size and its fluctuations. This is the final step in completing the CMF framework as a complete explanation of the origin of profits and how different business actions lead to greater profits.

HAPPY KIDS EAT HAPPY MEALS
The Value of Customer Loyalty

What does a c-moat look like in action? For an illustration, let's turn to McDonald's, which has for decades outperformed its peers in the fast food industry.

McDonald's has outshined its rivals in terms of financial performance. Even its largest and closest competitor, Burger King, has not come close to achieving its level of success. While both food chains provide a similar service to similar customers using similar products, their financial results have diverged significantly. To put this into numbers, in 2007, McDonald's averaged 65 percent higher sales per store while maintaining 150 percent more outlets than Burger King.[3]

In most blind taste surveys, McDonald's does not rank higher than its fast food rivals. How, then, has McDonald's managed to leave its competitors in the dust?

A key difference is a c-moat strategy that has successfully targeted a particular demographic: children. McDonald's has worked hard to become the most preferred option of this group.

To develop strong loyalty around kids, the company has created the Ronald McDonald and Hamburglar characters, installed playgrounds in many of its restaurants, and developed a menu system that makes ordering as easy as saying "I'd like a number three." Even restaurant counter tops are purposely placed a little lower in an effort to empower children to get in the habit of ordering meals for themselves.

McDonald's has also realized that a meal—even a fast food one—can be more than just a meal. To enhance the "eating experience," morning cartoons are bombarded with advertisement images of happy families sitting together eating Happy Meals. Promotions like Monopoly, where food items come with game pieces and prizes, turn ordinary dining experiences into a fun activity. McDonald's has spent considerable money to convince kids that it is where they want to be.

The campaign to win the hearts of children has paid off handsomely. In a 2007 paper published by the *Archives of Pediatrics & Adolescent Medicine*, now known as *JAMA Pediatrics*, an experiment was conducted involving sixty-three children, ages three to five.[4] In it, kids were given five pairs of identical food items. The catch of the experiment was that one item in the pair was wrapped in plain white paper, while the other identical item was wrapped in paper with the McDonald's logo on it. When asked which tasted better, kids overwhelmingly chose the foods with the McDonald's wrapping—in some cases by a ratio of three to one. Even McDonald's-branded carrots were twice as favored as plain carrots.

By securing such a high probability of being chosen by kids, McDonald's has been able to boost its performance well-beyond its rivals. While McDonald's still competes with other fast food chains in other demographic categories, the company has built a very reliable customer base from children. In 2006, it was estimated that as much as 40 percent of the company's television budget was aimed directly towards kids.[5]

Of course, there is an ancillary benefit to McDonald's targeting of kids. The company has realized that where children's hearts desire to go, adults will often follow. Ray Kroc, the company's CEO, summed it up: "A child who loves our TV commercials and brings her grandparents to a McDonald's gives us two more customers."[6]

WATCHING PATTERNS
Principle #1: C-Moats Grow Market Share

The following six sections outline three key business principles. Together, they form the core of the Customer Moat Formula and set the stage for understanding how businesses gain market share and profit margin.

The three principles are (1) c-moats grow market share, (2) c-moats increase profit margin, and (3) market share and profit margin are related in a trade-off that is managed by price.

● ● ●

The first of these principles is that *c-moats grow market share.*

In situations of all things being equal, as the probability of customers purchasing from a business increases, the more market share the business will gain.

This discovery was made early on by marketing researcher Andrew Ehrenberg. In the 1980s, during a consulting project, Ehrenberg was tasked to observe and analyze the viewing habits of TV watchers.[7]

Early into the project, Ehrenberg noticed something that was well known to many researchers: that the ratings for TV shows (i.e., the percentage of households watching a program) tended to follow a steady, predictable trend. A show's ratings would stay fairly consistent week to week, and a program with 4 percent viewership one week would have about a 4 percent viewership the next week.

As Ehrenberg delved deeper into the data, he noticed something else. While the overall ratings stayed fairly consistent week to week, the actual composition of viewing audiences altered dramatically. For most programs, fewer than half of the people that tuned in to watch an episode went on to watch next week's episode.

Major TV networks had been under the impression that a television audience was composed of a loyal group of watchers, an assumption that turned out to be false. Instead, a show's audience was determined probabilistically from a large pool of highly volatile viewers with relatively low loyalty rates.

Ehrenberg then discovered another intriguing pattern; even though audiences had weak loyalty, those shows that garnered a slightly higher number of repeat watchers (i.e., those watching two consecutive episodes of a show) held vastly higher ratings. Small differences in loyalty made a huge impact on ratings. In other words, even small increases in repeat watchers mattered greatly.

As Ehrenberg carried his research to other consumer markets, he discovered these same patterns occurring again and again. Outside the TV industry, he measured market share instead of TV ratings. In categories ranging from toothpaste to chocolate drink mix, from restaurants to newspapers, he found that companies commanding the highest percentage of repeat customers also held the largest market shares. The data showed conclusively that repeat loyalty was correlated to market share.

While Ehrenberg's discoveries were groundbreaking at the time, today we have the benefit of twenty-twenty hindsight to make sense of his observations. Shoppers are volatile groups of people that make purchases probabilistically from a set of choices. Even if a shopper likes a particular yoga studio, bakery, or package delivery company, it is likely that shoppers will continue to try out other vendors. With this said, however, the more often people choose to frequent a particular establishment, the more dollars they end up spending with it than with its rivals.

As a business drives up its intrinsic probability of being chosen (i.e., through widening its c-moat), it not only gain sales but denies sales to its competitors, thereby capturing greater market share.

THE MYSTERY OF VOODOO DOLLS AND SHRUNKEN HEADS
Businesses without Repeat Customers

In 2011, I was taking a stroll along Seattle's Alaskan Way waterfront, a place famous for the Alaskan cruise lines that originate from its piers. During my walk, I pondered Ehrenberg's research when a few souvenir shops happened to catch my eye.

When I encounter different businesses, I often try to deconstruct their c-moat strategies. This serves as a useful test—a personalized Monte Carlo simulation, if you will—for discovering any wrinkles that need to be ironed out in my theories.

On this particular day, I faced an interesting dilemma. In front of me was a set of stores operating in an industry that does not build customer loyalty in a traditional sense. For all practical purposes, souvenir shops do not create repeat customers. In Ehrenberg's research, repeat loyalty seemed to be a large driving force behind greater market share. By his logic, all of the souvenir shops should have been performing roughly the same.

I noticed, however, that one souvenir shop somehow stood in sharp contrast to its peers. It attracted far more customers. In fact, compared to its neighboring rivals, this store was hands down winning the market-share war. This shop offered the same assortment of goods as other shops—postcards, T-shirts, and mugs.

As I observed this store, I found out that what set it apart was a display of intriguing oddities—shrunken heads, crocodile skulls, and old fortune-teller machines—though these items were not for sale. Above the shop's entrance was a plaque inscribed "Ye Old Curiosity Shop."

The souvenir shop had obviously built up some sort of c-moat, as tourists were choosing it at a much higher rate than its rivals. It also accomplished the feat without the use of repeat customers. What did it all mean?

After much contemplation, I realized that a c-moat, at its most funda-mental level, represents the probability that customers will choose a business at *each and every purchasing decision,* regardless of whether that decision happens to be repeat or not.

In the case of souvenir shops, since a decision only occurs once, the most successful shop needs to be the best at boosting the odds of being chosen at first glance. With its clever marketing mix of mystery and intrigue, Ye Old Curiosity Shop had enticed more customers through its doors and gained a much higher probability of being chosen.

In most industries—like those Ehrenberg studied—chasing repeat customers still makes sense. When customers make multiple purchases over time, repeat loyalty increases the overall probability of being chosen in the future. Drivers buy vehicle insurance every six months, moviegoers go to the theaters every couple of weeks, and office workers purchase lunches on a daily or weekly basis.

The lesson is that, to build strong c-moats, we need to target customer decision points regardless of whether they are repeat decision or not. For each and every instance of a customer's purchase, we want to position ourselves as their top choice.

To accomplish this, it helps to plant seeds so that when the time comes to make a purchase, our business is already at the forefront. A car insurance company can send renewal reminders by email a week before policies expire. A movie theater can promote gift certificates right before holiday seasons as a way to get people to choose it during family get-togethers. And a lunch spot can hand out menus to office workers so that they have easy access to its offerings when lunchtime comes around.

The better a business targets people's specific decision points, the better the results.

KING OF THE HILL
Creating an Edge in Capturing Market Share

The classic story of King Camp Gillette is a great example of how fostering greater intrinsic loyalty can be used to capture market share. Gillette is famously known as the man who had one good idea and one great idea. The good idea was to create a razor system that used replaceable blades, a product that took him eight years to develop; the great idea occurred to him a decade later, to expand his user base by giving away his razors at cost.

In the 1880s, before razors entered the equation, Gillette set out on a personal quest to create a company built around one design principle: to create a loyal, repeat customer. At the time, Gillette was working for Crown Cork & Seal, a company that sold durable glass jars for preserving food. The bulk of Crown Cork & Seal's profits came from selling replacement cork lids; their business model was simple: sell a jar once and then sell lids forever. As Gillette devised his own scheme, his boss advised him, "Why don't you try to think of something like Crown Cork, which when once used is thrown away, and the customers keep coming back for more?"[8]

After years of brainstorming, in 1895 Gillette came up with his eureka product: a shaving razor that employed replaceable blades. During this period, people were using straightedge razors which required manual sharpening and honing on leather strops, a laborious and time-consuming process. Gillette's invention cut straight through the hassle by eliminating the need for re-sharpening.

There was only one major snag to Gillette's plan. The technology for producing a blade that was both thin enough for his device and strong enough to maintain a sharp edge did not yet exist. If Gillette wanted to realize his vision, he had to develop the technology himself.

After Gillette spent a decade on sizable investments and trial-and-error failures, he finally met an engineer who could help him develop a suitable blade. In 1903, Gillette finally debuted his shaving kit which featured one razor and one blade for $5—equivalent to $130 today.[9]

Sales trickled in modestly, but Gillette had achieved his vision of creating a loyal customer. People who purchased his razors found themselves reliant on a steady supply of its replacement blades. By the end of his first full year of sales, Gillette sold more than ninety thousand blades.[10]

It was not until a decade later that Gillette came up with his great idea. At the onset of World War I and in the midst of a depressed economy, Gillette expanded his user base by selling his razors to the U.S. military at cost.[11] Soldiers needed razors and the military was hard-pressed to pass up such a generous offer.

When the deal was struck, Gillette didn't reap immediate financial gains, but he did set the stage for future success by distributing his razors to a whole generation of users. Over the course of the war, he supplied more than 3.5 million razors and 32 million blades to troops.[12] Once the war ended and troops came home, each already owned a Gillette razor and only needed to continue purchasing Gillette's replacement blades.

It took two decades for King Camp Gillette to achieve the company of his dreams, but in doing so, he showed that the basic idea of creating a loyal customer could not only capture incredible market share but durably hold on to it. Gillette didn't only dominate the razor industry after World War I, but has continued to dominate it up to today. In 2005—almost a century later—his company maintained an astonishing 70 percent market share.[13] Gillette's tactics are deemed so successful that they are now commonly taught in business schools as the famed "razor-and-blade" strategy.

THE PRICE OF LOYALTY IN HEALTH INSURANCE

Principle #2: C-Moats Increase Profit Margin

The second principle is that *c-moats increase profit margin*. In essence, when a business holds a higher likelihood of being chosen by customers, it can enjoy a fatter profit margin.

This phenomenon is easily observed every day at movie theaters. For the duration of a moviegoer's visit, a theater enjoys a wide c-moat over them. When the moviegoer becomes hungry or thirsty—a desire that theaters are very good at implanting—then, as the only choice, the theater's concession stand can charge a hefty premium. A theater's wide c-moat allows it to sell drinks and food for far higher profit margins—albeit temporarily. Where else do people pay $6 for a soda that can be purchased for $3 at a convenience store across the street?

The link between intrinsic loyalty—whether driven by preference or lack of options—and profit margin is surprisingly a relatively new field of study. In 2002, three researchers (B. Strombom, T. Buchmueller, and P. Feldstein) published a paper titled "Switching Cost, Price Sensitivity, and Health Plan Choice."[14]

Here the researchers wanted to understand how consumers respond to price changes. Specifically, they wanted to know whether a loyal demographic behaved differently than a less loyal one. Their hypothesis was that these two groups would react differently to price changes.

To structure their study, the researchers attained statistical data on the University of California school system's 103,835 employees over a five-year period (from 1993 to 1997). They then examined this data to see how school employees picked their health care plans from a list of options provided by the school system.

To analyze this data, the researchers segregated it into annual snapshots. Within each snapshot, they then categorized employees into two distinct groups: incumbents and new hires.

"Incumbents" were people employed by the university for more than one year and were considered more loyal. To them, switching from an existing plan to a new plan would involve extra research compared to a renewal, and many of the incumbents had already become accustomed to visiting their particular health care providers. "New hires," on the other hand, were people employed by the university for less than a year. They were considered less loyal and were choosing health plans for the first time during the hiring process. With a clean slate to work from, they had no past loyalty.

During the study's 1993 snapshot, the University of California provided employees with seven health plans to choose from. While six of them didn't charge a monthly premium, the last carried a premium of $64.55. For the study's 1994 snapshot, the prices of the plans remained mostly unchanged except the last plan's premiums almost **doubled** to $114.55 per month. (*While not relevant to the results, during the 1994 snapshot, five of the six free plans remained free, while the sixth plan increased slightly to $14 per month.*)

The big question posed by the researchers was, "Does loyalty play a role in how much health plans can charge?" Would incumbents react differently to a price hike than new hires?

The outcome was stark. After the significant price increase in 1994 of the expensive plan, 6 percent of incumbents chose to stick with it whereas only 1.3 percent of new hires chose it. Incumbents were willing to pay the higher premium at *four times the rate* of new hires. It turned out that loyalty profoundly influenced the rate at which people were willing to pay higher prices for the same good.

THE SWEETEST REWARD
A Recipe for Mouth-Watering Profit Margins

Perhaps the greatest story of how intrinsic loyalty can be used to fatten profit margins comes from See's Candies, a cherished subsidiary of Warren Buffett's Berkshire Hathaway.

Every year, a few days after the Christmas, as the holiday season wraps up, Buffett receives an amazing present from See's Candies. While the gift does not come in a box and cannot be wrapped, it is perhaps the most amazing present that Buffett could wish for: See's Candies will quietly raise all its prices by a few pennies.

To the casual outsider, this small annual price adjustment is often glossed over as an ordinary business activity, but for Buffett's business empire, it has been the source of vast riches.

In 1972, Buffett purchased See's Candies for $25 million. At the time, the company was well established on the West Coast, with a fifty-year reputation for making high-quality confectioneries. Californians grew up eating its delicious chocolates on holidays and special occasions. People had been used to receiving and gifting boxes of See's Candies wrapped in their iconic white packaging featuring a portrait of Grandmother See—whose original recipes are still faithfully followed to this day.[15]

The many decades of accumulated loyalty was not lost on Buffett. In purchasing the company, Buffett realized that he was buying not only a quality product but a dedicated audience. Customers who bought from See's Candies were not going to skimp on quality just to save a few cents. Buffett framed their loyalty by saying, "Imagine going to your wife or sweetheart, handing her a box of chocolates and saying, 'Honey, I took the low bid.'"[16]

The strength of See's Candies' c-moat was reflected in how much Buffett paid for the company: a staggering three times its physical net worth, by far the highest premium Buffett ever paid for a business up to that point. Even though the purchase price was expensive, Buffett later explained in his folksy manner, "Price is what you pay; value is what you get."[17]

Immediately after the purchase was completed, Buffett put See's Candies' c-moat straight to work. He told management to continue operating as it always had with one exception: raise prices slightly at the end of each year.[18] In doing so, over the next 35 years the price per pound of See's Candies' chocolates has risen an average of 5.8 percent annually; the expense of making candies has risen roughly 4.7 percent annually.[19]

This small and steady 1.1 percent annual profit-margin increase has snowballed exponentially. In 1972, Buffett purchased See's Candies for $25 million, and in that year, it earned $4 million in pretax profits.[20] By 2007, without selling significantly more candy, See's Candies earned $82 million in pretax profits. Tallied over three and a half decades, the small confectionery company has netted Buffett a staggering $1.35 billion in cumulative profits, a 5,300% investment gain.[21] (A closer look at See's Candies' profit-margin strategy is in chapter 3.)

See's Candies was able to create wealth by simply exploiting its strong c-moat to raise profit margins, and this ability is shared by all companies that are able to create wide c-moats.

AN ECONOMICAL RELATIONSHIP

Principle #3: Market Share and Profit Margin Are Related in a Trade-off

The third and last principle is that market share can be traded for profit margin, and vice-versa. This trade-off is controlled by how we set prices.

Price holds a very special role in business strategy. This was why the definition of "c-moat" separates it out. In situations of all things being equal, price changes will impact market share and profit margin in an inverse trade-off.

Lower prices will provide greater market share and reduced profit margin. On the flip side, higher prices will lead to lower market share and increased profit margin.

As entrepreneurs, we face this trade-off when deciding whether or not to alter our prices. It is reminiscent of the old saying, "You can't have your cake and eat it too." The choice in front of us is, "Do we prefer to have a larger slice of cake or a better-tasting cake?" Do we to set prices low to gain market share or high to attain a fatter profit margin?

CUSTOMER MOAT FORMULA (PART 1 OF 3)
Piecing Together a Framework

The three principles have been laid out that form the core of the Customer Moat Formula (CMF). We can combine them to create a basic understanding for how businesses gain market share and profit margin.

PRINCIPLE #1: Wider c-moats grow market share.

PRINCIPLE #2: Wider c-moats increase profit margin.

PRINCIPLE #3: Market share and profit margin are related in a trade-off that is managed by price.

To help visualize the assembly of these principles, each has been represented graphically using the following figures:

FIGURE 1.1
C-moats Grow Market Share

FIGURE 1.2
C-moats Increase Profit Margin

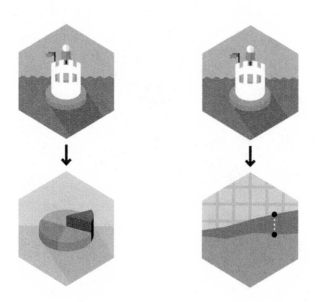

FIGURE 1.3 Market Share and Profit Margin Trade-Off

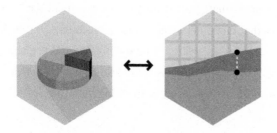

Combining them provides the following relationship, which serve as the core of the Customer Moat Formula.

FIGURE 1.4 Core of the CMF (Combining the Three Principles)

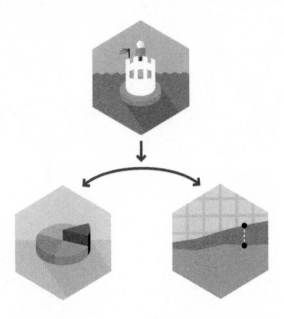

The CMF now lays out the basic relationship between c-moats, market share, and profit margin. It begins with the c-moat (i.e., the intrinsic probability that customers will choose a business). As this probability increases, businesses will gain either greater market share and/or higher profit margins. Businesses can also adjust the balance between these two outcomes by raising or lowering their prices.

With the CMF model established, we have the foundation to ask a more important question: "What are the actions that give businesses wider c-moats?" (This topic will be covered in chapters 4 through 12.)

The lesson of this chapter is that widening our c-moats is the most important task of our business. If our c-moat can be successfully widened, we will not be forced to choose between market share and profit margin but can enjoy the best of both worlds. The wider we grow our c-moat, the more we can have our cake and eat it too.

CHAPTER TWO

DEFINING MARKETS

Baseball legend Yogi Berra quipped, "You've got to be very careful if you don't know where you are going, because you might not get there."[1]

Before addressing the tools available for widening a c-moat, it helps to take a step back and determine who exactly we are trying to widen our c-moat around. What is our target market? How do we properly define this market? And what are its important attributes?

The primary objective of defining our market is to determine where we want our business to go. After all, we must have a destination before we can craft a game plan for getting there.

First and foremost, markets should revolve around a set of customers. Customers can be people, businesses, institutions, governments, or even the owners of a business—such as co-ops or private equity funds.

It is important to avoid defining markets around products. When businesses become product-centric, they run the risk of taking their eyes off the most important task: serving customers. Think back to all the businesses that fell into a trap of becoming enamored with their products. Remember how Sony manufactured the world's best portable CD players? Or how Kodak produced the best film? These products were great for a while, but what happened when new innovations served customers better?

Second, markets should be defined around a customer need. The trick is to choose needs that will continue to exist in the long run. Will people always need cupcakes or cable TV? Or, instead, will people always need a way to treat themselves or a way to enjoy high-quality entertainment? For strategies to be durable, they must be built around persistent needs. Fads come and go, but needs are forever.

A well-defined market thus has two key components: a set of customers and a set of needs being served.

Typically, markets are defined in a company's mission statement. If your business doesn't have one yet, don't worry; just be prepared to set aside a few days to think it over and a few quality hours to write it out. Mission statements should be crafted with great care as they set up a company's purpose and future direction. While mission statements might not be used on a daily basis, they are there to guide businesses through troubling times and when making life-altering decisions.

Some notable mission statements include Amazon's goal, "to be earth's most customer-centric company; to build a place where people can come to find and discover anything they might want to buy online."[2] Starbucks's mission statement is, "To inspire and nurture the human spirit—one person, one cup and one neighborhood at a time" by being a "third place for people beyond home and work."[3] And Google's mission statement is, "To organize the world's information and make it universally accessible and useful."[4]

These mission statements of highly successful companies all focus on customer needs; notice that none of them are tied down to a specific product. Will people always need a customer-centric place to buy anything they could possibly desire? Will they always need a third place to go beyond home and work? And will they always need to access the world's information in a useful, organized manner? The answer is a resounding, "Yes."

In 2000, Amazon faced a tough decision that forever affected its business. Internally, an idea was floated around to allow third-party sellers to list their products on Amazon's website.[5] Right beside Amazon's own product listing, a competitor would be given the ability to sell the same product and potentially undercut Amazon's prices. Within Amazon, a great debate raged as to whether this was wise. For many, it seemed insane that Amazon would invite competitors into its house and then give them the ability to compete for its sales.

It was a tough decision, but Amazon's CEO stuck to the company's mission statement. Today, third-party sellers are allowed to sell on Amazon, and they have become an integral part of the company. These sellers have transformed Amazon from being an online retailer to an online marketplace. The decision—while contentious—was the right move in solidifying Amazon's position as the place where "people can come to find and discover anything they might want to buy online."

So, what happens when mission statements, and hence markets, fail to be properly defined? Take RadioShack as an example. When walking into a RadioShack, we have probably been confused about the store's purpose and who it is trying to serve. After reading the company's mission statement, the reason becomes clear. RadioShack's mission statement is, "Through its convenient and comfortable neighborhood stores, knowledgeable sales associates help customers get the most out of their technology products."[6]

First off, is RadioShack actually serving a durable need? Will people always need neighborhood stores and sales associates to help them get the most out of their technology products? While this may have been relevant in the past, people today are no longer bound to their local neighborhood stores for technology purchases. We have access to large electronic warehouse stores such as Best Buy and Fry's or can simply shop online.

Second, RadioShack is defining itself around a set of products—namely, neighborhood stores and sales associates. While these features might be nice to have, are they actually the best way to serve customers? Are neighborhood stores and sales associates the most effective means to help people "get the most out of their technology products"? By listing products in its mission statement, RadioShack has essentially tied its hands and limited the methods in which it can serve its customers. Unsurprisingly, in 2015, RadioShack's identity struggles came to an end when it filed for bankruptcy.[7]

● ● ●

Once a business has a well-defined market (i.e., a customer and a set of needs being served), we can begin devising metrics for gauging its progress.

Consider the well-defined mission statement of a restaurant chain that goes, "To provide a dining environment for on-the-road truck drivers who need a comfortable home-like eating experience." Presented here is a clear vision for who the business is trying to serve and in what capacity.

With this well-defined market, the restaurant can create measurable benchmarks for tracking its progress. It can estimate the number of truck drivers that stop in versus pass by, it can use loyalty programs to keep tabs on repeat customers, and it can survey truck drivers on their dining experiences.

After we define our market, it is important to spend time thinking about which measurements can help us to gauge our progress in achieving our mission statement.

Take great care when structuring these measurements. Workers will focus their energies on reaching the measurable, quantitative goals that we set out. As such, it is important to avoid metrics that might accidentally narrow our c-moats.

An example of a poor measurement would be a daily sales target for waitstaff at a restaurant. This could push waitstaff to employ high-pressure sales tactics to get customers to buy expensive drinks and unwanted appetizers or desserts, an activity that would likely backfire in the long run and drive down repeat business.

Another poor measurement would be to reward managers of warehouse retailers like Wal-Mart purely for cost cutting. While costs should be contained, cost-cutting often goes a step too far with managers pushing workers into part-time positions that deny them benefits. This leads to unhappy workers, which severely impair productivity and customer service. A better measure would be to reward managers for revenue growth as well as keeping a lid on cost as percentage of revenue.

● ● ●

In many situations, we don't have the luxury of picking our own mission statement, such as when we join an existing business with an existing customer base. How then do we know which customer needs we are serving?

A little bit of reverse-thinking can help us sort out the situation. We can imagine what would happen if our business were to shut down tomorrow and ask, "Where will our customers spend the dollars that they would have spent with us?"

This exercise can yield surprising insights about both ourselves and our true competitors. A neighborhood sushi restaurant might realize that its biggest challenger is not a nearby sushi restaurant a few streets down but a popular Thai restaurant next door. A pastry shop may discover that its major threat is not Dunkin' Donuts but a board game cafe that has established itself as a popular hangout destination. And a car rental company may find that its biggest rival is not taxicabs or public transportation but hotel buses that shuttle people around.

Once we identify our real competitors, we can get a better feel for which customer needs we are currently serving and how we can position our offerings to be more effective.

FIVE POSSIBLE OPTIONS
How to Pick Successful Markets

In the winter of 1981, in the ballroom of New York's The Pierre, a hotel on Fifth Avenue, the newly elected CEO of General Electric (GE) was preparing to present his vision for the international conglomerate's future.[8] As Wall Street analysts anxiously awaited Jack Welch's speech, many wondered what this new leadership meant for the global empire.

Analyst meetings were typically used to provide quarterly updates, sales forecasts, and financial discussions of the business, but for his first meeting, Welch had something special in mind. He wanted to clarify to the audience how he envisioned GE's markets and what he thought would be the driver of their success or failure.

Welch told the attendees that those successful enterprises of the future would "search out and participate in the real growth industries and insist on being number one or number two in every business they are in—the number-one or number-two leanest, lowest-cost, world-wide producers of quality goods and services."[9]

For Welch, this was what winners of the future looked like. As GE's new CEO, he would do everything in his power to transform the company into a formidable player, even as it meant challenging decades of ingrained traditions and a rigid corporate culture.

To the analysts in the room, Welch's speech was a flop. They were not interested in his grand vision but instead were looking for quantitative numbers and financial predictions. What the analysts didn't realize at the time was that Welch's speech would be one of the strongest predictors of GE's future success, far more telling than any financial forecast or mathematical model.

Inside GE, Welch's strategy to dominate each of its markets became known as the "number one or number two, fix, sell, or close" rule. Welch had drawn line in the sand; these were the only five options for each of GE's business units.

In adhering to this rule, during his first two years, Welch sold seventy-one subsidiaries that no longer fitted his strategic requirement. Even the company's air conditioning division, which held a massive 10 percent market share, was sold. While the segment represented a sizable portion of GE's revenue, Welch reasoned that controlling the customer experience was too difficult. Air conditioners were shipped to third-party distributors where outside contractors purchased them and then installed them. With little ability to exert control over the distributors or contractors, the quality of end-user experiences varied widely and, many times, was far from positive.

For other business units, Welch invested heavily to bolster their market standing; 118 deals were struck to purchase companies that fortified existing business lines. The largest and most important acquisition was RCA in 1986. RCA, like GE, was a large conglomerate and the two overlapped in multiple markets areas. GE had an aerospace division as did RCA; GE owned a semiconductor business as did RCA; GE manufactured TVs as did RCA. Overnight, the buyout of RCA catapulted many of GE's business units into the coveted number-one or number-two spot.[10]

The purchase of RCA also came with ancillary businesses that did not meet Welch's strategic test. In the process, GE shed RCA's record business, carpet business, and insurance business.[11]

Twenty years after the first analyst meeting, the results of Welch's "No. 1, No. 2, fix, sell, or close" plan was apparent. When Welch took over as CEO in 1981, the company recorded $25 billion in revenue and earned $1.5 billion annually. By 2001, GE's sales had risen to $125 billion with earnings of $14 billion. Revenue shot up fivefold and profits nearly tenfold. GE's profit margin increased from an uninspiring 6 percent to an impressive 11.2 percent.

The lesson is that we should choose markets where we can become number one or number two. If we want to earn healthy profit margins, we need to be in markets where we can gain the widest c-moats.

What happens when we are not number one or number two is that we become susceptible to the competitive forces of our rivals. The profit margins of third-place-and-lesser competitors are dictated by how intensely the top two rivals compete. In a worst-case scenario, when the strongest rival decides to allocate all of its c-moat towards gaining market share, a price war will then ensue that squeezes the profit of weaker rivals. This effectively pushes them into sustaining massive financial losses and possibly pushes them out of the market altogether.

Therefore, we want to avoid being at the mercy of competitors by choosing markets where we can reasonably attain a status of having the number-one or number-two widest c-moats.

THE ECOLOGY OF COMPETITIVE ENVIRONMENTS

Niche Markets and Segmentation

When building our strategy, we want to pick markets where we can become formidable players. GE achieved this by leveraging its deep pocketbook and vast financial resources to consolidate its market share until it held the top spot. Another method of reaching the coveted number-one or number-two spot is to redefine our business around a smaller market and narrower set of customer needs.

Honing in on a smaller group of customers and needs is evocative of the age-old question, "Is it better to be a small fish in a big pond or a big fish in a small pond?" When c-moat strength is an issue, smaller ponds are often much better. While it might be difficult to compete in a large pond, if we can attain success in a small pond, we can later expand to a larger pond.

A backpack maker, for example, might produce high-quality backpacks but still struggle in the larger marketplace. One way to increase its chances of developing a wider c-moat is to focus on the needs of a narrower audience. The backpack maker can funnel its energy towards serving airline travelers who desire attributes such as wheels and handles to make walking through airports easier, or hikers who desire highly durable and waterproof backpacks, or bicyclists who desire thin, streamlined versions that are aerodynamic and can clip onto bikes. By specializing on a subset of customers and needs, a backpack maker can become a more effective problem solver and thus increase its chances of gaining the coveted number-one or number-two spot.

Surprisingly, an ideal place to learn about the value of specialization as a means for survival is about as far from the business world as possible, in the remote reaches of the Galápagos Islands.

In 1973, two experts in ornithology, Peter and Rosemary Grant, chartered a boat to Daphne Major, one of the more isolated islands in the archipelago. From a distance, Daphne Major is an imposing sight to behold. The island, surrounded by steep, sharp cliffs, has no shoreline, and its top is covered by a rough, rocky terrain. It is a challenging environment that seems hardly hospitable to life.

Despite the island's harshness, however, life does exist on it, and for twenty years, the Grants have documented it while completing one of the most detailed observational studies of a competitive ecosystem ever attempted. The full story is recounted in the Pulitzer Prize-winning book *The Beak of the Finch* by Jonathan Weiner.[12]

In the hostile world of Daphne Major, the Grants have recorded the lives of finches and how these birds have evolved over time. Of the approximately 1,300 finches that live on the island at any given moment, the two ornithologists have come to know each one intimately. They not only recognize the birds by sight, but they know each one's parents, grandparents, and great-grandparents. They know each one's physical measurements, their dietary habits, the survival rates of their eggs, and—with the aid of modern technology—their DNA. In studying these birds, the Grants have mapped out the evolutionary process of a species, unlike any study before.

With all this data, the Grants have corroborated many of Darwin's views on evolution and natural selection, but just as importantly, their studies have shed light on the competitive forces that can affect our businesses, some of which have great implications on our strategy.

Each year, the climate of Daphne Major oscillates between two major seasons: wet and dry. During the wet months, fruits and plants thrive and the finches feast like kings. As the dry season takes hold, the environment transforms into a harsh and barren landscape. The finches begin to scrounge for seeds. As the season progresses and the food supply further dwindles, the search for seeds becomes more desperate. It is during these scarce times that the shape of a finch's beak will determine its life or death.

The seeds available in the dry season vary in size and hardness; small grass seeds require only a small amount of force to break open, while larger seeds require up to twenty-five times the effort. With high competition for these resources, the finches have branched into specialized groups, each focusing on a differing seed type. As one of the Grants' researchers described it, "The biggest beaks eat the biggest seeds, the birds with medium-sized beaks eat medium-sized seeds, [and] the birds with the small beaks eat the smallest seeds."[13]

Birds with bigger beaks tend to have shorter beaks that reduce the energy needs for cracking open large seeds. Birds with smaller beaks have long, narrower beaks that make them more efficient at searching for smaller seeds among the nooks and crannies of the rocks.

By branching into subgroups, the finches have increased their ability to master different food supplies during scarce times. This adaptation has translated into survivability.

We can apply this concept to our own businesses. When positioning our c-moats around smaller markets, we will be better at dominating our food supply—i.e., our customers. In doing so, we increase our competitiveness while creating a stronger fallback during tough times. The trade-off is that we might be limiting the scope of our current market size—but that is something we can always expand upon later on.

Luckily our companies can metaphorically change the shape of their beaks *well before* undergoing a brutal natural selection process. At any time, we can choose to rearrange the DNA of our business by simply rede-fining our market and reshaping our strategy for targeting that market, and we can prepare ourselves well-before our survival is threatened.

Targeting narrower groups of customers will come in two forms: niche markets and segmentation. Niche markets are used offensively to break into new markets while segmentation is used to defend existing markets.

● ● ●

How do we enter an industry and challenge entrenched players? How can we successfully go up against larger, better-funded competitors? The answer lies in niche markets.

In the respective worlds of laptops and cereal, Panasonic and Nature's Path have both succeeded despite challenging more sizable, well-established industry players.

If we were to think about buying a laptop, the first brand that pops into our head is probably not Panasonic; in fact, this brand is likely quite far down on our list. Panasonic, however, has built a strong following among specific laptop users—those requiring portable, rugged computing solutions capable of withstanding real-world abuses.

In catering to this demographic, Panasonic has developed a line of Toughbook laptops designed to be the industry's most durable. These computers feature strong frames, shock-resistant hard drives, water-proof keyboards, and rugged outer shells. They are damage resistant and can withstand drops of up to six feet. Unsurprisingly, with its Toughbooks, Panasonic has vaulted itself into a strong position with customers in the military, construction, healthcare, and manufacturing industries. With its strong niche, Panasonic's laptop division has earned a gross profit margin 5 percent higher than the industry average.[14]

The other notable company, Nature's Path, has broken into one of the most difficult markets: cereal. This market has long been dominated by the big three—Post, General Mills, and Kellogg—which, combined, account for 85 percent of the industry's sales.[15]

Nature's Path has found an entry into this market by developing a niche around the underserved population of adults. While the big three have historically targeted children through heavy bombardments of advertising and sugary cereals, Nature's Path has focused on adults who desire quick, wholesome breakfast options that promote a healthier lifestyle. Nature's Path organic cereal line includes Flax Plus Multibran Flakes, Heritage Muesli, Optimum Power Blueberry Cinnamon Flax Cereal, and Multigrain Oatbran Cereal. By positioning itself as a top choice with adults, during a period when the overall cereal industry has achieved flat growth, Nature's Path has increased its revenue by 20 to 30 percent annually.[16]

When working on our own business—whether we are a small start-up or just looking for a way to create a foothold in an industry—narrowing the scope of our focus will greatly improve our odds of success.

One way to discover a niche market is to observe how industry players are serving different customer groups and their specific needs. After an analysis, if any group seems underserved, it may present an opening for us to develop a niche market.

● ● ●

While niche markets are primarily an offensive maneuver, specialized targeting can also be used to play a defensive game. The process of segmentation allows companies to divide their existing customer base into smaller subgroups. This helps intensify the focus that each subgroup receives and prevents rivals from being able to drive a wedge in the customer base.

One business that has mastered the art of segmentation is 3M, a company best known for its Scotch tape and Post-it notes. Founded in 1902 as an ambitious sandpaper manufacturer, 3M had its start when it purchased a rare mine that could produce the "sand" for its sandpaper. In developing the mine, the company's founders were quickly humbled when they discovered that the mine was a dud; the rock in it only looked similar to the one for making sandpaper but was ultimately unusable. The setback almost destroyed the company, but its bad luck eventually turned into good fortune. To stay afloat, 3M was forced to learn how to produce sandpaper using materials sourced from different suppliers. As these materials varied greatly in their physical properties, 3M became a leading innovator at formulating adhesives that could bind differently textured products together.[17]

In the 1920s, 3M reached its first breakthrough with a waterproof sandpaper called Tri-M-ite. The product solved a nightmare problem for the burgeoning automotive industry. Manufacturing cars required huge quantities of abrasives, most of which disintegrated upon getting wet on the assembly line. Tri-M-ite became an industry game changer.

Into the 1950s, 3M redefined its mission to better address the needs of its different customers. The company set itself a goal of creating "a special adhesive for each specific industrial job"—a unique solution to each manufacturer's specific problems. To accomplish this, 3M developed more than one thousand specialized adhesive formulas that served different purposes, with about 350 in regular production.[18]

To enshrine a culture of specialization, 3M has come up with its "30 percent rule": 30 percent of the company's revenue must come from products introduced in the last four years.[19] This has pushed the company not only to continually innovate new products but to expand existing product categories that can increase the company's effectiveness at solving different customer problems.

In 1980, when 3M hit upon the blockbuster product of Post-it notes, people found the 3x3-inch sticky note pads useful for everything, from taking messages to making grocery lists, bookmarks, and labels. Since then, the 30 percent rule has helped 3M segment its market and improve its ability to address each individual need.

Today, Post-its come in a variety of shapes, sizes, colors, and lines; there are Post-it bookmarks, Post-it "Sign Here" arrows, Post-it easel pads, Post-it removable labels, and even entire Post-it bulletin boards. With such customer-centric problem solving, it is no wonder that 3M continues to expand its retail shelf space.

CHAPTER THREE

THE ART OF PRICE SETTING

I n 2008, I went home to Louisiana to help my family turn around their business. After arriving, I quickly realized that the topic of price was not only a tough subject to broach but one that caused us great distress.

For decades, we built our strategy around a false perception that low prices are key to driving customer loyalty. In adopting this thinking, we developed a habit of maintaining cutthroat margins. Our game plan was essentially to compete for customers through "cheapest-price loyalty"–a rather fickle creature in hindsight. Breaking this mindset was one of our toughest challenges.

Under cheapest-price loyalty, we gained market share by having virtually no profit margin. This meant that we never accumulated any type of cash cushion. For years, our strategy pushed us to tiptoe around the edge of bankruptcy. By the time I arrived, we stood with one foot over the edge.

Our mistake was the same that many businesses face: we overemphasized cash flow while discounting profits. Cash flow is an important indicator of a company's ability to pay its bills; it is the amount of cash a business takes in versus the amount of cash it pays out. If a business can always take in more than it pays out, then it is on solid financial footing.

A business's cash flow can originate from three different sources: earning profits, selling a company's assets (e.g., shares of stock or equipment), and incurring debt.

Unfortunately for us, with a zero-margin pricing policy, we achieved positive cash flow through the years by slowly accumulating debt. Over the course of decades, this debt became substantial.

When I took account of our finances, I learned that we had piled on debt from a variety of sources. We had business loans, personal loans, delays in payments to suppliers, and a growing accounts receivable. At one point, things were so shaky that we even borrowed money from our largest competitor while paying an exorbitant interest rate. We squeezed as much cash as we could from all possible sources and as we exhausted our ability to finance more debt, something had to give.

Without enough cash flow to pay our bills, we were left with only one viable option: to raise prices. This was an emotional decision for us, especially after years of being ingrained with a belief that the path to customer loyalty was through having the cheapest prices.

Raising prices seemed counterintuitive—and, to be honest, it was incredibly scary.

We had backed ourselves into a corner. Since our zero-margin strategy led us to accumulate debt while also preventing us from building a cash cushion, if our customers defected from a price hike, it would be game over for us. With no choice and also no extra funds to weather a possible misstep, raising prices was a make-it-or-break-it moment for us.

Luckily, my intuition guided us through this rough period. I believed that our business held a valuable yet hidden asset, one that was not captured in its financials: a very strong standing with our community of customers. While I couldn't quantify the value of this asset, I knew it was precious. Today, I realize that it was the basis of our c-moat.

Even though we had always tried to garner loyalty through low prices, I suspected the devotions of our customers ran far deeper. We had been a staple in the community for over twenty-five years. We knew our customers, their families, their children, and we held a strong reputation for going above and beyond in helping people solve their problems. My hunch was that, if we raised prices slightly, our customers would stick around, and they did.

We eventually became comfortable with the idea of raising prices, especially given our decent c-moat. We provided a solid service, good value, and held a strong reputation; we didn't need to rely on low prices as a sledgehammer tool for keeping customers returning.

Of course, when we raised prices, we did encounter an occasional groan and a lost customer here and there, but these cases were few and far between. In fact, after raising prices, our business grew busier. We suddenly had funds that could be plowed back into improving efficiency and further enhancing customer satisfaction. For us, increasing prices was crucial in both our success and survival—and, not to be discounted, it allowed us to sleep much sounder at night.

Years later, I came across a saying that helped explain our emotional challenge to raising prices: "The greatest fear in life is the fear of the unknown." For many decades, we defaulted to a cutthroat pricing scheme because we didn't actually know what would happen if we were to raise prices. Emotionally, low prices felt like the safest option—even though in retrospect it was neither safe nor wise.

What we should have done was to bring more of the unknown into the known. Rather than being fear-driven, we should have tried to understand the subtleties of pricing and its potential effects on our business.

This chapter sheds light on the mechanics of pricing. In it we will analyze when it is beneficial to raise prices, when it is beneficial to lower prices, and how these actions affect our market share. After reading this chapter, we will be able to wield price, not as an enigmatic black box, but as a strategic tool.

● ● ●

To understand pricing, we must go back to the definition of "c-moats." A c-moat is the intrinsic probability of a customer choosing a business, outside the influence of price.

There are in reality nine fundamental factors that influence a customer's behavior: the eight moat builders and price. While the eight moat builders are used to widen c-moats, price is the tool for determining how much of a c-moat gets allocated to market share or profit margin.

In other words, c-moat are how we create value for our business; pricing is how we choose to capture that value, through either more market share or higher profit margins.

● ● ●

Setting prices is partly art and partly science. When choosing the price for our goods and services, we are juggling the competing interests of different parts of our business. It can be a delicate balancing act.

Some aspects of our business will benefit from higher prices while others benefit from lower prices. On the higher side, there is the ability to bolster cash reserves, reward shareholders (through greater dividends and stock buybacks), and gain funds that can be reinvested to widen the c-moat. On the lower side, there is the ability to maintain market share, squeeze the profitability of rivals, and regulate the long term ecosystem of our competitors.

A very important question must be considered before we attempt to alter our prices: "To what extent will a price change impact the buying behavior of our customers?" Will the impact on customers be large or small?

Once we know the pros, cons, and the tradeoff of altering our prices, we can determine the best course of action for being successful in the long run.

VISUALIZING THE ALLOCATION OF PRICES
The Token-Bucket Method

For most endeavors, the odds of success will be greatly improved if we can visualize a path to it. The question is, "How can we visualize an abstract activity like price setting?" While it is easy to envision riches, it is a bit more difficult to picture the actions that get us there.

Fortunately, the Customer Moat Formula provides an easy technique for visualizing this process: the token-bucket method.

The token-bucket method starts from a business's point of view. As a business's c-moat is widened, it is rewarded with tokens. The wider the c-moat, the more tokens received. These tokens can then allocated into two possible buckets: a market-share bucket or a profit-margin bucket.

When businesses gain tokens, the tokens will be automatically allocated into the buckets. How they are allocated will depend on which moat builder was used to widen the c-moat. For example, a business that improved its customer satisfaction will have people coming back more often, thus leading to tokens being added to the market-share bucket. On the other hand, a business that lowered its cost of providing the same great service will have tokens automatically placed in its profit-margin bucket.

After this automatic allocation, tokens can be manually moved between buckets through the changing of prices. Price increase will transfer tokens from the market-share bucket to the profit-margin bucket, and price decreases will do the opposite.

● ● ●

So, how do we set prices to have the correct proportion of tokens between the two buckets? This is where pricing becomes an art. There is no single correct answer as it depends on a business's circumstances and goals. It is, however, *always* the responsibility of management to align a business's pricing policies to its strategic priorities. For this reason, price setting should take place only at the highest levels of management.

Amazon, for example, has decided to place nearly all its tokens into the market-share bucket. The company essentially maintains a zero profit margin. From 2012 to 2014, Amazon's profit totaled negative $6 million on sales of $225 billion.[1]

While Amazon holds a few strategic advantages—such as a slightly lower cost structure, tremendous selection, and quality of service—at its core, the company is still a retailer competing with other retailers on price. In fact, most of the products found on Amazon are identical to those available at other stores. Because of this, it is hard for Amazon to raise its prices without customers defecting to other retailers. As such, it currently makes more sense for the online giant to chase market share rather than a higher profit margin.

To Amazon's credit, the company has worked hard to strengthen its c-moat and overcome the challenges of a price-sensitive industry. Ventures like the Kindle e-reader, Amazon Prime membership, and cloud computing services are all aimed at keeping customers more loyal. While the verdict is still out on how much intrinsic loyalty Amazon can garner, no one doubts its ambition to dominate its customers' lives. If the online retailer does discover a way to develop a wide c-moat, it can use its market share clout to earn massive profits.

On the opposite end of the allocation spectrum, the technology giant Apple has skewed its tokens heavily towards the profit-margin bucket. For its fiscal 2012 results, the company's net profit margin after tax was an astounding 26 percent, translating to $41 billion of earnings.[2]

While Apple has established a massive c-moat and has enough ammunition to place tokens into both buckets, the company has actively chosen to forgo extra market penetration in favor of heftier profit margins. When we purchase an Apple product, we know that we are paying a high premium.

FIGURE 3.1 Visualizing the Token-Bucket Method

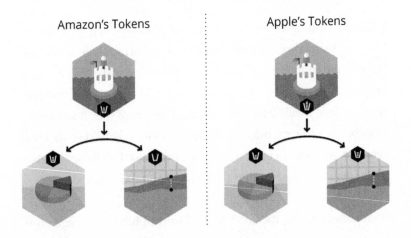

Amazon's Tokens   Apple's Tokens

How we choose to allocate our own tokens will depend on how we view our position in relation to competitors and whether we can raise prices without mass defection.

There is a flip-side lesson to the token-bucket analogy. If we find ourselves ceding ground to competitors, our c-moat will narrow and we will be forced to remove tokens from our buckets. As such, we will face a dilemma of whether to remove tokens from our market-share bucket, our profit-margin bucket, or a combination of both.

The best defense is to protect our tokens by continually widening our c-moats and increasing the intrinsic loyalty of our customers.

SNOWBALLING SMALL CHANGES
A Billion Little Reasons to Raise Profit Margins

So, why would we want to allocate more of tokens to the profit-margin bucket? The reason is fairly straightforward: profits, and potentially vast profits.

In the grand scheme, raising profit margins is the greatest lever that a business possesses for managing its profit. From a mathematical viewpoint, small changes in "profit margin" have an outsized affect on our bottom line.

Profits are a valuable, all-purpose resource. They can be used to create financial reserves (i.e., to insure against turbulent times when cash flow dips negative), to reward shareholders (i.e., through dividends and stock buy backs), and to be reinvested in further widening our c-moats.

Many businesses underestimate the vast impact that small price changes have on profit margin. Even seemingly insignificant adjustments can translate into enormous wealth gains.

To understand this, we can refer to the classic profit formula: *profit = price - cost*. This equation—albeit a simple one—masks an often overlooked pricing lesson: that price changes have a large multiplier effect on the bottom line.

The best way to illustrate this is by playing the what-if game and asking, "What if we raised prices by just a tiny bit?"

The following table shows a profit statement for a typical business earning a 5 percent profit margin. The columns show the "what-if" effects of small incremental price increases.

TABLE 3.2 The Effect of Price Increases on Profit

	BASE 5%	+1%	+2%	+3%	+4%
REVENUE	100%	101%	102%	103%	104%
COST	95%	95%	95%	95%	95%
PROFIT MARGIN	5%	6%	7%	8%	9%
INCREASE IN PROFIT	-	+20%	+40%	+60%	+80%

From the table, we can observe that a mere 1 percent price rise has boosted profits by an incredible 20 percent. This multiplier effect is the reason that pricing power is so valuable to businesses.

The mileage gained from raising prices will depend on each company's particular situation. Naturally, a 1 percent rise will impact a 5-percent-margin business far more than a 1 percent rise will impact a 20-percent-margin business.

To explore how small price adjustments affect the profitability of your business, simply create a customized "what-if" spreadsheet with your company's current numbers plugged in and the potential effects of 1 percent price increases. This exercise is well worth the time and will be a powerful motivator in getting you to work to widen your c-moat.

● ● ●

With the what-if game, we can reverse-engineer Warren Buffett's incredible feat of transforming See's Candies from a good but ordinary business into a phenomenal money-making machine. How did Buffet convert a $25 million investment into $1.35 billion in profit?

The following page is a what-if spreadsheet of See's Candies that begins with its 1972 financials–the year Buffett bought the company. The table assumes a profit-margin increase of 1.1 percent annually over the next thirty-five years until 2007.

To model this profit-margin increase, we use an annual price rise of 5.8 percent (which is taken from the actual average price increase per pound of See's chocolates) and an annual expense rise of 4.68 percent (which is taken from the actual pace of inflation over the period). How does the 1.1 percent profit-margin increase stack up over time?

TABLE 3.3 See's Candies: "What-If" vs. "Actual" Price Increases
Dollars in millions.

	1972 *Actual*	1977 *What-if*	1987 *What-if*	1997 *What-if*	2007 *What-if*	2007 *Actual*
REVENUE	$31	$41	$73	$128	$225	$383
COST	$27	$34	$54	$85	$135	$301
PROFIT	$4	$7	$19	$43	$90	$82
PROFIT MARGIN	13%	17%	26%	34%	40%	21%
CUMULATIVE PROFIT	$4	$33	$162	$470	$1,170	$1,350

Our table predicts that See's Candies would earn $90 million in 2007 with a cumulative profit of $1.14 billion. Actual earnings for the year were $82 million with a cumulative profit of $1.35 billion—an impressively close estimate, and not to mention a staggering sum of money.

Buffett's genius was that he realized that small profit-margin increases could compound over time. After all, raising prices was the one request he made to management after buying the company. In incrementally increasing See's Candies' profit margin, Buffett snowballed the company's earnings from $4 million per year to $85 million. Buffett summed up his billion-dollar lesson in Berkshire Hathaway's 1991 Annual Report: "In our See's purchase, [we] had one important insight: We saw that the business had untapped pricing power."[3]

As a note, the divergences between See's Candies' actual revenue versus its predicted revenue were due to a few factors. One is that See's Candies sold more candy over the years, which has increased its sales slightly. The other is that much of this increase has come from selling chocolates at bulk discounts which offer lower margins. Combined, these two factors account for the 21 percent margin versus the predicted 40 percent.

IN DEFENSE OF MARKET SHARE
Pricing Out the Competition

A compelling argument was just laid out for allocating tokens to the profit-margin bucket—after all, who doesn't want to earn vast riches? What reasons would we have for preferring the market-share bucket instead?

Placing tokens in the market-share bucket is generally a tactical move for defending market position. There are a few instances where this defense is particularly advantageous.

The first is when a business's c-moat exhibits weakness. Here, it is wise to keep market share high with the intention of later converting that market share into a wider c-moat—hence, Amazon's strategy of maintaining a low profit margin until it develops greater loyalty.

A newly opened pizza restaurant, for example, might craft delicious pizza pies, but if no one knows of the pizza shop's existence, it will be difficult for it to attain success. By sacrificing profit margin early on, the restaurant is able to lure in more customers. Only after the parlor has established a critical mass of loyal customers and a strong c-moat should it consider raising prices.

This was the tactic of King Camp Gillette when distributing razors to the U.S. military. By allocating his tokens to the market-share bucket (and sacrificing profit margin), he laid the groundwork for a much larger customer base in the future. After the war ended, his massive market share allowed him to reap huge profits from a generation of users.

The second advantage of putting tokens in the market-share bucket is that it squeezes the financial resources of competitors. This should only be performed if it reduces a rival's desire and/or ability to reinvest in their businesses. This tactic can backfire if it causes competitors to redouble their efforts, so be sure to place tokens in the market-share bucket carefully and in way that avoids stoking the flames of competition.

When we grab market share, rivals will respond by giving up market share and/or lowering their profit margin. In either scenario, rivals will be forced into a tougher financial scenario, something we can use to our advantage.

Before we maneuver to squeeze competitors, it is wise to hold the number-one or number-two widest c-moat. If a price war breaks out, the weakest competitor will be hurt the most. Imagine a business that ranks third place or below in a consumer preference. When the top two preferred options lower prices, customers will default to them much more; as such, weaker options will face enormous pricing pressure.

The third reason to grab market share is to play a longer-term strategic game. When companies maintain high market share and low profit margins, they make their markets unattractive to potential competitors. Outside investors will observe the industry's low profit margin and be less inclined to plow money into creating a rival. In other words, low profit margins act as a ceiling on competitor profits, thus paring down the number of future rivals. Just picture the razor thin margins of Amazon, Costco, and Wal-Mart. Very few investors would want to create a new competitor to challenge their already low margins. In the current environment, it would be a money-losing proposition.

PRICE SENSITIVITY OF CUSTOMERS
Estimating the Magnitude of Trade-Offs

The benefits of both the profit-margin and market-share buckets have been laid out. The next pricing question—and the perennial elephant in the room—is, "If we change prices, what is the tradeoff that we face?" In other words, if we raise prices, how many customers will defect? And alternately, if we lower prices, how much market share will be gained? When shifting tokens between buckets, we want to know, "How sensitive will our customers be to the price change?"

Price sensitivities come in a variety of degrees. Picture two identical vending machines sitting next to each other. Both machines are stocked with the same Coca-Cola sodas. The difference is that one machine sells bottles for $2, while the other sells bottles for $1.90.

With no discernable difference between the two, which machine will people choose? The odds are that people will overwhelmingly pick the $1.90 sodas. Price sensitivity is high.

For moderate price sensitivity, suppose that the $2 machine is stocked with Coca-Cola products, while the $1.90 machine is stocked with Pepsi products. Would a 10¢ price difference be enough to sway Coca-Cola drinkers to purchase Pepsi products? Here, it depends on the strength of each drinker's personal preference, but on average, we can safely assume that people will be less price sensitive than in the previous example.

And on the low end of price sensitivity, if the $2 machine stocked Coca-Cola products, while the $1.90 machine stocked mini-shots of a protein smoothies, would a 10¢ difference be enough to entice Coca-Cola buyers to switch to the protein smoothie? Highly unlikely.

These examples demonstrate not only the variability of price sensitivities but that price sensitivities are based upon two factors: the comparability of alternatives and individual consumer preferences.

Understanding these two factors is therefore the key to understanding how price changes affect our customers. But how do we gauge these subjective factors?

Fortunately, we don't need to know the precise details of each customer's alternatives and preferences; a decent estimation will carry us quite far in formulating a pricing strategy.

To appraise the price sensitivity of our customers base, we want to employ a "divide and conquer" approach. We want to break our customer base into logical groups that exhibit similar behaviors and face similar alternatives. Once we do this, we can gauge how each group will respond to a price change and estimate the overall price sensitivity of our customer base.

The following is a three-step process for estimating the price sensitivity of a customer base. It will help us determine whether or not it is a good idea to raise or lower prices.

We begin by asking, "How much are we willing to affect our profit margin to achieve our desired goal (i.e., gaining market share or boosting profit margin). Once we know this, we can figure out the impact on our prices and estimate how customers will react to it.

STEP #1: Which bucket do we desire to put tokens into, and how much are we willing to affect our profit margin to achieve this goal?

By now, we should know which bucket is strategically most important to us. Are we contemplating a higher profit margin or increased market share?

If opting for a higher profit margin, we want to know how much the change will impact customer prices. Suppose our desire is to raise the margin from 4 percent to 5 percent. This increase entails a 1 percent price rise for customers.

If our goal is to gain market share, we want to know how much we are willing to sacrifice our profit margin to achieve the goal. Here, suppose we are willing to reduce profit margin from 10 percent to 8 percent. This entails a 2 percent price drop for customers.

STEP #2: How will the resulting price change affect customer purchases? Also, can we segment our customer base into smaller groups based on similar behaviors and alternatives to improve accuracy?

The goal is to understand how customers will react to the price change. To gauge the effect, it is helpful to categorize customers based on similar price sensitivities.

As an example, a public bus system has many types of users: long-distance commuters, short-distance commuters, weekend errand runners, late-night bar hoppers, tourists, etc. Each group holds its own set of alternatives and price sensitivities. If we can estimate the effect of a price change on each group, we will have a good estimation for the overall outcome.

To maintain accuracy, we want our subgroups to represent as much of our total customer base as possible. There is a useful term in consulting called MECE (pronounced mee-see) which stands for "Mutually Exclusive, Collectively Exhaustive." We want our customer subgroups to be MECE. Combined, the groups should be mutually exclusive to each other so that don't accidentally double count some customers, and we want these groups to be collectively exhaustive so that they represent 100 percent of our customers, not 70 percent.

Beyond breaking customers into MECE groups, accuracy can be improved by splitting a customer base into more subcategories. A restaurant might think of its customers as a breakfast crowd, lunch crowd, and dinner crowd and then analyze how a price change affects each group. The restaurant might be able to improve accuracy by further subdividing its breakfast crowd into "casual weekday early birds," "grab-and-go weekday breakfasters," and "weekend brunchers."

STEP #3: How do these price sensitivities of each group add up? What will be the overall effect of the price change on our market share?

Given the price increase or decrease, how will each subgroup react to it and where will their behavior fall on the "C-Moat Scale of Price Sensitivity" chart? (This chart is found on the following page.)

For each subgroup, we want to empathize with their objectives and alternatives. Does a group at a gym join for health reasons, or because they want to be a part of an active community, or as a way to meet single people? It is important to understand each group's motives. This determines how they perceive their alternatives. Depending on the type of gym member, alternatives could range from buying home exercise equipment to joining running clubs to signing up for singles mixers.

To use the C-Moat Scale of Price Sensitivity chart, just find the description that best fits the "Customer Point of View" if prices were to be raised or lowered.

The higher the absolute number on the scale (1 to 5), the bigger the reaction to a price change. The plus sign on the scale indicates a gain in market share, and the minus sign indicates a decrease. Example: The -4 rating translates to a massive loss of market share caused by a price rise. The +2 rating translates to a minor market-share gain due to a price decrease.

TABLE 3.4 The C-moat Scale of Price Sensitivity: Estimating the Reaction of Customers to a Price Change

	SENSITIVITY CATEGORY	MARKET SHARE IMPACT	CUSTOMER POINT OF VIEW
Price Lowered by X%	+5	Maximum Gain	Lower price creates desire to choose option as often as possible; news of price change will likely be shared with others.
	+4	Massive Gain	Lower price benefits lifestyle; becomes the preferred option; alternatives seem less appealing.
	+3	Moderate Gain	Lower price incrementally improves lifestyle; moves up a few notches in rank compared to alternatives.
	+2	Minor Gain	Lower price lingers in the back of the mind; begins to slightly impact decisions.
	+1	Minimal Gain	Lower price is noticed but does not affect behavior.
	0	None	
Price Raised by X%	-1	Minimal Loss	Higher price is noticed but quickly forgotten.
	-2	Minor Loss	Higher price creates minor second guessing of buying decisions; occasional skipping of purchases occurs; small cracks in loyalty appear.
	-3	Moderate Loss	Higher price causes alternatives to seem compelling; purchases are made grudgingly; resistance to purchases builds.
	-4	Massive Loss	Higher price leads to actively seeking other options; unhappiness looms; near-permanent defection is likely.
	-5	Maximum Loss	Higher price is a non-starter; purchases are made as a last resort.

Once we know where each subgroup falls on the C-Moat Scale of Price Sensitivity, we have a good feel for how a price change will affect our overall customer base.

As a general rule of thumb, when trying to gain market share, we want customer price sensitivity to be high (i.e., the +3 to +5 range). When raising prices to improve our profit margin, we want customer price sensitivity to be low (i.e., the -2 to 0 range).

● ● ●

In 2011, Netflix showed us the vast importance of gauging customer price sensitivities before enacting price changes. On September 1st, the company switched its pricing model from a bundled service–which included DVD rental and online streaming–to a DVD-only service and a streaming-only service. The bundled service, which previously cost $10 per month, now cost $7.99 for DVD rental and $7.99 for streaming–entailing a combined price hike of almost 60 percent. Within a matter of months, Netflix lost eight hundred thousand subscribers and its stock price plummeted 77 percent.[4]

Netflix did a poor job in estimating the reactions of their customers. For many, the 60 percent price hike was seen as a tactless move to extract money, and people responded by abandoning the otherwise beloved brand.

Netflix could have avoided this misstep by estimating the price sensitivities of its different customer groups. To do so, its customer base could have been broken into three types of watchers: DVD only, online only, and DVD and online combined. How would each subgroup react to the proposed price change?

DVD-only watchers and online-only watchers might be slightly dismayed at the loss of a service. However, since they did not often use the other service, they would save $2 under the new system. For the most part, it would be an acceptable trade-off.

But what about the 12 million subscribers, or roughly half of Netflix's customer base, who used both services? These customers would be confronted with a tough choice: either pay 60 percent more or be forced to unsubscribe from one or both services. Psychologically, Netflix had boxed consumers into choosing between an extortionary price hike or having something taken away from them.

The result was that more than forty thousand comments were logged on Netflix's Facebook page with many people promising to cancel their subscriptions. In a newspaper interview, one engineer from North Carolina, complained, "I can definitely afford it but I dropped them on principle."[5]

The Netflix debacle shows us that even large companies are not immune to serious pricing mistakes. While Netflix eventually recovered from its error, it was not before experiencing severe backlash.

The C-Moat Scale of Price Sensitivity and its three step process helps us understand the effects of price actions on customers. As an added precaution, we can test price changes on small scales before committing them to broader rollouts. We can also opt for gradual rises; or in Netflix's case, grandfathering in existing users for a period of time.

When in doubt about raising prices, it is wise to temporarily err on the side of market share. While this sacrifices profit in the short run, it buys time for greater strategizing. Once customers are lost, it can take twice as much effort to win them back.

THE TACTIC OF FUZZY PRICING
Discovering Profit in Imperfect Information

The University Village shopping complex sits on the outskirts of the University of Washington. Among its stores, Starbucks operates a concept café. At first glance, this café seems like any other Starbucks store; it does not stand out except for a slightly updated interior design. This store, however, is a testing site for many of Starbucks's new ideas, such as the Clover brewing system, Starbucks Reserve coffees, and in-store fresh-baked goods.

Of the store's more intriguing experiments, one has involved its menu. A large chalkboard hangs above and behind the counter as it displays the handwritten names of the café's beverage offerings: espressos, lattes, mochas, Frappuccinos, Reserve coffees, etc. The menu feels friendly and rustic. It takes a minute before patrons start to realize that there is a subtle omission to the menu: prices.

For most companies, not listing prices may seem counterintuitive, but for this Starbucks store, it has been effective at lowering customers' price sensitivities. Starbucks has experimented with getting people to think about its cafés as a lifestyle rather than a competing seller of coffee. When people enter, Starbucks greets them with friendly faces, offers them tasty beverages, and provides them a relaxing ambiance;

the last thing Starbucks wants on people's minds is a price comparison. Perhaps surprisingly, without prices being listed on its menu, this café is rumored to be one of the chain's best-performing stores.

● ● ●

When altering prices, we are changing the trade-offs that people face. There are two types of trade-offs: real and perceived. A real trade-off is that when people spend more money on one thing, they have less money to buy other things. If our usual lunch spot raises prices by $3, we will have less money to spend for other things. Just as important, however, is the perceived trade-off. After the $3 price rise, does the usual lunch spot still offer good value? Or does it suddenly seem like a poor value? This perceived trade-off is the fuzzier side of pricing and it is something we can manipulate to our benefit.

Interestingly, we can view prices as snippets of information that affect people's decisions. How customers react to this information can be skewed by how they perceive it. As such, businesses have the ability to either obscure this pricing information or bring it to the forefront. And because information is digested imperfectly, they can help customers take it in through a manner that is more beneficial to them.

As an example, a trip to Disney World is expensive. If people realized the total price tag of a trip beforehand, they might choose not to go. To change people's perception, Disney World offers good deals on its admission tickets knowing that the tickets mask the hidden price of hotels and other expenses—such as food, drinks, and souvenirs. By presenting only a small part of the true expense, Disney is able to encourage people to choose it more often.

In addition, Disney World skews the perception of its ticket prices. If the theme park wants to sell tickets for $129 per day, it can set prices higher, such as $159, and then offer a $30 discount. This way, people perceive that they are getting a good deal. While this concept is basic, the lesson is that businesses have the ability to alter how people perceive prices.

This fuzzy attribute of pricing is known as the "price information impact." It represents the extent to which we want our customers to perceive our prices.

● ● ●

When lowering prices to gain market share, we want the price information impact to be high. The goal is to advertise prices as much as possible and force a price comparison each time a consumer makes a purchasing decision. Advertisements for McDonald's Dollar Menu and Subway's $5 subs are attempts to force a price comparison each time someone is deciding on where to grab a meal. A person might still eat at Wendy's or Burger King, but in the back of their mind, they are contemplating whether it is a good deal compared to what they could have gotten at McDonald's or Subway.

On the flip side, when businesses want to raise prices, the goal is to have the price information impact be as low as possible and to have prices fade into the background.

Coca-Cola is a master at raising prices because it has learned how to keep its price information impact low. For decades, the soft drink company has consistently raised prices with only minimal complaints from customers.

Coca-Cola drinkers would likely balk at price increases if they paid close attention to price per ounce. To reduce this possibility, Coca-

Cola has employed a clever mix of packaging sizes that make direct price comparisons between its products difficult. In a typical grocery store, a shopper can find Coca-Cola in twelve-pack 12-ounce cans, twenty-pack 12-ounce cans, eight-pack 8-ounce cans, six-pack 22-ounce bottles, and two-liter bottles. This variety of package sizes, container volumes, and even measurement units has made it difficult to calculate and pin down the price of Coca-Cola.

As such, Coca-Cola is able to roll out its price increases from one packaging size to another in a way that customers will barely take notice. These price hikes can also be timed with promotions to distract buyers from noticing what's going on. With this strategy, Coca-Cola has impressively been able to raise prices on customers with minimal backlash.

Another way of reducing price information impact is through bundling. While it is easy to compare the price per pound of strawberries, blueberries, and raspberries, it is far tougher to determine the relative value of a fruit cup. Baskets of goods create uncertainty in price perceptions as direct comparisons are less readily available. This is especially useful when the individual components of a basket can be priced high as it shifts customer reference points so that the bundles appear to be better value.

The Wall Street Journal, for example, sells its print subscriptions for $28.99 a month and digital subscriptions also for $28.99 a month. To receive both, it costs only $32.99.[6] While each component may be overpriced, does the bundle present a good deal? If we used the individual subscriptions as our reference point, the bundle is an exceptional value. By skewing price perceptions, the newspaper is able to squeeze a little more pricing power from its products.

Another tactic for reducing price information impact is to employ back-loaded pricing. This is similar to how Gillette sells its razor for a lower margin and then earns a tremendous margin on its disposable blades. The company reduces upfront prices while raising backend prices, thus skewing people's perception of the true price.

Even though the tactic of back-loaded pricing is not always a bad thing, some companies take it too far. Comcast is notorious for its use of it. The cable giant offers one- and two-year contracts with the first six months at a steep discount. While it heavily advertises its introductory rates, the fine print hides that prices dramatically shoot up after the introductory period. To many people's chagrin, they discover this only after they've been locked in.

And last, but not least, price information impact can be lessened by simply prepping customers for a price rise before it happens. Giving customers a heads-up can mentally prepare them for the increase. The purpose is to avoid abrupt changes that might force people to reevaluate their shopping habits.

When announcing price raises, it is good practice to attach a reason to the event. This softens the blow to consumers. People are generally reasonable and understand that prices have to go up; what they don't appreciate is the feeling of being taken advantage of. By providing a reason, we can frame how people interpret the price change. From a psychological standpoint, providing a reason is more important than the actual reason itself. People just need something to help them mentally justify the new price. It could be as simple as saying, "We are raising prices to continue providing the best service to our customers."

CHAPTER FOUR

TRANSFORMING STRATEGY INTO ACTION

I t is said that the distance between strategy and implementation is the middle of the ocean. Molding the world to fit a vision is not an easy endeavor.

To get past the paper stage of strategy, we need to become action-oriented. Fortunately, the Customer Moat Formula was designed with this in mind. There are eight tools at our disposal that help us widen our c-moats: the eight moat builders.

Thus far, the CMF has laid out *why* c-moats are important and *how* price allocates the rewards of our c-moats. The eight moat builders now provide us with concrete steps on how to go about widening c-moats.

The eight moat builder tools can be applied universally across all businesses regardless of industry or size. In fact, every business already employs some part of the toolkit—whether already realized or not. This is because all businesses fundamentally share the common goal of getting customers to choose them more often.

Oftentimes—as with my own family's business—the moat builders are applied in an intuitive, haphazard manner. While one might get lucky and hone in on one or two important factors, this trial-and-error approach can create uncertainty in the results. It leaves a lot of untapped potential on the table. To achieve greater success, it helps to use all the levers.

Naturally, different businesses will be exposed to different industry dynamics. How each chooses to use the moat builders will vary accordingly. Some industries will rely on a particular moat builder more heavily than others.

Regardless of industry, it is best to use each moat builder to the greatest extent possible. Remember, the goal is to have the widest c-moat and to create the greatest intrinsic loyalty; this means employing every tool at our disposal to get customers to choose us the most often.

● ● ●

Before moving on, it is useful to reiterate a point: "price" is not a component of our c-moats, but "cost" is most definitely a component.

Price affects customer behavior, but it is not a structural business advantage. As such, it is not a component of our c-moats. (There is a minor exception to this which will be discussed in this chapter.) In general, businesses have the freedom to set their prices at any level they desire; they can choose to sell a product for 10¢ or $10 billion. These prices themselves do not imply that one company is superior to another.

Costs, on the other hand, are definitely a structural business advantage and an integral component of our c-moats. Many factors go into widening a c-moat. Some of these include having higher customer satisfaction, stronger brand influence, and better location. One factor—which is hidden from customers—is cost. When a business lowers its cost of producing a product without diminishing its value, the business has fundamentally gained a competitive edge over its peers. Lower costs give companies a fundamental advantage in getting customers to choose them more often.

For the remainder of this book, "costs" refers to a business's expense of serving customers. The cost from a customer perspective is called "price."

THE BLUEPRINTS OF ACTION
Drafting a New Set of Tools

The eight moat builder tools originated during the early stages of this book's research. In deciphering the nature of how businesses earn money, I decided that rather than taking random stabs in the dark, I would adopt a more holistic approach. Using a brute force methodology, I combed through tens of thousands of pages of research and documented every business attribute or action that I came across. I compiled them into a master list and I began to categorize them according to similar traits.

With this list in hand, I knew that I had all the pieces of the puzzle. The million dollar question was, "How do I organize these elements into a single framework? And what was the invisible glue that connected the pieces together?"

The key discovery was that once I set aside the role of pricing and its related variables of market share and profit margin, I was left with a collection of actionable steps that various businesses had taken to increase their competitiveness.

These leftover variables not only fit a pattern of being actionable, but they were held together by a common theme: they affected the *probability of patronage* for a business. They shared a common goal of swaying purchasing outcomes in a *probabilistic manner*. And while somewhat counterintuitive for me at the time, I realized that the action of creating low costs is also a powerful method for affecting consumer buying decisions—albeit indirectly.

As I sorted these actionable variables into groups, I came to classify them into four broad categories: Operations, Scale, Positioning, and Industry Control. Combined, these OSPI (pronounced ah-spee) categories represent the building blocks of all business's c-moats.

OPERATIONS: The primary way for businesses to compete for loyalty is by providing value to customers. Operations represent how businesses effectively manage their three internal resources to create and deliver value. The three internal resources are workers, processes, and physical assets.

SCALE: Scale also involves providing value to customers. Scale differs from Operations in that value is derived externally from other customers and not from a business's three internal resources. For Scale, value is dependent on customers creating a benefit for other customers.

POSITIONING: Another way to increase intrinsic loyalty is by positioning a business closer to its customers—whether physically or emotionally. This involves geographically and mentally positioning a business to be central to a customer's life. (*While this moat builder is technically a hybrid of the other OSPI classifications, it becomes a more useful tool when we separate it out as its own category.*)

INDUSTRY CONTROL: The final way to create loyalty is by shaping the alternative choices available to customers. Industry Control is about reducing the competitive forces that vie for customers. This can be accomplished by either eliminating rivals or locking out rivals' access to customers. Industry Control actions will be highly regulated by governments as they attempt to control the playing field of competitors.

Combined, the four OSPI categories are a set of maps for describing different aspects of our business. Much how a street map, satellite map, terrain map, and population map each illustrate a unique geographical perspective, each category of OSPI sheds light on a different method for how businesses hold on to their customers.

DIGGING DEEPER, WIDER C-MOATS
Exploring the Eight Moat Builders

OSPI describes the types of actions that businesses can use to widen their c-moats. To convert these broad categories into action-oriented tools, each one has been split into two *moat builder* tools. The following is an overview of the eight tools.

TABLE 4.1 The Eight Moat Builder Tools

O	S	P	I
LOW COST	ECONOMY OF SCALE	LOCATION	SUPPLY
HIGH SATISFACTION	NETWORK EFFECT	BRANDING	DISTRIBUTION

OPERATIONS

The two tools of the Operations category are the Low Cost moat builder and the High Satisfaction moat builder. They both deliver value to customers through wielding the three internal resources of a business: workers, processes, and physical assets. The Operations moat builders utilize these three resources to innovate cheaper and better ways to meet customer needs. Each tool represents a different side of the value coin: while the first strives to minimize cost, the second works to maximize customer satisfaction.

MOAT BUILDER #1: LOW COST

The purpose of the Low Cost moat builder is to lower a business's cost structure without sacrificing customer satisfaction. This is done by improving the way we manage our internal resources.

As an example, Ikea, the world's largest furniture retailer, has been an industry leader in using this moat-builder technique. The company has used it operational prowess to construct functional, modernist furniture using inexpensive materials. To further lower costs, the company has constructed giant warehouse stores to minimize overhead expenses. Customers are asked to pick up their own purchases, which reduces the need for extra workers. The company also limits its furniture selection to bestsellers, which keeps inventory churning and storage costs lower. With its attention focused on low cost, Ikea has been able to sell furniture profitably while still maintaining low prices.

MOAT BUILDER #2: HIGH SATISFACTION

The goal of the High Satisfaction moat builder is to improve a customer's experience without significantly raising costs. Again, the three internal resources are used to achieve this.

Disney World is a champion in this field. The company has delivered an amazing experience to its theme park visitors at a price that is within reach. At the time of this writing, a four-day pass was $65 per day—an affordable amount even when taking into account the hidden expenses.[1] To deliver its grand experiences, the company has used its resources to create enjoyable interactions with highly trained staff, fun rides, and inspiring architecture. Every detail of a family's visit has been carefully planned. Disney World's hotels feature two peepholes for their doors, one for adults and one for children. The texture of the pavement changes as visitors pass through different sections of the theme park. And perhaps most impressively, the Disney World complex itself is built on top of a first-floor structure that conceals the mundane activities of trash collection, worker transport, and deliveries. In using its resources, Disney World treats its visitors to something that is truly magical.

SCALE

The two tools of the Scale category are the Economy of Scale moat builder and the Network Effect moat builder. Similar to the Operations moat builders, they deliver value by lowering cost and improving satisfaction. They differ in that the value originates from other customers, and not from a business's internal resources. With these two tools, customers are the ones creating a benefit for other customers.

MOAT BUILDER #3: ECONOMY OF SCALE

The Economy of Scale moat builder lowers the average cost of serving customers as more customers are served. This tool works when the expense of adding a new customer is lower than the current average expense of serving customers. Generally speaking, the larger the customer base, the lower the cost per customer.

An important distinction between the Economy of Scale moat builder and the generic term "economy of scale" is that this moat builder tool is about *adding customers* to lower cost, it is *not* about adding quantity to lower cost.

Intel, the computer chip manufacturer, relies heavily on the Economy of Scale moat builder to be successful. Producing a single CPU processor requires immense sums of money spent on design, engineering, and manufacturing. For the Pentium CPU, these expenses were estimated to run in the billions of dollars.[2] After the initial startup costs, the cost of producing an additional CPU chip is only a few dollars. As more customers purchase Intel's CPUs, the company is able to spread out its development and equipment expenses across its customer base. As such, billions of dollars of expenses can be shared across hundreds of millions of customers, and Intel can sell its CPUs for a few hundred dollars each while still being highly profitable.

MOAT BUILDER #4: NETWORK EFFECT

The Network Effect moat builder raises the average satisfaction of customers as more customers are served. In short, customers can often be used to increase the happiness of other customers.

Amazon employs this moat-building technique through its online product-review system. This massive database of customer-generated reviews has become one of the most significant draws for getting consumers to shop on its site. In actively fostering a community of helpful reviewers, Amazon has leveraged its customers to help other shoppers make more-informed purchases, thus improving outcomes. As Amazon's database of reviews has grown, a positive-feedback cycle has been created where the more that people shop on Amazon, the better a place Amazon becomes for shopping.

POSITIONING

The two tools of the Positioning category are the Location moat builder and the Branding moat builder. Their goal is to influence the probability that customers choose a business through a sense of physical and mental nearness. This works in two ways: through geography and branding.

MOAT BUILDER #5: LOCATION

The Location moat builder uses geography to affect people's buying decisions. When customers are physically closer to a business, the higher the probability they have for choosing it.

In the retail world, Walgreens has used this moat builder tool to position itself as a convenient place to buy basic goods and drugs. By offering multiple stores scattered throughout a region, Walgreens has become a quick and easy place to shop. While the company's prices are rarely the lowest, its convenience has helped the company become highly successful.

MOAT BUILDER #6: BRANDING

The Branding moat builder is about creating mental associations with consumers to affect their purchasing outcomes. Brands and reputations can act as powerful motivators in swaying customer decisions.

TAG Heuer, for example, has become a lifestyle brand that is coveted by some luxury shoppers. When it comes to telling time, there is no discernable difference between a TAG Heuer and a $10 quartz watch. TAG Heuer, however, has established a strong reputation for craftsmanship, style, and high social status. By reinforcing these mental associations, TAG Heuer has created a dedicated following. Customers who admire these attributes are more willing to buy its watches, even at higher prices.

INDUSTRY CONTROL

The two tools of the Industry Control category are the Supply moat builder and the Distribution moat builder. They increase a business's probability of being chosen by influencing the set of alternatives that are available to customers. This can occur in two ways: affecting the supply of competitors or altering the distribution pathways that lead to customers. When employing these two tools, caution is required; their usage will fall under government regulations. Some actions will be condoned—and perhaps even encouraged—while others will be considered illegal and anticompetitive.

MOAT BUILDER #7: SUPPLY

The Supply moat builder is a blunt but effective tool for increasing customer loyalty. It does so by eliminating the competition. If a business can get rid of its rivals (or reduce their desire to compete) then customers will choose it at a higher probability.

The pharmaceutical industry employs this moat-building technique legally every day. When pharmaceuticals attain patent rights on drugs, they are granted temporary monopolies by the United States Patent and Trademark Office. As such, drug companies can use their patents to prevent competition from eroding their market share or profit margin—at least for a few years.

MOAT BUILDER #8: DISTRIBUTION

The Distribution moat builder increases customer loyalty by making it difficult for competitors to access customers. This is accomplished by developing a pathway to customers that rivals cannot piggyback. The stronger the pathway, the more rivals can be excluded from reaching a business's customers.

Coca-Cola is highly regarded in this arena. The company has created a strong distribution platform by developing an extensive network of vending machines and soda fountain machines. These selling channels are exclusive to Coca-Cola's beverages and cannot be accessed by competitors. With these avenues in place, Coca-Cola has been able to keep competitors at bay and make it harder for them to create a foothold with customers.

ANALYZING GOOGLE'S STRATEGY
Eight Layers of Defense

Google serves as an excellent case study for showing how all eight moat builders can be used to create a very formidable strategy. In the highly competitive environment of the Internet, the technology company has managed to achieve phenomenal success.

During its start-up days, Google was rooted in a simple premise: search results on the web could be made more relevant if the value of web pages could be determined. To calculate a page's value, Google employed a novel approach of counting the number of external links referring to a particular page. The more links to it, the more valuable it was assumed to be, and the higher it ranked in search results.

Google's search engine quickly overtook the popularity of other web page portals, which were typically Internet directories curated by people. Google's automated algorithm provided people's queries with highly relevant answers from across the entire Web.

Since those early years, Google has continued to extend its dominance. Today, more than one billion unique visitors access its services each month, or roughly 14 percent of the world's population.[3] This figure is made more impressive by the fact that only 42 percent of the world's population has Internet access.[4] For the United States alone, Google provides more than 67 percent of Internet searches on PCs and 83 percent of searches on mobile devices.[5]

How did Google dominate this market so thoroughly? The eight moat builders will help us break down its strategy.

LOW COST MOAT BUILDER: Most people would not describe Google as a "low-cost" company, but the Internet giant is built upon a low-cost computing model. During Google's start-up days, cash was a scarce resource and the company fought to keep up with its growing computer demands. This shortage in resources was so severe that it would leave a lasting impression on the company's founders. To ensure that Google would never again face such limitations, the founders prioritized maximizing computing ability at the lowest possible cost.

Today, Google works to squeeze the greatest computing performance per dollar spent. Its server farms are often built in temperate climates where air conditioning is not required, and hence less electricity is needed. Locations are also chosen where electricity is abundant and cheap.

Server farms themselves are designed around mass-produced parts. Computers are typically bare-bone systems consisting of a motherboard, CPU, RAM, and hard drive attached to an inexpensive board and connected to a network. The backup power supply is a cheap car battery.

In one design, cargo ship containers are used to house a few hundred of these computers each. The containers serve as economical clusters of computing power. The hardware in them is hot-swappable, so when a computer breaks, it can simply be unplugged and replaced. Impressively, Google is able to manage a server farm of tens of thousands of computers using only a handful of employees.[6]

HIGH SATISFACTION MOAT BUILDER: In terms of high satisfaction, Google's greatest core competency is its ability to direct resources towards effective problem solving. Its goal is not only to organize all of the world's information, but to make that information universally accessible and useful. In working towards this end, Google has developed an array of tools: web search, book search, image search, video search and hosting, mapping, language translation, e-mail, and the list goes on.

Staying ahead of the curve in each of these arenas is not easy. To speed up the innovation process, Google often rushes beta versions of its products to market. The assumption is that the key to success is to get a product out, receive feedback, and then work as quickly as possible to improve it.

To encourage the flow of new ideas, the company has a policy to allow employees 20 percent of their time to pursue personal projects.[7] As a result of this, Google has the ability to harvest a wide breadth of ideas from its workforce while capably developing the most promising of them. Few businesses, even in the technology sector, have been able to match Google's pace of both innovation and execution.

ECONOMY OF SCALE MOAT BUILDER: Scale lies at the heart of Google's business model. Answering a single search query requires a staggering amount of technology. The entirety of the World Wide Web must be crawled through, indexed, ranked, and then sorted. Armies of algorithms have to sift through all the information before returning a single most relevant search result, and all within tenths of a second. While the infrastructure costs are enormous, when spread over trillions of searches, Google is able to lower its underlying cost per search to fractions of a penny. Google has leveraged the vastness of its customer base to keep costs low for users.

NETWORK EFFECT MOAT BUILDER: To create a network effect, Google leverages its customer base to improve the quality of its search results. The company tracks which keywords are used in searches and which results users click on. In doing so, as more people use Google to search, the better Google predicts which information they are looking for. Google has amassed the world's largest database of search queries, and as customers add more information to this database, the company is able to further improve its ability to serve customers.

LOCATION MOAT BUILDER: While the Internet is considered a virtual world, it is underlied by a tangible system of wires, cables, and switches. How fast Google provides search results is dependent upon the speed at which data travels over this network. To combat slowness and bottlenecks, Google strategically locates its data centers around the world to be physically closer to its users—it has literally shortened the distance between people and the data they are seeking. This has shaved off precious milliseconds of wait time. In a society where people increasingly expect instant responses, even split-second delays can negatively affect users' impressions.

Some of these latency issues have been cleverly bypassed by Google when it realized that users spend precious split-seconds of time deciding which link to click. To make use of this time, Google's Instant Search and Chrome web browser work together to preload popular search terms and results to web browsers as users are typing in their search queries.[8] This advanced level of predicting and pre-caching has significantly reduced people's web page load times.

BRANDING MOAT BUILDER: The holy grail of branding is to your company's name become synonymous to its product or service. Today, people don't just search for information; they "Google it." Google has become so ubiquitous with online search that in 2006 it was formally added to the dictionary.[9] With its powerful brand recognition, it is no surprise that many people mentally default to Google as their search engine of choice.

SUPPLY MOAT BUILDER: On the Internet, anyone can become a potential rival. To maintain its dominance, Google has systematically been paring down its field of potential competitors. By purchasing search-related players, the company has consolidated its position as the Internet's de facto search service. These purchases have included YouTube (video search), DoubleClick (search advertising), AdMob (mobile search advertising), IAC (flight search), Where 2 (map search), Zagat (restaurant review search), and many more. These additions not only bolster Google's offerings, but, importantly, they weed out potential future rivals.

DISTRIBUTION MOAT BUILDER: "Click and a user is gone." This is how Google likes to describe the Internet's competitive environment to regulators. While this might have been truer in Google's early days, the company has since developed channels to its customers that make it much harder for users to click elsewhere. With products such as Chrome (web browser), Android (mobile operating system), and Chromebook (computer), Google has distributed its services to consumers in a way that rivals cannot piggyback. These offerings anchor Google's services into people's lives and allow the company to keep its customers one more step away from its competitors.

In wielding the eight moat builder tools, Google has transformed itself into a juggernaut. Google has carved out a dominant stronghold in a highly competitive and rapidly changing field. While a rival can still make inroads against Google's customer base, it would likely involve an uphill battle against the giant on all eight fronts. Google has gained phenomenal success by having every one of its business decisions geared towards increasing the intrinsic probability that customers choose it.

THE PRICE C-MOAT PARADOX
Price's Influence on the Moat Builders

Which came first, the chicken or the egg? This age-old paradox similarly exists in business strategy. The difference is that instead of chickens and eggs, it's between c-moats and prices.

In chapter 3, "The Art of Price Setting," we discussed how c-moats create value for businesses and how price is the mechanism for capturing that value. It turns out that in some special situations, prices can also affect the strength of our c-moats.

Specifically, prices have a feedback effect on three of the moat builders: Economy of Scale, Network Effect, and Branding.

The first two, Economy of Scale and Network Effect, are Scale driven tools; this means that they use customers to benefit other customers. Lower prices can lead to greater market share, thus translating to a larger customer base and greater value creation (i.e., lower cost or higher satisfaction). In effect, this means that lower prices can lead to a stronger Economy of Scale and/or Network Effect. The amount of this benefit is highly dependent on how much market share can be gained.

The third moat builder affected by price is Branding. Specifically, this can be witnessed when we encounter the economic quandary of

Giffen goods—a situation where raising the price of a good leads to more sales. In most situations, raising prices reduces sales, but why can the opposite sometimes occur?

The reason is due to price's influence on the Branding moat builder. In select cases, higher prices can bolster a brand's image, leading it to greater overall market share. When this occurs, there are actually two forces at work. On one side, higher prices are creating a loss in market share; on the other side, higher prices are strengthening the brand's image, thus widening its c-moat and improving its market share.

When more market share is gained (from the Brand) than lost (from the price trade-off), a Giffen good will exist.

So when do Giffen goods occur? Typically, they show up when businesses need to correct an imbalance in how their brands are perceived. In the minds of customers, products and services should be within certain price bands. When prices fall below this normal range, a disconnect occurs that could potentially hurt sales.

For example, if a luxury designer sold its handbags at a 60 percent discount to its peers, people might question the brand's integrity, which would lead to lower sales. Adjusting prices to be inline with its peers would likely add confidence to the brand and improve sales.

In the same vein, if a convenience store sold tuna fish sandwiches for 49¢, most people would be wary of such a cheap item and highly suspect of its quality. If the store raised its sandwich price to $1.49, people would have less doubt. When prices are set too low, they can negatively impact a brand's image and perceived quality.

When a price disconnect occurs, the situation can be remedied by simply raising prices. Just remember that raising prices beyond the normal price band will not bolster sales; Giffen goods only exist to the extent that they correct a low-price imbalance. Once prices are raised beyond this imbalance, the higher prices will simply lead to the trade-off between market share and profit margin.

CUSTOMER MOAT FORMULA (PART 2 OF 3)
Attaching the Eight Moat Builders

We can now amend the Customer Moat Formula to include the eight moat builder tools.

The CMF takes us from the eight actions that widen c-moats to how c-moats provide us greater market share and/or higher profit margins. The two-way arrow represents the smaller feedback effect that prices can sometimes have on our c-moats.

FIGURE 4.2 CMF with the Eight Moat Builders and the Token-Bucket Method

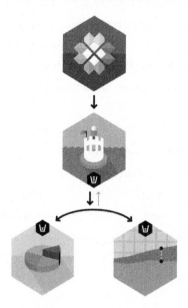

In Part II of this book, we will delve deeper into each moat builder tool and learn how to wield them. Then in Part III, we will wrap up the the Customer Moat Formula by introducing the final variable of *total market size*. This then completes the CMF as a model for understanding the origin of how our actions turn into profits.

Before we jump into Part II, there are a few useful tips to help us apply the eight moat builders more synergistically as a unified business strategy, rather than a piecemeal one.

TIP #1: Always concentrate on the intrinsic probability that customers are choosing a business. There might be limited control over a particular customer's purchasing decision, but the more important concern is to always increase the *likelihood* of being chosen.

TIP #2: High-pressure sales tactics may drive sales temporarily, but for companies to prosper in the long term, it is often better to foster repeat customers. It takes tremendous resources to convince new customers to try a business; keeping existing ones is usually more cost-effective. This follows the military advice, "Don't pay for the same territory twice." Once you gain a customer, make sure to keep them.

TIP #3: The purpose of the eight moat builder tools is to help businesses break their strategy into smaller, more manageable pieces. In rare instances, a company can utilize just one moat builder to become successful; for the vast majority, however, it is better to apply all the moat builder tools. By systematically implementing each tool to the greatest extent possible, we can position ourselves to be far more formidable forces. Each moat builder is like the leg of a stool—the more legs, the stronger the platform.

TIP #4: Observe how competitors are implementing the moat builder tools. Steve Jobs quoted Picasso by saying, "Good artists copy, great artists steal."[10] What Steve Jobs meant was that good companies copy the best practices of others, whereas great companies incorporate these best practices into their own system. We don't want to merely copy the best; we want to become the best.

TIP #5: Prioritize actions based on effectiveness. The Pareto rule is that 80 percent of the difference usually comes from 20 percent of the change; focus on the 20 percent of decisions that will have the greatest impact on the c-moat. As in baseball, the best way to improve the batting average is to swing at the easiest, fattest pitches. Once we hit all the easy decisions out of the ballpark, only then should we spend time working on the more difficult swings that require a little more skill and finesse.

PART II

THE EIGHT MOAT BUILDERS

———————— ◆ ————————

"In a corporation the role of a leader is often not to force the outcome, but to force execution."

ERIC E. SCHMIDT

CHAPTER FIVE

LOW COST (O)

The Low Cost moat builder uses
the three internal resources of a business
to reduce the cost of serving customers.

● ● ●

Chapter Overview: The Low Cost moat builder is about lowering cost in a business's operations. Improving cost efficiency can take many forms, from reducing waste through frugality to a much deeper attack on waste through rooting out poor processes. Cost efficiency can also be structurally embedded into workforces by creating incentive programs that promote controlling costs. In addition, a good business plan can lay the foundation for creating a low-cost business model.

n 1737, Benjamin Franklin quipped, "a penny saved is a penny earned."[1] He was giving advice in Poor Richard's Almanack to help people understand their personal finances. His point was simple: the path towards wealth accumulation is to spend less than what one earns. Regardless of a person's income level, this mathematical principle holds true for all those wanting to grow wealthier over time.

While Franklin's advice made great sense to individuals, what does it mean for our business? Should our businesses likewise strive to save pennies?

Of course the answer is a resounding *yes*. To put Franklin's advice into a proper business context, however, it helps if we can tack an amendment to it: "A penny saved is a penny earned, *and if desired, that savings can be passed on to customers through lower prices to gain greater market share.*"

● ● ●

The first weapon in our arsenal of tools is the Low Cost moat builder. It saves us money by eliminating waste and finding more effective ways to employ our resources. Importantly, these savings provide us the ability to offer greater value to our customers.

A business's operations consist of three components: its workers, processes, and physical assets. These are the building blocks of production. Our task is to answer, "How can we structure these three elements to become a low-cost provider of goods and services?"

Note: The goal is to become a "low-cost provider of goods and services," not necessarily a "low-price provider"—a very important distinction.

When using the Low Cost moat builder, there is one caveat: cost reductions should not be achieved in ways that erode customer satisfaction. It is counterproductive to lower costs if at the same time the cost savings drive customers away.

In 2007, Circuit City made this epic blunder. In the midst of ceding ground to rivals, the electronics retailer decided to recapture its competitiveness by embarking on a deep cost-cutting campaign. With a surprise announcement, the retailer issued immediate plans to lay off the top 9 percent of its highest-paid sales force.[2] The logic behind this action was that it saved the company the most money with the fewest layoffs.

From a customer's point of view, however, Circuit City had just fired all the workers best at answering technology questions and helping with purchases. Customer satisfaction and sales plummeted. While Circuit City achieved some cost savings, it also alienated a huge portion of its customers. Only a few months later, the company shuttered its doors.

When implementing the Low Cost moat builder, we need to remind ourselves not to cut costs at the expense of our customers. Instead, we need to cut costs to provide *more* to our customers. To do this, one question should always be kept in our mind: "How can we lower the cost of serving our customers without reducing their satisfaction?"

THE MINNOW THAT SWALLOWED THE WHALE
Waste Not, Want Not

The power of frugality is often vastly underrated. Each dollar that is wasted could have been a dollar added to the bottom line. Leaving lights on overnight, printing more pages than needed, buying equipment that doesn't get used–tiny expenses can add up to large unnecessary costs. Over time, these wasteful habits not only squander profits but can significantly reduce a business's competitiveness.

Developing a culture of frugality aligns organizations to be more cost-conscious. It is no coincidence that many of the world's most successful businesses–such as Costco, Wal-Mart, Amazon, and Berkshire Hathaway–were founded by penny-pinching personalities (respectively, James Sinegal, Sam Walton, Jeff Bezos, and Warren Buffett).

The power of frugalness is perhaps best exemplified by the story of Thomas Murphy, who in 1985 performed a remarkable feat in the television broadcasting industry. As CEO of Capital Cities Broadcasting (Cap Cities), Murphy announced from his thirty-person office located across from St. Patrick's Cathedral in New York that he was buying the American Broadcasting Company (ABC) for $3.5 billion in cash.[3]

The purchase of ABC was the largest deal in broadcasting history up to that date, and it marked the first time that one of the three major networks changed ownership. What made the purchase even more remarkable was that when Murphy joined Cap Cities thirty years prior, Cap Cities consisted of only one local UHF TV station in Albany, New York, and it was in the middle of bankruptcy.

In 1954, Murphy, who had just turned twenty-nine, ran into Frank Smith during a cocktail party. Smith was a friend of Murphy's dad and in a casual conversation told him, "I'm going into a little crapshoot in Albany, New York, and I'm looking for someone who would be a good salesman, and maybe a pretty good manager, to run a television station up there. Maybe you know someone who would be a good fit for the job?"[4]

After the party, Murphy ran through his list of friends and their qualifications when it dawned on him that perhaps Smith was actually offering him the job. Murphy had no previous experience in broadcasting but was nonetheless drawn to the idea of being in control of something. After consulting with his dad, he applied for the position and a week later became the new chief operating officer of Cap Cities.[5]

Smith wasn't lying when he described the television station as a crapshoot. The little UHF station was in the midst of bankruptcy reorganization, and as Smith put it, "We'll either make it or not make it in five years. If we make it, you'll be worth a quarter of a million dollars in five years; if not, you'll be young enough and you can go back to what you're doing and you'll have terrific experience."[6]

Those first years were tough but critical in shaping Murphy's views about money. Low costs were not a desire as much as a necessity. As such, Murphy kept the purse strings tight and ran the station with a skeleton crew. Even so, during his first year, Murphy lost $30,000.

Murphy went to the company's shareholders twice to ask for additional funding. By the end of his third year, he had burned through $1 million in additional capital, but he had finally stopped the financial bleeding. The station posted a $20,000 profit.

Reflecting on those early years, Murphy later commented, "We always ran the operation with a very limited number of people. We never had any more people than we absolutely needed . . . Over time, that barebone culture stayed with us."[7] Murphy had learned the value of a hard-earned dollar and he carried this lesson to all his endeavors. Any waste of money was considered a squandering of precious resources.

One legendary episode cemented Murphy's reputation as a penny pincher. At the Albany station, someone suggested that the building was in dire need of repainting; it looked far too shabby for the potential advertisers that drove up. Murphy agreed with the assessment, but instead of allowing the entire building to be repainted, he only approved funds for painting the two sides of the building that people would see.[8]

Fortunately, the broadcasting industry turned out to be decently profitable. Once a broadcasting station was properly set up, it required very little money for its upkeep. The industry was also insulated from competition due to government regulations. With the combination of a decent business model and Murphy's low-cost discipline, Cap Cities began accumulating its profits as excess cash.

As the fortunes of the Albany station improved, Murphy found a way to put this surplus capital to work. When he collected enough proceeds, he used it to purchase other poorly run stations. He then indoctrinated these stations with his low-cost philosophy, and eventually they, too, became cost-efficient and began churning out excess cash.

Since the Federal Communications Commission (FCC), the main regulatory agency of TV stations, held a five-station ownership limit, Murphy established a trend of selling his smaller, well-run stations to purchase larger, poorly-run ones. Once these larger stations were brought up to snuff, the process was repeated until Cap Cities owned one of the largest, most profitable collections of broadcast stations in the United States.

In 1985, when Murphy announced the purchase of ABC, Cap Cities was recording $940 million in revenue and $135 million in post-tax profits for its past year.[9] In contrast, ABC was four times larger than Cap Cities but only slightly more profitable. ABC had revenue of $3.71 billion and post-tax profits of only $195 million.[10]

Beneath ABC's bloated cost structure, Murphy saw a hidden gem. In a telling difference between the two operations, Cap Cities ran its Philadelphia station with less than half the employees of ABC's Chicago station.

When the purchase of ABC was announced, Wall Street was deeply skeptical of the outcome. How could Cap Cities gobble up a business that was four times larger than itself? Murphy, however, was confident that his strategy of frugality could be applied regardless of ABC's size. In Murphy's words, "I was told it would never work . . . but it worked; the minnow swallowed the whale."[11]

Ten years after the Cap Cities/ABC merger, the newly combined entity saw its earnings more than double to $729 million per year—and this was after Cap Cities was forced to shed some of its stations as part of FCC's merger approval. Impressed with the strong performance, The Walt Disney Company proposed to buy Cap Cities/ABC for

$19 billion.[12] When this deal was completed, original investors in Cap Cities reaped an investment return of 8,500 to 1. For those who purchased Cap Cities stock after it became publicly traded, they earned a return of 1,700 to 1.[13] The lesson of Murphy's legendary result is, "When it comes to resources, waste not, want not."

THE FIVE WHYS OF TOYOTA
Eliminating Waste at the Root Cause

While frugality is effective at reducing cost at the surface level, creating a truly world-class low-cost operation requires an even deeper attack on waste. The perception of waste should not only include unnecessary expenditures but poor businesses processes as well. In other words, bad workflows and ineffective systems should be considered forms of waste.

Think about a house painter who buys 20 percent more paint than is needed—this is an obvious form of waste where frugality can help. On a subtler level, however, waste can also occur when the painter does not know how to take fully take advantage of the paint. With bad techniques and processes, the painter might be using excessive paint or creating inconsistencies that need to be re-touched later on. These hidden inefficiencies are also forms of waste.

To our frustration, many of us experience this type of inefficiency in our daily lives when calling customer service centers. Sometimes during these calls, we will get redirected two or more times before reaching the right person who can help with our problems. In this situation, call centers are clearly mismanaging their resources. Each unnecessary transfer drains a business's resources while also lowering customer satisfaction; it is the epitome of how poor processes can destroy value.

Toyota has attained worldwide success by reducing this type of waste. The company strives to eliminate all process inefficiencies in its factories, and this led it to develop some of the world's most advanced manufacturing processes, such as Lean Manufacturing, Kaizen (a.k.a. continuous improvement), Just-in-Time, and the Toyota Production System.

Toyota's attack on waste took root in the 1930s when it adopted the operating philosophy of Taiichi Ohno, one of the company's most influential engineers. Born in 1912, Ohno began working for the Toyoda Spinning and Weaving Company at the age of twenty.[14] During his time in the textile industry, Ohno realized that Japan lagged far behind the rest of the industrialized nations in terms of productivity. The disparity was so large that it was estimated that foreign workers could out-produce their Japanese counterparts by nine to one.[15]

Ohno concluded that the ultimate cause for this discrepancy was waste. If waste could be reduced, it logically followed that a business's productivity must rise. For Ohno, reducing waste would be the key, but it would also only be the first step. If Japan truly wanted to compete on the world stage, Ohno believed that waste needed to be stamped out in all its forms.

Fujio Cho, an employee of Ohno's for fifteen years, recalled, "It was [Ohno's] creed that the top priority was to eliminate all waste, and by waste he meant anything that was unnecessary at that moment, be it goods or actions. He was trying to make himself hate any form of waste, and he thought when he became unable to find or detect any waste in his company it would be time for him to quit."[16]

In 1943, the Toyota Motor Company absorbed the Toyoda Spinning and Weaving Company, and with the transaction, Toyota inherited Ohno's vision for a waste-free future. Within the automaker, Ohno embarked on a campaign to eliminate all waste by addressing problems at their root causes.

Ohno's basic technique for problem solving was to ask "Why?" at least five times. This traced issues back to their source. If a machine broke down, he asked, "Why?" If the bearings got stuck, he asked, "Why?" If the bearings weren't being lubricated, he asked, "Why?" And so on, until an underlying cause could be discovered and solved once and for all.

While this problem-solving technique required intensive up-front effort, Ohno felt that the investment paid off in the long run. To him, it was more wasteful to battle the same symptom again and again when he could treat the disease.

On one occasion, Ohno assigned Nanpachi Hayashi, a newly hired worker, a problem to solve. The factory's paint shop was experiencing quality control issues with three out of ten units needing to be brought back for refinishes and touch-ups. On the shop floor, Hayashi noticed that workers were having a difficult time moving the defective car units back into the paint shop. He decided to attach a motor to the shop's conveyor system to increase its efficiency.[17]

When Ohno discovered this, he became furious. Ohno tore the motor off the conveyor and then made Hayashi move all the car bodies by himself for the remainder of the day. After the grueling experience, Hayashi was told that his responsibility was to, "create a system so that no failures occur; that no rejects will be made."[18] Instead of ensuring high quality, Hayashi had made it easier for poor-quality processes to persist.

The aspiration to be waste-free has pushed Toyota to innovate. In the mid-1960s, Toyota's Motomachi plant, which used giant contoured dies to manufacture auto parts, wanted to raise its production levels. The plant requested funds to build a new warehouse for holding the extra parts. Ohno was sent in to consult on the project. Upon arriving, he immediately refused the request. To Ohno, warehouses were used to store excess inventory, and excess inventory was a form of waste. Instead of granting the new warehouse, Ohno ordered the factory to cut its production batch sizes in half.[19]

At the Motomachi plant, workers spent two hours on average changing dies, and on larger production lines, this could run four to eight hours. Cutting batch sizes in half meant switching dies twice as often. Plant workers were soon frantically working overtime just to maintain production levels. They quickly realized that the only way to survive in this new environment was to shorten their die-changing times.

After six months of attacking the problem, factory workers figured out how to cut die changing times down to ten minutes. The result was a factory that not only produced more parts because less time was spent switching out dies, but it could manufacture parts in small batches almost on demand, which eliminated the need for an extra warehouse. In searching for ways to minimize waste, the plant's workers innovated a far more efficient production system.

Today, being waste-free is still core to Toyota's culture. Every worker at its factories has a responsibility to prevent any flaws from slipping through or persisting. The company's *andon* process gives each person the power to stop the production line by simply pulling a cord or pushing a button. When production is halted, teams are deployed to the problem site to find a lasting solution to the issue. With such a setup, Toyota has been able to refine its operations over the years and is now able to manufacture top-quality cars with minimal need to go back and fix them.

(Note: *Beginning in 2009, Toyota has faced headwinds in maintaining its high quality levels. These problems have largely stemmed from the company extending its manufacturing base into countries outside Japan where its factories have not yet established strong production cultures.*[20])

Toyota has been impressive in stamping out waste and process inefficiencies. In doing so, it has become the world's eleventh-largest company. In the 1940s, the label "Made in Japan" was synonymous with junk, and the country's cars were no exception. Under Ohno's tutelage and desire for a waste-free future, Toyota has transformed itself into a world-class competitor and, in 2008, attained the title of "world's largest automaker."[21]

THE "DEAL" WITH COSTCO
Rules for Low-Cost Cultures

How do we implant a desire within our workforces to care about low costs? Of course, as leaders, we can—and should—lead by example, but we should take things one step further by creating a culture that promotes low costs.

As the founder of Costco, James Sinegal has managed to do just that. During his time as CEO, he often toured Costco's many warehouse stores—he was reputed to visit up to twelve per day.[22]

On a typical walk-through, he receives feedback from store managers by barraging them with questions: What's new today? How are the in-stocks? What did we do in produce last week?

On one particular visit, Sinegal walked past a display of dress shirts, when he paused and doubled back to them. With a worried look, he wondered out loud, "I'm anxious to see how it does." The shirts were all Hathaway brand and they came in only one size, 34/35-inch sleeve. He then bent over and picked a piece of trash off the floor. Sinegal's hands-on approach has set the tone for the company and how workers stay connected to customers.[23]

Costco has become a retailing phenomenon. Its massive box stores hold a reputation for selling a selection of bulk goods at deep discounts: 1,875 Q-tips for $6.99, four pounds of jelly beans for $4, ninety ounces of Palmolive dish soap for $5.99, seventy-two frozen Eggo waffles for $8.09.[24] While the variety is not large, the quality is excellent and it is paired with extremely low prices. Even disciplined shoppers find it difficult to resist its temptations.

In the brick-and-mortar retailing environment, staying ahead of the curve is not easy. Competitors can quickly copy operational efficiencies, making advantages short-lived. Despite this arms race to efficiency, Costco has consistently remained ahead of its peers. Since its first store opening in 1983, Costco has grown to become the fifth-largest retailer in the United States. On a per-store basis, the company averages twice the revenue of its nearest competitor, Wal-Mart.

The driving force of Costco's success is more than just Sinegal's hands-on approach and great leadership. While he has been known to directly haggle with suppliers—he once called the CEO of Starbucks to demand lower prices when he noticed a fall in global coffee prices—he has also realized that the entire company needs to work together as a team if it wants to best serve customers.[25]

To create a culture of cost efficiency, Sinegal has baked a clever rule into Costco's operations: "No product can be marked up by more than 14 percent of its cost (15 percent for private label)."[26] This "low-markup rule" means that Costco can increase its earnings in only two ways: either reduce its operating cost or sell more goods.

To achieve the former, Costco tries to run a tight ship. The company keeps a lid on its expenses by having easy-to-maintain box stores, skylights to lower electricity costs, and wide industrial shelving to display goods cheaply.

The backend supply chain is similarly streamlined. Cashews, once packed in round containers, now come in square containers which has saved the company 560 truckloads of space.[27] When goods are delivered to a Costco location, truck drivers are handed restaurant-style pagers at the gate entrance. As such, trucks can dock and be unloaded, and then the pager goes off, signaling that the driver can take off again all without the driver needing to leave the cab. This time-saver is estimated to save $7 million in labor costs annually.[28]

To address the second way of increasing earnings—i.e., selling more goods—Costco knows that its success rests on finding the best deals for customers. Preferential pricing from suppliers is key to achieving this. While Costco does receive pricing leverage from its large-volume orders, to gain an even sharper negotiating edge, Costco has developed a way to turn the heat up with its private label brand, Kirkland Signature.

What makes Kirkland Signature special is that while typical private label brands are considered lower quality versions of their premium counterparts, Kirkland Signature emphasizes a level of quality that is almost on par with its branded rivals.

Case in point: Kirkland Signature beer. Sold in twenty-four-packs, this case of beer contains four varieties: German Style Lager, Pale Ale, Amber Ale, and Hefeweizen. In a blind taste test, Kirkland Signature beer was compared to its name-brand equivalents: Samuel Adams Boston Lager, Samuel Adams Boston Ale, Sierra Nevada Pale Ale, and Paulaner Hefe-Weizen. While the name-brand beers scored slightly higher as being a little more flavorful, clean, and complex in character, the Kirkland Signature beers held up quite well and were, for many tasters, a preferred choice. According to taste testers, the Kirkland Signature beers were very "party-worthy." The difference is that Kirkland Signature beer sold for $19 per case while the branded beers were priced around $35 per case.[29]

With such a strong house brand, Costco has placed enormous pressure on its suppliers to further lower their prices. According to vice president and CFO Richard Galanti, in categories where Kirkland Signature had been introduced, "It didn't take very long for the national and regional brands to come down [in price] because they were losing drastic market share."[30] Liquid soap dropped prices 6 to 10 percent. Plastic utensils dropped 12 percent. Branded water dropped 7 percent.[31]

The cleverness of the "low-markup rule" is that it has forced Costco to find ways to reduce operating costs and sell more to its customers. Perhaps its greatest achievement, however, is that it aligns the company's interests with those of its customers. For Costco to win, customers must win.

As we look to our own business, how do we create a desire in our workforce to care about low costs? How do we measure costs, incentivize workers to care about costs, and empower workers to innovate ways to reduce costs? Whether we use a combination of stock rewards, profit sharing, clever rules, or simply ask workers to track cost data, we want to have strong internal systems that create a culture of delivering the most value to our customers.

FLYING A SIMPLER ROUTE AT SOUTHWEST

A Game Plan for Low Costs

"We always do things this way." "It's just the way it has always been."
Have you ever asked a question and received these responses? If so,
alarm bells should be sounding off in your head. Resistance to new
ideas is a sure sign that times are ripe for change.

When reflecting on the stories in this chapter, a pattern emerges.
Thomas Murphy built his success in the broadcasting industry, a
sector which had accumulated decades of wasteful habits and bloated
costs. Toyota managed to leapfrog American automakers in part
because Detroit became paralyzed in maintaining a status quo within
its operations. And Costco achieved its success in a retail environment
that had become enamored with low prices rather than low prices for
high-quality goods. When industries get stuck in a rut doing the same
things the same way, it is a sign of great opportunity.

In 1971, Herb Kelleher saw a chance to shake up a sector that had
long become accustomed of doing the same things the same way:
the passenger airline industry. Kelleher founded Southwest Airlines
as a new type of carrier that could challenge tradition. With an
unorthodox way of operating, Southwest would go on to smash
industry records by achieving three and a half decades of consecutive

profitability–a feat previously unimaginable.

During Southwest's first thirty-eight years, the company lost money in two, 1971 and 1972–its two founding years. In 1992, Southwest was the only major U.S. carrier to earn a profit, and in 1993, it would be one of two.[32] The former CEO of American Airlines, Donald Carty, said this about Southwest: "Our major competition over the last fifteen years was other people doing the same thing we do. That's not the case anymore."[33]

As CEO, Kelleher has been as unconventional as his airline. One particular scene captures his essence perfectly. During a publicity event at a boxing arena, Kelleher was sitting at a table in the middle of the boxing ring. Across from him was seated the CEO of Stevens Aviation, a competitor. The two engaged in a spirited battle where the winner would receive exclusive rights to use the slogan, "Just plane smart."

The event deciding the outcome? An arm-wrestling match. To add to the fun, Kelleher had just turned sixty-one the week before and tried to win the match while smoking a cigarette with his other hand. In the end, Kelleher lost the contest, but the CEO of Stevens Aviation let Southwest use the slogan anyway; it turned out to be great PR for both companies.[34]

The business plan for Southwest Airlines took shape in 1966 during a conversation between Herb Kelleher and Rollin King. At first, Kelleher was skeptical of the King's proposal but eventually came around. King argued that the airline industry was grossly inefficient and pitched the idea of creating a new type of carrier. During their discussion, they concluded that a new airline could be successful if it achieved a basic task of "[getting] your passengers to their destinations when they want to get there, on time, at the lowest possible fares and [making] darn sure they have a good time doing it."[35]

The plan's guiding principle would be low costs. Airlines by nature have expensive cost structures: planes, airports, and crew. Operational logistics are also dauntingly complex. Most airlines at the time employed a "hub and spoke" system, where planes flew into one airport around the same time, passengers hopped onto connecting flights, and then the planes flew off again. On paper, this system seemed reasonable as it allowed passengers to get to their destination with only a short layover. In the real world, however, this system's implementation led to a nightmare of challenges.

The first problem was congestion. To efficiently get people to their connecting flights, all planes need to land and take off at roughly the same time. This meant traffic jams on runways and gates getting crammed to capacity during peak hours while the airport sat idle at other times.

The second issue was that if a small percentage of flights got delayed or canceled, the holdup could ripple throughout the system. A snowstorm in New York could cascade delays across the United States. If enough dominos fell, the entire system plunged into crisis.

With a blank slate to work from, Kelleher and King didn't need to cater to every demographic. They just needed their service to be fast, reliable, and cost-efficient for their particular customers. With this in mind, they decided that they could most benefit the niche market of those flying direct between major metropolitan areas. (Please refer to chapter 2 for more information on niche markets and segmentation.)

In serving this group, the first thing they could do was abandon the hub-and-spoke system. Flying nonstop routes between major cities held two important advantages. First, it ensured fuller planes because demand was already high on these routes. Second, customer satisfaction would rank higher as layovers could be eliminated.

The next decision was to operate mainly out of second-tier airports rather than the first-tier airports that were commonly used by major carriers. The passenger facility charge (PFC) at these secondary locations was up to 33 percent less than their top-tier counterparts.[36] Simply put, they were cheaper to fly out of, and as an added bonus, these airports tended to be closer to city centers and had less runway congestion.

Avoiding congestion and reducing delays would later play an important role for the company. It was discovered that if crews could implement a fast enough turnaround time on the ground (the time between arriving at a gate and departing from it), then a typical plane flying five or six routes a day could save enough time to squeeze in an additional flight or two.[37] This boosted revenue by 16 percent or more.

The last decision for keeping costs low would be unprecedented. The entire airline's fleet would operate only one model of aircraft—with the Boeing 737 eventually being chosen. While other carriers managed fleets of six or more types of planes, this new airline would have only a single model aircraft.

From a mechanic's perspective, the expertise and spare parts required to maintain one type of plane—as opposed to six—was vastly cheaper. From a pilot's view, each pilot could now fly every route and plane in the fleet. And from a customer's standpoint, if a plane was taken out of commission for any reason, another plane of exactly the same size and type could be seamlessly substituted. While Southwest potentially lost some bargaining power when purchasing new planes, the logistical benefits far outweighed the cost.

As revolutionary as Southwest's business model was to the industry, at its core, it was a common sense approach to achieving lower costs. By ignoring the status quo, Kelleher and King developed a better plan for serving customers from the ground up. The result was an airline that took the industry by storm.

Rivals have felt the impact of Southwest's low-cost strategy. When Southwest enters a new territory, airfares often fall by up to two-thirds. When routes began between the California cities of Oakland and Ontario, prices dropped 60 percent while traffic shot up threefold.[38] When flights opened up to Philadelphia, fares between Philly and Chicago dropped from $390 to $200.[39] For flights to Phoenix, a last-minute ticket plummeted from $1,180 to $299.[40] On average, flying into Boston became 40 percent cheaper.[41]

In running our own businesses, we must avoid a mentality of always doing things the same way. Andrew Grove famously wrote, "Only the paranoid survive." We must not be held back by past ways of doing things, and instead we must embrace change. Only through constant change can we increase the value that we deliver to customers.

The successful businesses of the future will hold a low-cost edge over their rivals. We need to envision what those businesses will look like and how they will disrupt the status quo. We should then work fast to become them before our competitors do the same.

CHAPTER SIX

HIGH SATISFACTION (O)

The High Satisfaction moat builder uses
the three internal resources of a business
to enhance the customer experience.

● ● ●

Chapter Overview: Customer experiences are a key driver of whether people decide to choose a business again. The bedrock of creating satisfying experiences is consistency. Unhappy interactions make it difficult to develop repeat customers; consistency's purpose is to prevent poor experiences from occurring. Once consistency is established, businesses can work towards raising the average level of customer satisfaction. This is accomplished by becoming a more effective problem solver, breaking down the barriers between customers and solutions, and going above and beyond in making each customer experience memorable.

Why do so many of us continue buying goods on Amazon, eating at Chipotle, and search using Google? We probably do so because we had good experiences with them in the past. Likewise, if we desire our own customers to continue returning, we must provide them with compelling reasons to do so.

The High Satisfaction moat builder is the second tool in our arsenal. It widens our c-moat by elevating the customer experience and increasing the probability that we get chosen.

The customer experience is more than any single product or service; it encompasses every point of interaction between a business and its customers. It is through this holistic experience that customers determine whether or not to return again.

Similar to the Low Cost moat builder, the High Satisfaction moat builder works to improve the effectiveness of a company's operational resources. This means structuring a business's workers, processes, and physical assets to maximize customer satisfaction.

That being said, higher quality experiences should not be attained through spending ever larger sums of money. If improving quality requires a significant bump in costs, then a business is not offering more value as much as it is offering a more expensive product. Products with high price points are fine, we just need to realize that value is what ultimately drives customer purchases.

To implement the High Satisfaction moat builder, we should ask, "How do we elevate the customer experience without substantially increasing our costs?"

COMING UP SHORT AT STARBUCKS

The Bitterness of Poor Quality

On February 26, 2008, Starbucks broke a cardinal rule of business, "Never send your customers into the arms of your competitors." But for three and a half hours, the company did just that. That Tuesday evening, all 7,100 Starbucks stores, with their 135,000 baristas, closed up shop and directed their customers elsewhere.[1] It was a bold move for a coffee chain that was struggling to survive.

Twenty years earlier, in 1987, Starbucks had skyrocketed to success by introducing European-style espresso drinks to the U.S. By the mid-1990s, the chain expanded to become a national presence. In the early 2000s, growth began to stall. To counteract the slowdown, management embarked on an ambitious plan to build more stores.

As management shifted its attention to adding new stores, customer satisfaction steadily eroded. By 2008, the slide finally caught up, and over the course of two years, Starbucks's earnings plummeted 96 percent. The company's stock price dropped 78 percent.[2]

Magazines that once heralded Starbucks as a poster child of success were all but pronouncing its demise. Articles came out with titles like "Coffee Jitters" and "Starbucks: The Decline of the Empire."[3] Starbucks fell into a deep crisis and a realization crept in that the company might not survive its downward trajectory.

In desperation, Starbucks called on Howard Schultz, the original founder of the company, to once again take helm of the company. Upon being re-handed the reins, Schultz realized that Starbucks had been coming up short with customers. In a leaked internal memo, he admitted that the company had lost much of its friendly mom-and-pop feel and that its cafés felt more like sterile chain stores.[4] Pushing for sales had taken priority at a sacrifice to quality and friendliness.

The decision by Schultz to temporarily close the entire chain was his way of getting back to basics. Exceptional customer experience has always been one of Starbucks' most important differentiators.

During the closures, employees were retrained in the basics of quality and service. Baristas practiced pulling espresso shots and were quizzed, "How did the shot turn out? Was it too long? Was it too short? Was the color correct?" Bad espresso drinks were created so workers could try the difference for themselves.[5] One executive explained, "The machine is really a tool . . . ultimately the barista is still the artist."[6] To maintain quality customer experiences, Starbucks needed good artists.

The Starbucks experience began with its beverages, but other details were just as important, such as the coffee's smell. To preserve the aroma, workers were trained on how to properly open bags of coffee beans, the value of keeping food covered, and to avoid wearing perfume that might interfere with the aroma experience.[7]

To promote positive interactions with customers, the company created a board game depicting different customer scenarios. The purpose of the game was to teach employees how to empathize with various customer moods. The payoff was that sometimes a Starbucks employee could understand a person's mood and then offer a product that could help make their day a little better. If the company gained a sale while making customers a little happier, it was a win-win situation.[8]

Of course, the temporary store closures came at a cost. Dunkin' Donuts and Caribou Coffee experienced a spike in their sales, and Starbucks sacrificed an estimated $4 million in revenue.[9] But Schultz believed that the timeout was a critical reaffirmation—to both employees and the public—that Starbucks was committed to providing the best customer experience.

The renewed focus on customer experience has led to tangible results. In 2008, a rather rough year for the company, Starbucks announced closures of six hundred underperforming stores, same-store sales declined 3 percent, and net earnings fell 53 percent (from $673 million to $315 million). From 2010 to 2012, Starbucks rebounded with full force. The company was able to add two thousand new stores, same-store sales grew an average of 7.5 percent annually, and earnings reached a record $1.38 billion in 2012.[10]

In 2009, as Starbucks put behind its darkest chapter in history, Schultz wrote in the company's annual report, "I would like to offer my heartfelt thanks to everyone who touches Starbucks. To our people, who stepped up to the challenge of delivering an exceptional customer experience, to the farmers and suppliers who grow our coffee, to our business partners around the world, to our shareholders for their continued support, and ultimately to our customers—for inviting us into their lives and for giving us the opportunity to earn their loyalty and trust every day."[11] The company's turnaround was a team effort, but Schultz understood that it was ultimately the customers' trust and loyalty that determined its success.

"THE CUSTOMER IS ALWAYS RIGHT"
Consistency as the Bedrock of Satisfaction

How do we create highly satisfying experiences for our customers? The first step is to create consistency within our operations. While consistency won't improve the average customer experience per se, it still does something important: it reduces the rate of poor experiences.

According to the White House Office of Consumer Affairs and 1st Financial Training Services, when customers receive rude or discourteous treatment, 96 percent of them will not complain to the offending business. Of these dissatisfied people, 91 percent will choose not return. On top of this, each one will go on to share their poor experience story with nine to fifteen other people.[12]

The lesson is chilling: bad experiences not only permanently lose existing customers, but they potentially lose future customers as well.

The following illustrates why poor experiences are so detrimental. Imagine a popcorn stand located inside a movie theater. The stand gives moviegoers a satisfactory snacking experience 85 percent of the time; the other 15 percent of the time, the popcorn is stale and unsatisfactory. While the majority of moviegoers are satisfied, the 15 percent of dissatisfied customers becomes a growing concern. They are unlikely to purchase popcorn again in the future.

Over time, as the population of moviegoers cycles through the theater, the percentage of customers willing to buy popcorn shrinks. With a 15 percent attrition rate, the original 100 percent of people who buy popcorn will dwindle to 85 percent, then to 72 percent, then 61 percent, and so on.

If our strategic goal is to increase the rate at which customers choose our business, then poor customer experiences pose serious headwinds. We should weed out poor experiences and prevent them from happening.

The growing clout of the Internet has increased the power of customers to voice their dissatisfaction. Review sites, blogs, and social media allow customers to not only tell nine or fifteen people but to share their poor experiences with the whole world.

In 2014, a bad customer interaction was recorded on audio when a customer tried to quit Comcast's services. The conversation was posted online and went viral. The damage created by the publicity was so extensive and swift that, to prevent further fallout, the company's senior vice-president was forced to apologize directly to the customer.[13]

Ideally, we should always strive to provide satisfying experiences to 100 percent of our customers all the time. While this goal might not be fully achievable, it will ensure that we do our best not to let anyone fall through the cracks. We should never give customers a good reason to prefer our competitors.

This brings us to the phrase, "The customer is always right." Logically, common sense tells us that the customer is not always right. What is missing from the phrase, however, is that it actually refers to a customer's feelings. A person's feelings will always be the absolute truth, and it will be reflective of their experiences. Importantly, these feelings are what impact a person's future purchases. As such, the focus is not whether a customer is right or wrong; it is whether a customer *feels* like they are being taken care of.

● ● ●

Consistency takes great effort to achieve. We can simply imagine the difficulty of preparing the exact same-tasting meal twice. Even when we follow the same recipe, use the same ingredients, and work with the same equipment, our results will rarely be identical.

When it comes to this difficult task of preparing food, McDonald's has strived to be at the forefront of delivering a consistent, dependable meal—regardless of whether people are eating in a restaurant or on-the-go, during rush hours or during off-peak times, or in the United States or Japan.

Consistency is core to McDonald's culture as well as its success. As mentioned in previous chapters, the company's food does not often win awards in the taste category; what the company does excel at is being consistent at creating a good customer experience.

This quest for consistency is perhaps nowhere as apparent than with its star product—french fries. Delicious french fries are a hallmark of the McDonald's experience. Ray Kroc, who was the CEO and driving force behind the chain, put it this way: "A competitor could buy the same kind of hamburger we did, and we wouldn't have anything to show. But the french fries gave us identity and exclusiveness because you couldn't buy french fries anywhere to compete with ours. You could tell the results of the tender loving care."[14]

In the 1950s, McDonald's began its research on how to cook a consistent-tasting french fry. During those days, cooking fries was a rather unpredictable process. Batches were tossed into frying oil, and sometimes they turned out perfectly while at other times randomly undercooked on the inside. There was no way to tell until they were eaten. Over the next decade, McDonald's would spend more than $3 million (roughly $24 million today) trying to invent a better french fry.[15]

Early research pointed to the deep fryers as the problem. When bags of cold potatoes were dropped in, the oil temperature of different fryers recovered at different rates. This inability to control cooking temperature created wide variations in the final product. Fred Turner, who was responsible for quality at McDonald's, recalled with some chagrin, "I found myself carrying a damn thermometer with me on all my store visits to calibrate the temperature of their fry vats."[16]

Even when fryers were optimally calibrated, different batches still led to different results. This was despite using the same equipment, the same temperature settings, and even potatoes sourced from the same supplier.

The company stumbled upon its first big breakthrough when someone discovered that potatoes sitting in the basement made better-tasting fries than those cooked right after delivery. It turned out that sugar content of potatoes played a key role in how they cook. If the sugar content was too high, fries would brown on the outside before cooking on the inside. By storing potatoes in a cool room, some of these sugars were allowed to burn off (i.e., to be "consumed" by the potato), ensuring that fries turned golden brown only after being completely cooked.

The second breakthrough was learning that a potato's *solid content* (i.e., the ratio of solids to liquids) affected a fry's crispiness. As solid content varied, so did texture. This discovery took place in a time when french fries accounted for less than 5 percent of the potato crop—versus 35 percent today.[17] Most potato farmers had not even heard of the term "solid content." The idea was so novel that McDonald's had to visit each of its farmers to convince them of its importance while teaching them how to measure it using hydrometers.

Then, in the late 1950s, Louis Martin, an experimenter at McDonald's, solved the elusive cooking problem that plagued so many bad batches of fries.[18] After years of experimentation, he noticed one day that when cold fries were put in the fryer, the oil temperature dropped by an amount depending on the quantity and temperature of the cold fries. What Martin discovered was that when the oil temperature rose three degrees above the lowest point reached, he ended up with a perfect batch of fries each and every time. For an incredibly elusive problem, the answer turned out to be ingeniously simple. Soon afterwards, McDonald's installed temperature gauges with alarm settings on all its fryers.

Perfecting french fries was undoubtedly a daunting task, but it has been integral to the McDonald's experience. While the company continues to refine its recipe, it is the relentless pursuit of keeping every customer visit a happy one that entices people to keep returning. Today, McDonald's sells over three billion servings of french fries annually—definitely no small potatoes.[19]

● ● ●

Beyond our products, consistency should permeate our services as well. In the same way that Costco embedded a low cost culture into its operations, we want to instill processes and incentives that promote a high level of customer satisfaction.

Home Depot has a great story from its formative growth years, and how it developed a system that delivered high-quality service.

In 1979, Home Depot opened its first two stores in the Atlanta metropolitan area. The premise was that a large one-stop shop could offer better convenience to customers. With this setup, construction workers and do-it-yourselfers could eliminate the hassle of hopping from one specialized retailer to another (i.e., separate lumber stores, hardware stores, plumbing stores, electrical supply stores, etc.).

Besides convenience, Home Depot also offered affordable prices and outstanding customer service. The customer service philosophy of its founders was, "Whatever it takes." They personally delivered this guarantee by walking through their stores and talking with customers.[20]

The stores became a huge hit, and soon Home Depot expanded to more locations. As the company grew larger, its quality of customer service began to falter. Once the ninth and tenth stores opened, the practice of walking through each store became less feasible; the founders had spread themselves thin and the decline in quality showed.

To regain a high level of customer satisfaction, the founders came up with a ingenious solution. At the entrance of each Home Depot store, they placed a sandwich board that displayed the message, "Are you satisfied? If not, contact the store managers, _____ , or call me, Ben Hill, director of consumer affairs, at 800-553-3199."[21]

The brilliant thing about Ben Hill was that he was not a real person. Instead, "Ben Hill" was a code word within the head office. Everyone understood that calls for Ben Hill were actually customers calling in with a complaint.

The policy was to expedite these calls to the highest-ranking person in the office at that moment. No matter what the person was in the middle of doing, it was their personal responsibility to handle the call. The founders adhered to this rule so strictly that it didn't matter if they were about to sign a multi-million-dollar deal; the priority was to first take the call and resolve the customer's problem.[22]

Ben Hill was instrumental in delivering exceptional customer service in two aspects. First, when unhappy customers called, the head office could immediately know about the issue and take care of it. It served as a direct line to upper management; no layers of managers or bureaucracy stood between customers and solutions. If a product was out of stock or there was a delivery issue, the head office could immediately direct the resources necessary to resolve the problem.

Second, Ben Hill motivated store managers to provide the best possible experience for customers. If a store manager failed to deliver good service, the outcome would be numerous phone calls to Ben Hill. The last thing a store manager would want is to have their boss receiving a large number of complaints.

Ben Hill serves as a model for how systems can promote consistent, excellent service. Great experiences are built on developing processes that support them. For Home Depot, a little ingenuity, a few sandwich boards, and a telephone line has made all the difference in the world. What are we able to do to instill great service within our companies?

BEHIND TOYOTA'S
PROBLEM-SOLVING WHEEL
Putting Yourself in Customers' Shoes

Once a foundation of consistency has been laid, businesses can move to the more primary function of helping people solve their problems. The better a business becomes at this task, the greater its importance.

Customer problems exist in a variety of shapes and sizes. When a person buys a kitchen appliance, are they looking for functional cooking equipment or do they desire a way to personalize the look of their kitchen? When a person visits a coffee shop, are they searching for a beverage to keep them awake or do they desire a temporary escape from the office?

People face a wide range of issues and before trying to solve these problems, the first task is to know which ones are worth solving. In other words, how do we prioritize our efforts?

The main tool at our disposal is empathy. The best way to know what our customers care about is to walk in their shoes.

In 2000, Yuji Yokoya, one of Toyota's engineers, was handed the monumental challenge of turning around the fortunes of the Sienna minivan. Three years earlier, Toyota had introduced the Sienna to the

North American market, but sales failed to take off and since its launch were steadily declining. The public's impression was that the van was small, underpowered, and uncomfortable. Yokoya's job was to redesign the van.[23]

Upon accepting the task, Yokoya decided to bypass the usual focus groups, marketing analysts, and number crunchers.[24] Instead, he wanted to get to the heart of Sienna's driving experience. He did so by personally embarking on a fifty-three-thousand-mile road trip—equivalent to four times the distances between the North and South Poles. On this journey, Yokoya would pass through every state in the United States, every province in Canada, and every *estado* in Mexico.[25]

It took only thirty minutes into his trip when Yokoya realized that the driver seat was uncomfortable. Seats are the initial feel of a vehicle and an integral part of the driving experience—especially for a vehicle geared towards long road trips. Yokoya decided that in the van's redesign, it needed to have the most comfortable seats of its peers. Money would not be a limiting factor even if he had to cut costs in other areas. Sienna's seats would not only be the best in class but they would accommodate a wider range of body types.[26]

Updates to the passenger seats were also in order. On the road, Yokoya witnessed families on road trips becoming practically buried under their luggage. To alleviate this issue, the new van would feature additional room and a flexible seating arrangement. The van's width increased by 4 inches and its length by 5.9 inches.[27] Two basic seating options were introduced: a seven-passenger setup and an eight-passenger setup. The difference between the two versions was whether the center row featured two or three seats.[28]

To create versatility, all center- and back-row seats could be removed so that the interior layout could be customized to fit each individual's needs. To further increase the number of possible configurations, the back row offered a 60/40 split. One thoughtful feature of the eight-passenger setup was the ability to shift the center seat of the middle row forward by thirteen inches; this gave adults in the front better access to infants while on the road.[29]

As his journey progressed, Yokoya experienced many little nuances that drivers face. While crossing the Mississippi River into Memphis, Tennessee, crosswinds on the bridge were so intense that they pushed the vehicle into the next lane. The redesign would feature improved side-wind stability, smaller gaps between parts, and plastic shielding in wheel wells to redirect air. In Santa Fe, California, parallel parking was such a nightmare that the turning diameter of the van would be reduced by three feet. In Mexico, the sun beat down so harshly that sunshades would be standard in addition to the normal privacy glass.[30]

While driving along the Alaska Highway, which is mostly gravel, Yokoya found the noise level so high that it was nearly impossible to hold a conversation. For the redesign, cabin noise would be drastically reduced by adding more padded surfaces and sound-absorbing foam. In an innovation, the carpet would be engineered to have tiny holes that absorb certain frequencies while allowing others to dissipate.[31]

Back in New York City, the combination of bumper-to-bumper traffic and bad drivers resulted in a massive number of dents. To handle the abuse, Sienna's bumpers were strengthened to withstand a five-mile-per-hour impact, twice the industry standard.

Beyond these improvements, Yokoya also offered a few customizable options: an entertainment center for those with kids, all-wheel drive for those living in steeper terrain, and upgraded wood and leather trim for those wanting a more luxurious feel.

With the multitude of improvements, Yokoya's redesigned Sienna went on to become the best-selling minivan of its class. In 2002, the older Sienna model sold 80,915 units. In 2004, the first full year of sales for the new Sienna, sales soared to 159,119.[32] While Yokoya proved to be a strong problem solver, his great achievement to empathize with customers enough to know which problems were worth solving.

● ● ●

In putting ourselves in customers' shoes, we should also become aware of any roadblocks between them and the solution. For the Sienna minivan, the challenge might not be the van's design but how customers finance its purchase. As such, dealerships can boost sales by offering a wider range of financing options as well as educating customers on the full trade-in value of their current vehicle.

In its earlier days, Wal-Mart overcame an important roadblock that discouraged many people from buying its merchandise. The problem was that the retailer was known for its low prices, but its cheap prices were also associated with low quality. To prevent this negative perception from interfering with sales, Wal-Mart instituted one of the first 100 percent money-back satisfaction guarantees. This was instrumental in allowing customers to focus on Wal-Mart's low prices rather than needing to worry about being stuck with poor-quality purchases.

In 1992, Gillette discovered a surprising roadblock as it was about to launch a new razor system geared towards females: Gillette Sensor for

Women. Before the product's launch, Gillette analyzed the behavior differences between men and women while shaving—and the results turned out to be significant.

In the study, Gillette discovered that men who cut themselves tended to blame the blade, but women who cut themselves were more likely to blame themselves.[33]

During a press conference, Gillette released its findings to the public. The reaction was a burst of laughter from both men and women in the audience. They found it funny as to how overly serious and over the top Gillette seemed to take the simple task of shaving. For Gillette, however, the findings uncovered a real problem. The implication was that women might not replace their razor blades as often as men, and as a result, they would receive subpar shaving experiences.

To address this issue, Gillette funneled money into a marketing campaign that was coordinated with the product's launch to get women to replace blades more frequently. After eighteen months on the market, Gillette Sensor for Women became an official blockbuster by selling nearly as well as the men's version. Impressively, the razor reached nearly 10 percent of the U.S. female population.

When it comes to effective problem solving, we can keep in mind Alan Kay's sage advice, "Perspective is worth 80 IQ points." The more we can empathize with our customers and the more time we can spend in their shoes, the better we can become at solving their problems.

EASTER EGGS

The Details of Great Experiences

So far, consistency showed us how to weed out poor experiences, and empathy showed us how to become effective problem solvers. How do we take things one step further to make customers' experiences truly remarkable? What is it about some companies that make us want to stick with them and keep us desiring to return?

The common thread is that these companies probably did something to delight us beyond our expectations. Whether it is a mint placed on our pillow, a large selection of mustards at a hot dog stand, or a free car wash after an oil change, experiences can be greatly enhanced when we receive something both appreciated and out of the ordinary.

To elevate customer experiences above and beyond, we can use the "Easter egg" approach to create small surprises that impress people.

Easter eggs are small details or bonuses that provide a wow effect. They can be anything a customer discovers to their delight, such as Google's doodles, Disney hotels' second peepholes for children, or Five Guys' free peanuts while waiting.

A popular lunch spot in Chicago is Potbelly Sandwich Works, which is known for its toasted subs. Among its best-selling products are its milkshakes, which feature a fun Easter egg. When customers order a milkshake, they receive it in a typical to-go cup with a lid and straw. To make the shake stand out, Potbelly slips a small flower-shaped shortbread cookie around the straw. While this cookie costs a few pennies at most, it helps transform an ordinary drink into a memorable treat.

A real estate salesperson has also found a novel way to increase the satisfaction that families get when purchasing a new house. When all is said and done, she knows that people aren't buying a house as much as they are buying a home. So after each sale, she gathers together with the family and plants a small tree in the backyard. This way, as the tree grows, the family grows—it is a powerful symbolic gesture. While the family might not need another house for many years, they are highly likely to refer this salesperson to others because of their positive experience.

Easter eggs also play increasingly critical roles in the success of digital businesses. In Xbox's *Halo* video game series, what makes the single-player mode so much fun is not just the gaming action but the Easter eggs nestled throughout the virtual world. *Halo 4* features voice cameos by Conan O'Brien, hidden radios that play the theme song to *Red vs. Blue* (a popular TV-show parody of *Halo*), and skulls that, when discovered, unlock game features. As players explore the game's different levels, they are treated to fun surprises along the way.[34]

One of the greatest executions of Easter eggs comes from Amazon's early days. In 2001, when the company was still in its infancy, the postage rate of first-class stamps increased from 33¢ to 34¢. In a memorable move, founder Jeff Bezos included a set of ten 1¢ stamps with every shipment.

In a letter attached to the stamps, Bezos wrote, "We can't wash your dishes. We can't pick up your dry cleaning. We can't change the light bulb in your refrigerator. We can't make your tuna salad just the way you like it. Then I realized there was one thing we could do that we've never done before—spare you the hassle of an extra trip to the post office! Sure, we're only talking 10¢ in value, but hopefully the time you'll save will be worth much more."[35] After receiving a letter like this, how likely would you shop again at Amazon?

The conventional wisdom is, "Don't sweat the small stuff." In business, our job is to do the opposite; we want to pay attention to every detail. Customers will be more loyal to those companies that strive to improve the details of their experiences. Just consider Apple's products. While Apple's devices do not consistently lead in terms of speed, processing power, or capacity, Apple has still managed to outshine the competition because it is willing to nitpick over every tiny user detail. The result is a far smoother and more rewarding customer experience.

When creating Easter Eggs, we want to provide small wow effects that impress customers. Try to make these experiences as memorable as possible and remember the motto: "A good business solves customer needs; a great one surpasses their expectations."

CHAPTER SEVEN

ECONOMY OF SCALE (S)

The Economy of Scale moat builder
leverages customers to provide
a low-cost benefit to other customers.

● ● ●

Chapter Overview: Since the Industrial Revolution of the 1700s, Economy of Scale (EoS) has transformed the landscape of production in our society. It has exponentially lowered the cost of bringing goods and services to market. EoS has been a powerful tool for lowering costs, but it also has a lot to be desired when used as a business strategy; its use has been associated with three dangerous pitfalls. To avoid these pitfalls, this chapter shows us how to wield EoS as a customer-driven tool rather than a quantity-driven tool. Additionally, two techniques are introduced to help us better implement and know when to implement EoS. And lastly, as our society shifts towards an information economy, we will examine the role that EoS is playing in the Digital era.

Before delving into the specifics of the Economy of Scale moat builder, it helps to overview the difference between the two Operation moat builders (Low Cost and High Satisfaction) and the two Scale moat builders (Economy of Scale and Network Effect).

While the Operations moat builders employ a company's internal resources (i.e., workers, processes, and physical assets) to create value for customers, the Scale moat builders leverage a company's customer base to improve the value provided to other customers. In simple terms, the former is independent of what happens to the customer base, whereas the latter is directly dependent on it.

As a newspaper company, *The New York Times* relies on both Operations and Scale moat builders. On the Operations side, internal resources are used to produce well-written, compelling articles that enhance reader engagement and loyalty. On the Scale side, as more people subscribe to the paper, its larger customer base allows it to lower the average cost to each reader (i.e., production expenses are spread out among more people). In this way, for only $2, anyone can pick up *The New York Times* newspaper and read up on hundreds of thousands of dollars' worth of reporting.

The two Scale moat builders are Economy of Scale and Network Effect; they work respectively to lower cost and increase customer satisfaction. Their effectiveness *scales* with the size and composition of the customer base.

The table on the following page overviews the difference between the Operations and Scale moat builders.

TABLE 7.1 The Operations and Scale Moat Builders

	OPERATIONS *Is Independent of Customer Base*	SCALE *Is Dependent on Customer Base*
COST EDGE	Low Cost moat builder	Economy of Scale moat builder
SATISFACTION EDGE	High Satisfaction moat builder	Network Effect moat builder

The rest of this chapter is dedicated to the Economy of Scale moat builder, and the next chapter will explore the Network Effect moat builder.

● ● ●

The Economy of Scale moat builder is a powerful tool for lowering costs. The caveat is that when misused, it can act as a double-edged sword. Because EoS's advantage scales with the size of a customer base, it also tends to magnify our mistakes.

The challenge can be likened to captaining a small ship and then switching to pilot a much larger vessel. While the larger vessel is more efficient at ferrying goods and people, navigating obstacles becomes more difficult. The greater momentum reduces maneuverability, and this reduced nimbleness reduces room for error. When upgraded to larger ships, we should be wary that if we don't steer carefully, we risk becoming the next Titanic.

Even with the potential downside, EoS is an essential tool for lowering costs and should be implemented across all businesses—albeit with great care.

So how does EoS work? It acts to lower the average cost of serving customers as more customers are served. This reduction comes from increased efficiency (e.g., division of labor), the ability to spread out fixed costs, and being able to source supplies at greater discounts.

A basic example of EoS can be found in our home kitchens. When preparing dinner, it is more efficient to cook four servings rather than one. When larger quantities are involved, we can prep more efficiently, use our fixed assets better (such as pots and pans, oven, and stove), and buy ingredients at cheaper bulk prices. All this helps us to lower the cost per serving.

So, what would be the hidden icebergs of this scenario? The danger is when we end up overproducing—a problem that increases our average cost per serving.

In the kitchen, we might be fixated on achieving a lower cost per serving, but to realize the savings, we need to eat most of what we cook. If we prepare too much food and discard the leftovers, we inadvertently raise the average cost per serving—the opposite of what we are trying to achieve.

In the business world, overproduction is a real threat and can lead to massive losses. For many industries, profit margins hover in the 3 to 10 percent range; if our kitchens represented businesses in these industries, a mere 10 percent of food waste could be enough to turn a profitable enterprise into a money-losing one.

When employing the EoS moat builder, it is essential to keep our eye on the real target. The winner is not the one who reduces *per-unit* cost; it is the one who reduces *per-customer* cost. When focusing too much on *per-unit* cost, we can easily fall into a state of overproduction that negatively impacts customers.

When implementing EoS, the question we want to pose is, "How do we add customers in a way that reduces our average cost of serving them?"

FROM PIN FACTORIES TO EXPERIENCE CURVES
A Short History of Economy of Scale

In 1776, economist Adam Smith wrote the most famous example of EoS in his book *The Wealth of Nations*. As the United States was experimenting with its new political system, across the Atlantic, England was engaged in its own revolutionary struggle. Britain's economy was in a state of upheaval as new methods of production were tearing away at its social fabric.

The invention of the steam engine and large-scale manufacturing quickly altered the economic landscape. In a few short years, productivity didn't just triple or quadruple but increased by factors of hundreds to thousands. Factories replaced traditional job roles that had been passed down from generation to generation.

In *The Wealth of Nations*, Smith captured this transformation. Even with immense productivity increases, Smith realized that not all the changes were good. He witnessed oppressive working conditions, the rise of child labor, and the commoditization of labor. In this brave new world, society was struggling to determine what was morally acceptable or not.

In describing the surge in economic output, Smith wrote what has become the most famous example of EoS–the story of the pin factory.

In *The Wealth of Nations*, Smith described a pin factory in its most basic form–a one-man workshop where a single laborer produced pins. Here, a person took a heavy-gauge metal wire, sharpened one end, clamped it, sized it, cut it, fashioned the other end for attaching the pin head, and so on. Smith wrote, "A workman not educated to this business . . . could scarce, perhaps, with his utmost industry, make one pin in a day, and certainly could not make twenty."[1]

With industrialization, it was discovered that adding more workers could improve production–sometimes by whole orders of magnitude. Each additional worker meant that a greater specialization of work could take place. In a pin factory employing multiple workers, "One man draws out wire, another straightens it, a third cuts it, a fourth points it, a fifth grinds it at the top for receiving the head . . . making a pin is, in this manner, divided into about eighteen distinct operations."[2]

In a ten-person factory, Smith witnessed how division of labor revolutionized production. With ten people, the factory produced as many as twelve pounds of pins per day, an equivalent of 48,000 pins, or 4,800 pins per worker.[3] Production skyrocketed 240-fold from the original twenty pins per worker.

This enormous rise in output also carried an ancillary benefit in the form of lower fixed costs. With more pins being produced, the over-head cost attributable to each pin declined. If a pin factory paid $10 of rent per person per day, a one-person factory producing twenty pins would pay 50¢ in rent per pin ($10 / 20 pins = 50¢ per pin). In a ten-person factory, the rent expense dropped to 0.2¢ per pin ($100 / 48,000 pins = 0.2¢ per pin).

The lesson of the industrial age was that EoS was an undeniable force in lowering per-unit cost.

● ● ●

Two centuries after the publication of *The Wealth of Nations*, Bruce Henderson, the founder of the Boston Consulting Group (BCG), finally formalized EoS into a workable, strategic business model.

In 1966, he introduced the concept of "the experience curve."[4] The experience curve—which mostly mimicked the effects of EoS—stated that as a business produced more units of an item, the business could become a cheaper manufacturer of that item.

What made Henderson's experience curve special was that it also predicted the amount of cost reduction given a certain rise in quantity. By plotting EoS's effect along a mathematical curve (with the x-axis being *quantity*, and the y-axis being *average cost per unit*), Henderson transformed an abstract theory into a usable, quantitative model.

For business strategists, this would be a seminal moment. For the first time, there was a tool for measuring and controlling a business's competitiveness. In a hypothetical scenario, if two toaster companies vied for dominance, the experience curve showed how many additional toasters one needed to manufacture to gain a certain cost edge (i.e., drive down the *average cost per unit*).

The experience curve also implied a second-order effect.[5] If a business could lower its costs by producing in greater quantities, then by extension, it made sense that the company with the largest market share held the greatest cost advantage. Once a business gained the largest market share, it could perpetuate its dominance by using its lower-cost edge to gain even more market share.

To Henderson, this appeared to be the smoking gun: if a company gained the most market share, it could dominate its industry. For a while, this was how he envisioned the strategic goal of all businesses: to attain the greatest market share.

In the early 1970s, Henderson received an opportunity to put his market-share theory to the test. A situation presented itself when Texas Instruments (TI) introduced the world's first handheld electronic calculator. TI was seeking advice on how to win in this burgeoning market as its competitors were close behind. For Henderson, it was a perfect litmus test for the experience curve and its market-share effect.[6]

Forty years before coming out with the electronic calculator, TI was founded as a seismic exploration company that helped oil companies improve their drilling fields. In the 1940s, as World War II ensued, the company branched into military electronics and, after the war ended, began manufacturing semiconductor chips.

By 1967, TI patented its first handheld electronic calculator, a device that could add, subtract, multiply, and divide. It was a milestone. Previous to this, electronic calculators were large, unwieldy devices, and handheld calculators were limited to mechanical instruments such as slide rules, Curta calculators, and old-fashioned pencil and paper. TI's calculator bridged the divide.

On BCG's suggestion, TI embarked on a campaign to dominate the industry by taking on greater market share.[7] Calculator production would be ramped up to lower costs; TI would subsequently use its lower costs to drop prices and gain even greater market share.

In 1970, a handheld electronic calculator carried a retail price of $400. During the next two years, TI hammered prices down to $159.99. In another three years, prices further plummeted to $49.95.[8] In five years, TI successfully torpedoed electronic calculator prices by 87 percent.

To support these aggressive pricing maneuvers, TI went from selling three million calculator units in 1971 to forty-five million in 1975, at times growing unit sales by 40 percent *per month*.[9]

The experience curve predicted a steep drop in costs—which is exactly what happened. The problem was that by 1975, after five years of intense production, TI was suffering a $16 million quarterly loss.[10] Competitors failed to get the message that they were losing market-share and should give up. Instead, they buckled down, redoubled their efforts, and slashed prices in a brutal price war. Rather than dominating the industry, TI had stoked the flames of intense competition. Adding to its woes, TI's explosive growth numbers enticed newcomers into the field.

For Henderson, the direct link between market share and success was all but broken. Market share didn't determine competitiveness, and gaining it was not a panacea strategy. Michael Porter, a Harvard Business School professor and former BCG consultant, commented on the flaw: "[Henderson's] experience curve doctrine was hyper-confrontational, with only one relevant dimension, namely market share. If you really believed it, you would wreck every single industry, by single-mindedly cutting prices to build share."[11]

In 1989, Henderson concluded, "chasing market share is almost as productive as chasing the pot of gold at the end of the rainbow. You can never get there ... To grow and prosper, however, you must expand the market in which you can maintain an advantage."[12]

Today, we have the benefit of 20/20 hindsight; we can see what was wrong with Henderson's market-share approach. While his core point of lowering costs was highly-relevant, the problem was that he based competitiveness on solely one factor: lowering cost through EoS. Every other business aspect was neglected.

Today, we can understand EoS in the context of the eight moat builder tools. EoS is only one method among many for influencing the intrinsic probability that customers choose a business.

In a world where EoS was our only tool, and the same went for all our competitors, it would be a quick race to the bottom. The outcome would be high production, strong downward pricing pressure, and immense industry oversupply. With such a setup, no one would come out ahead.

When employing the EoS moat builder, we should use it in conjunction with other moat builder tools. By itself, EoS does not create a durable-enough edge for a business to prosper in the long run—especially when consumer preferences, technologies, and competitive dynamics change. As such, the EoS moat builder should viewed as a powerful method for bolstering performance, not as the main source of driving competitiveness.

THE THREE SCALE TRAPS
Pitfalls of Quantity-Driven Mindsets

When implementing the EoS moat builder to ramp up scale, we need to steer clear of three potential icebergs. In essence, when we increase production, we are committing ourselves—as well as tremendous resources—towards a strategic path. Once we gain momentum on this path, it is more difficult to navigate our businesses to avoid these obstacles.

The three dangers are harder to see when we adopt the mindset of "more is better." The challenge is that we are programmed to want more in life—more sales, more customers, more EoS. In business, however, the truth is that more is not always better, and in fact, in many instances, "more" is detrimental to our ability to compete.

The key distinction is that while we want to produce in larger quantities to drive down *per-unit* costs, larger quantities also need to drive down *per-customer* costs. As we saw earlier with TI, greater production can also inadvertently push our rivals to act more aggressively. To avoid these pitfalls, it is important to adopt customer-driven approaches to EoS instead of quantity-driven ones.

The following are the three common dangers associated with EoS–especially when using quantity-driven mindsets. Collectively, these pitfalls are referred to as the "Three Scale Traps."

SCALE TRAP #1: Greater quantities are not necessarily cheaper per customer.

Imagine Bluth Airlines, a hypothetical company that owns a single 180-passenger plane. It flies a single route between Chicago and New York. Its customers are happy and the airline operates at full capacity.

Feeling great success, Bluth Airlines wants to expand its capacity. Will it be wise to for the airline to purchase another plane and double its capacity?

From a production standpoint, a second plane means a lower cost per seat. This second plane can also piggyback on existing support functions, such as the ground crew, terminal gates, reservation desks, etc.

While the idea of a new plane *sounds* good, the more important question is, "Will this additional plane reduce per-customer costs?"

If customer demand is estimated to be 100 percent for both planes, the answer is a shoe-in, "Yes." If demand is predicted to be only 70 percent for both planes, then the answer is an emphatic, "No." In the latter, Bluth Airlines will significantly increase its per-customer cost as each customer has to pay for 1.42 seats of capacity (100% of seats/77% of customers).

While Bluth Airlines can easily lower its *per-seat* costs, that does not necessarily translate to lower *per-customer* costs. When ramping up scale, it is important to factor in the cost of overproduction and excess inventory.

SCALE TRAP #2: Greater quantities may lead to increased competition.

To continue with Bluth Airlines, suppose the company forecasts that 85% of its seats will be taken after adding a second plane. It also calculates that 85% utilization is the breakeven point where it makes sense to purchase the additional plane.

A few months later, Bluth Airlines flatlines at 70% utilization. Within the company, panic ensues as its *cost per customer* has skyrocketed. What went awry in Bluth Airlines' calculations?

While the logic of Bluth Airlines' decision sounded good, it assumed that competitors would react passively to losing market share. In reality, when competitors see their sales eroding, there is a high likelihood that they will respond.

The best case scenario is that rivals do nothing and Bluth Airlines can reach its 80% forecast. In a worst case scenario, rivals decide to severely slash prices to defend market share.

If the latter occurs, Bluth Airlines faces a dilemma. Being 10% shy of its prediction, the extra capacity has significantly increased its cost per customer. The company has two unhappy choices: either lower prices to fill capacity (which further aggravates a price war and squeezes profit margins) or raise prices (which offsets the higher per-customer cost but further erodes the already smaller-than-expected customer base). Neither choice is desirable.

When ramping up production, it is easy to underestimate or even fail to take into account our competitors' reactions. We want to avoid unwittingly pushing rivals into a price war that changes the calculus of our investment. Before embarking on increasing our scale, it is important to estimate the worst case scenario of how our competitors will react and adjust our plans accordingly.

SCALE TRAP #3: Greater quantities may reduce our financial flexibility.

The danger of this last trap can be summed up: "Scaling up is much easier than scaling down." Hiring workers, borrowing money, purchasing equipment, and signing leases—once we enter these long-term commitments, they become hard to unwind.

The greater these commitments, the more we rely on future revenue to pay them off. This can reduce our company's financial flexibility and weaken our ability to handle unforeseen obstacles.

While taking on long-term commitments is necessary for growth, to counteract the reduced financial flexibility, businesses need to maintain a cash cushion that buffers against hard times and/or ensure that the c-moat is strong enough to withstand some loss of market share or profit margin.

"To finish first, you must first finish," goes the car racing advice. When ramping up scale, we don't want to overextend our finances such that minor errors or small economic declines can become fatal crashes. It is necessary to maintain a responsible level of financial strength so that we can avoid any chance of a meltdown.

DISCOVERING DOUGHNUT HOLES IN THE STRATEGY
Growing Pains with the Scale Traps

In 2000, the craze of Krispy Kreme swept through America like wildfire. Seemingly overnight, the doughnut chain became the hottest food sensation as people clamored to get their hands on its sweet treats. I wasn't immune to the hype; I personally drove forty minutes just to visit my first Krispy Kreme store. With my friends raving about it for months, upon arriving, I understood what all the hype was about.

On first blush, Krispy Kreme stores seem rather ordinary. They sport clean, white cafés where people can enjoy fresh doughnuts and coffee. Counters display neatly lined rows of doughnuts that showcase their variety: Original Glazed, Chocolate Iced Glazed, Dulce de Leche, Glazed Lemon Filled, Cinnamon Apple Filled, New York Cheesecake, and Caramel Kreme Crunch. The overall setup is simple but pleasing.

It is as customers venture to the back of the stores where they discover the real magic. From behind a glass wall, visitors can gaze upon an automated contraption of conveyors, cookers, and specialized gadgets that work harmoniously in assembly line fashion to transform raw dough into fresh, piping-hot doughnuts.

The process starts with a yeasty dough from which a machine

punches out perfectly shaped rings. From there, the rings are placed in a humidifier and proofer where they rest while they rise. After leavening, they take a journey on a conveyor that delivers them to a long pool of hot cooking oil onto which they are gently floated. As the rings drift down the pool of oil, they sizzle on one side and puff up while cooking golden brown. At the pool's half way point, a mechanical flipper turns them over so that the other side can receive equal treatment.

After being fully cooked, a different conveyor lifts the piping-hot rings out of the oil and takes them around the room to cool. As they reach the optimal temperature—still warm but not too hot—the doughnuts undergo a final treatment: they pass beneath a white waterfall of sugary glazing.

Needless to say, the process is mesmerizing to watch and the smells are heavenly. And each bite of a hot, fresh Krispy Kreme doughnut is blissfully delicious. Even Willy Wonka would have been impressed.

Krispy Kreme captured people's imagination and found itself a sudden success. After gaining national media attention, word of its doughnuts spread rapidly across the country.

To capitalize on its surging popularity, the company decided to expand its footprint. To fund its growth, the company courted Wall Street investors by becoming a publicly traded company in 2000.

Over the next few years, locations started popping up across the U.S. On the opening day for the Las Vegas location, people were so eager that a line started forming at 5:30 a.m., and by the end of the day, the store had sold 72,000 doughnuts.[13] Krispy Kreme appeared unstoppable.

Both Wall Street and management held lofty expectations for the chain. Pushed by a combination of overconfidence, greed, and pressure to perform, Krispy Kreme's ambitions grew larger; the company wanted to grow even faster.

New locations couldn't be added quickly enough, so to attain a faster growth rate, Krispy Kreme began distributing its doughnuts to third-party outlets such as grocery stores, cafés, and gas stations. Sales exploded.

Selling doughnuts to third parties was not a new thing, but this new push was significant in terms of its scale. By 2003, Krispy Kreme averaged 67 percent of its revenue from third-party outlets.[14]

The idea behind third-party sales was that Krispy Kreme could increase its revenue per store by churning out more doughnuts and then selling them through other outlets. Each store's revenue could grow faster while only incurring incremental bumps in cost.

The problem was that these distributed doughnuts didn't provide the fresh, delightful experiences that people had come to expect and love. By the time these third-party doughnuts reached people's hands, many were stale and hours old. Krispy Kreme's magic began to fade.

In 2004, over twenty thousand third-party outlets carried Krispy Kreme doughnuts, and these outlets were saturated with subpar doughnuts.[15] The public's love affair with Krispy Kreme suddenly evaporated and demand plummeted.

With heavy debt load from its expansion and a narrowing c-moat, Krispy Kreme was forced into a desperate choice. Severe excess capacity and lower demand meant that the company was faced with two painful alternatives: either scale back or go bankrupt. In an effort to prevent the latter, the company closed many of its stores at steep losses. The company's stock price collapsed from $49 to $1.15 per share.

In the end, Krispy Kreme narrowly avoided bankruptcy, but it would take a whole decade for the company to sort out its debt problems. Even today, the company remains a shadow of its former self.

The parable of Krispy Kreme illuminates the dangers of quantity-driven approaches. When we produce more, are we actually serving our customers better? Are we widening our c-moat or are we inadvertently narrowing it? In the case of Krispy Kreme, selling to third-party outlets lowered its per-unit cost, but at the same time it sacrificed its customer experience and reputation in a big way.

When implementing its ambitious expansion strategy, Krispy Kreme leapt straight into the first and third scale traps: it ended up with a higher per-customer cost due to overproduction, and it reduced its financial flexibility to dangerous levels.

● ● ●

Krispy Kreme is not alone in its poor implementation of EoS. The scale traps have also posed a challenge for America's automaker. For decades, the American auto industry has relied on large-scale batch manufacturing to achieve lower costs per vehicle. In this process, a massive number of a particular vehicle model was produced, and then another model, and so on.

At year-end, the problem of this system became apparent. When a model failed to sell out, dealerships sat on piles of unwanted inventory.

To move these vehicles off-lot, automakers were faced with two tough choices: either heavily discount the vehicles or dispose of them.

On the discount side, automakers held year-end fire sales using deep price cuts to incentivize buyers—sometimes pushing vehicles to sell at losses. In a bit of irony, these price cuts did not harm competitors as much as they harmed the automaker making the discount; after all, the closest competitor to a discounted vehicle is not another rival's car but the newer model of the vehicle being discounted.

On the disposal side, American automakers employed a clever—albeit horrifying—trick to get rid of their excess inventory. Many automakers purchased car rental companies as a means to offload their unwanted inventory. Losses were still associated with this practice, but it was a way to get rid of cars that was less severe than straight-up disposal.

Buying car rental companies was tantamount to an insane "fix" for what was essentially an overproduction issue. If Taiichi Ohno, Toyota's anti-waste expert, had witnessed what American automakers were doing, he would have been horrified.

Thankfully, many American automakers today adopt flexible production systems, like *demand pull*, which benefit from EoS while minimizing the risk associated with overproduction. With demand pull systems, vehicles can be built in tiny batches, sometimes with different models alternating one after another on the assembly line. In this manner, when a dealership logs a sale, the information can be passed directly to the factory floor where a similar vehicle can be produced to replace it.

● ● ●

As the world's largest retailer, Wal-Mart has cleverly exploited the scale traps for its own gain. The company has learned how to push suppliers into the scale traps as an effective way to control them.

Newer and smaller suppliers are the most susceptible to these practices. Inexperience makes these companies prone to make the mistake of believing that "more is better." Wal-Mart capitalizes on this naivety by promising large-volume purchase orders.

Wal-Mart even goes as far as helping small suppliers secure loans and teaches them how to make the investments necessary for ramping up production. After all, a large-scale supply chain is needed to satisfy the demands of the world's largest retailer.

The trick is that once a supplier has borrowed funds and made large investments, Wal-Mart knows that it has gained the upper hand. The supplier is now heavily reliant on the retail giant for sales. As the percentage of sales coming from Wal-Mart increases, the more power shifts in Wal-Mart's favor. When 20 percent of a supplier's sales originate from Wal-Mart, it is a different scenario than when 80 percent of its sales originate from Wal-Mart. As the retailer positions itself as an indispensable buyer, it is able to dictate the terms by simply threatening to switch suppliers. Wal-Mart becomes the tail that wags the dog.

To further erode the supplier bargaining power, Wal-Mart is also reputed to withhold ninety days' worth of accounts payable.[16] In other words, the retail giant pays for goods ninety days after delivery to its warehouses. If for any reason Wal-Mart decides to delay or challenge these payments, it can force its supplier into a painful cash crunch—a potentially fatal situation. This helps keep suppliers on a tighter leash.

The lesson is to be cautious when ramping up scale especially when it severely reduces financial flexibility. Wal-Mart pushes its suppliers to deplete their cash buffers while weakening their c-moat by placing them at the mercy of one customer. We should never put ourselves in a predicament where our survival relies on one customer. In such situations, we have to ask, "Who holds the cards in the relationship?"

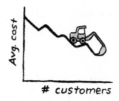

MINING FOR VALLEYS
Customer-Driven Techniques for Applying EoS

Now that we are aware of the potential dangers of Eos, how do we go about implementing it in our businesses while sidestepping the scale traps? First, our decisions should be based on *gaining customers*, and not *adding production quantity*. We want our decisions to be grounded by customer demand, and not some arbitrary increase in supply. Second, we want to gain customers in a way that always lowers our average cost of serving them.

By doing these two things, we avoid falling in the first and second scale traps. To circumvent the third, we just need to be disciplined in maintaining a financial buffer—in the form of cash cushions, lines of credits, or strong-enough c-moats that can be sacrificed if needed.

There are two techniques to help us implement the EoS moat builder: *leverage customer demographics* and *stay within the cost valleys*. These will aid us in using customers to lower our average cost.

TECHNIQUE #1: Leverage customer demographics.

Not all customers are created equal. Different customers will have different needs, and we can use this variation to our advantage. Sometimes, having the *right type* of customer is more beneficial than having a greater number of customers. In other words, "What groups of customers can help us lower the cost for our overall customer base?"

In recent years, many sit-down restaurant chains—such as Outback Steakhouse, Chili's, and Olive Garden—have introduced drive up services that allow people to order meals ahead of time and then pick them up. The recognition is that what limits a restaurant is not its kitchen but its seating. By serving people who don't require seating, these chains make better use of their underutilized kitchens. In targeting this demographic, they offer special to-go menus, customized food containers, and reserved parking spaces.

Another example of finding the right type of customer is in the passenger airline industry which courts express shippers to help lower costs. While passenger airlines work to keep their seats filled to full occupancy, they have learned that there is untapped potential in their cargo holds. Any underutilized space can be used to ship packages at very little additional expense. By working with express shippers, airlines have been able to take greater advantage of this otherwise wasted capacity.

Lastly, iron-ore mining companies have learned to branch into side industries that can beneficially piggyback from their low-cost transportation infrastructures.

Iron ore is the main ingredient in steel making and can naturally be found around the world in high-grade deposits—a form that can be sent straight to the blasting furnaces. The challenge is that these high-grade deposits are often located in remote areas. While iron ore is cheap, shipping the heavy rock to steel mills is not.

To cost-effectively deliver millions of tons of ore, mining companies have built energy-efficient transportation systems that link their mines to steel mills around the world. The infrastructure can easily cost billions of dollars and includes privately-owned railroads, roads, shipping ports, ocean container ships, and even power plants.

To make better use of these sizable investments, mining companies have targeted industries that benefit from low-cost, high-volume transportation systems. These industries include forest goods (e.g., tree logging) and fertilizer (e.g., pot ash). In entering these businesses, iron ore companies have boosted their EoS and maximized the use of their capacity.

When we try to increase our EoS, we want to determine which customer demographics will be most helpful for lowering our average cost per customer. If we can locate where the excess capacity lies, then we can find the right customer demographic to make better use of it.

TECHNIQUE #2: Stay within the cost valleys.

Investments are necessary for growth. A café might sufficiently serve twenty customers per hour with one espresso machine, but at thirty customers per hour, the café will need to contemplate buying another machine. This can require a significant bump up in equipment costs.

The key is to recognize that costs do not usually scale smoothly downward as we gain more customers. Instead, when customers are added, costs can often spike up before coming back down.

FIGURE 7.2 Perception vs. Reality (Economy of Scale)

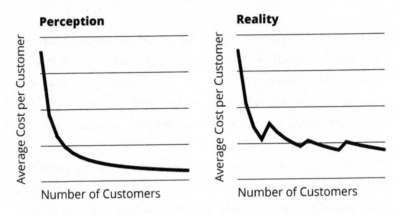

As such, it is helpful to know where these cost spikes occur and the degree of their magnitude. By knowing this, we are provided with a good sense of how EoS is working within our business.

To chart these cost spikes, it is helpful to graph out our average costs—which is nicknamed "The Peaks and Valleys Chart." We start by figuring out the marginal cost of serving each additional customer (shown in Figure 7.3). As the coffee shop serves more people, it incurs costs along the way for growing its capacity, such as buying espresso machines, getting a refrigerator, and adding more seating.

FIGURE 7.3 Marginal Cost of Each Additional Customer at a Hypothetical Coffee Shop

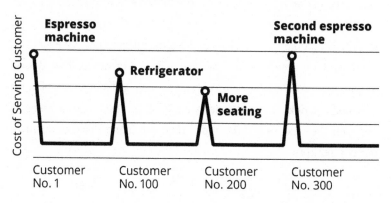

Once we know where these cost points occur, we can take the marginal cost chart, and from it, calculate the average cost for a given number of customers by adding the total cost of serving customers and dividing it with the total number of customers. Depicting this gives us the average cost chart(i.e., the "Peaks and Valleys Chart").

FIGURE 7.4 Average Cost per Customer at a Hypothetical Coffee Shop (Peaks and Valleys Chart)

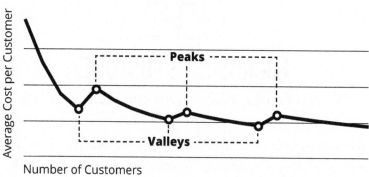

As we serve a greater number of customers, we can tell that sometimes our average costs will bump up; these are the peaks. To stay

competitive, we want our businesses to remain in the valleys of this chart as these areas provide us the greatest cost advantages.

If adding customers requires us to cross over a large peak of expenses, we must determine whether the peak is worth climbing. If we decide to continue crossing the peak, we should have a strong game plan for reaching the next valley as quickly as possible. The longer it takes us to reach the next valley, the more time we spend disadvantaged to our competitors.

• • •

To summarize the overall plan for implementing the EoS moat builder, there are four guiding principles: keep decisions customer-centric, maintain a level of financial flexibility, target customer demographics to make best use of excess capacity, and focus on staying in the cost valleys when adding more customers.

MICROSOFT'S FORTUNE

The Economics of Information in the Digital Age

There is an old academic saying that goes, "Information is expensive to produce but cheap to reproduce." Today, this is truer than at any other time in our history. Information is becoming increasingly valuable and yet vastly cheaper to reproduce. The Digital Age is pushing our society increasingly towards an information-based economy, and this holds wide implications for EoS's influence in our world.

During Thanksgiving weekend in 1980, a pivotal moment in this transformation occurred when a tiny Seattle start-up received a long-
awaited package in the mail: a prototype IBM personal computer.[17]
With the new device, the three-year-old company began its journey to
become one of the most incredible businesses of the Digital Age.

Only three years earlier, Bill Gates had dropped out of college to form
a company named Microsoft. At the time, Gates was unsure where
his venture would take him, but he realized that a dramatic shift was
taking place in the world. Advanced computing devices were the wave
of the future, and to run their complex hardware, they needed equally
sophisticated software.

For those early years, Gates focused his attention on expanding a
programming language called BASIC (Beginner's All-purpose Symbolic
Instruction Code) as a tool for creating more-advanced software.

Then, in 1980, opportunity fell into his lap. Two IBM executives
approached him with a proposal.[18] IBM was the world's largest
computer maker and in the midst of developing a new computing
device geared towards the average consumer, a personal computer.
To run it, however, IBM needed an operating system. The company
encountered difficulties securing a version of this software and
needed one before the product launched. If Microsoft could supply a
low-cost operating system, IBM agreed to bundle it with its PCs and be
its largest purchaser.

At the time of the offer, Gates had little experience with operating
systems, but the opportunity was too significant to pass up. Gates

jumped at the deal.

As soon as the ink dried on the contract, Microsoft sprung into action. Gates' first task was to secure a piece of software from his rival Tim Paterson at Seattle Computer Products. Microsoft licensed Paterson's QDOS, which stood for Quick and Dirty Operating System. QDOS itself was a bare-bones product with limited functionality, but it offered Microsoft a significant starting point. Later on, in July 1981, Microsoft would purchase the full rights to the operating system for $50,000.[19]

After adding numerous enhancements to QDOS, Gates dubbed his version MS-DOS which stood for Microsoft Disk Operating System. IBM packaged it under the pseudonym PC-DOS.

When IBM launched its personal computer, it became a runaway success. The IBM PC sold fifty thousand units in the first eight months and it cemented Microsoft's future.

What people in the technology industry didn't realize was that Microsoft was being handed one of the greatest EoS businesses of the Digital Age. Under the bundling agreement with IBM, PC-DOS was sold for $40 each.[20] The cost of producing an additional copy of the software was just the price of a floppy disk, or about one dollar. As IBM made PC-DOS popular, Microsoft expanded its software to other computer makers. Microsoft would go on to sell over one hundred million copies over the next decade and a half.[21] Even after its development cost, the company essentially profited more than $30 on each new copy sold, which translated to billions of dollars.

Currently, digital technology is continuing to alter the dynamics of EoS in our society. In the past, brick-and-mortar stores could only serve so many customers before building another store, and factories could only produce so much before making costly additions and facility enhancements. With digital goods, however, the cost of producing software and data can occur once and be sold to countless individuals with almost no additional cost. Programmers can create mobile apps from home and then distribute them to a billion users, or a website can host a viral video that reaches the entire world overnight.

The Digital Age is fundamentally changing information's ability to scale, and the speed at which the EoS moat builder can help businesses grow and profit is far greater than at any previous time in our history.

To prepare ourselves for the future, we want to ask, "How do we take advantage of this technology trend?" How do we use the information highway to lower the cost of serving our customers? Every business will be affected by society's adoption of digital technology. The question is, "How do we embrace this technology, and how do we position ourselves to capture its ability to drive down costs?"

Some examples are how Uber's car riding service makes use of excess car capacity to drive down the cost of cab rides, and AirBnB's ability to utilize extra housing capacity to drive down the price of hotel stays. When we can employ technology to take advantage of otherwise wasted resources, we can create powerful scale businesses that lower costs for customers.

CHAPTER EIGHT

NETWORK EFFECT (S)

The Network Effect moat builder
leverages customers to improve
the experiences of other customers.

● ● ●

Chapter Overview: Sometimes customer satisfaction originates from other customers; when this dynamic occurs, it is called a Network Effect. To create a Network Effect, businesses should develop systems that promote customers to improve the experience of other customers— with bigger customer bases often translating to better experiences. One easy-to-create Network Effect is through information sharing, which allows people to share content with each other in a way that improves purchasing outcomes and decisions. In addition, Network Effects can take the form of two-sided matchmaking (i.e., brokering between two distinct customer groups) and community building (i.e., creating social interactions). Importantly, many Network Effects also exhibit the game theory attribute of "first-mover advantage."

n 2007, a small, fast-growing tech company was seeking funding to fuel its expansion. To raise money, the company placed 1.6 percent of its stock on the auction block and disclosed having revenue of $145 million for the past year. While profit numbers weren't provided, everyone in the industry surmised that the company was losing money.

When the final bid rolled in, the 1.6 percent minority stake would sell for $240 million, valuing the tech company at a whopping $1.5 billion.[1]

Wall Street was shocked. Even by the most speculative standards, the price tag defied logic. To put it in perspective, it was equivalent to buying a lemonade stand for $10,000, knowing that the stand sold only $100 in beverages during the past year and lost money while doing so.

As crazy as the deal appeared, however, the company held one valuable asset that wasn't captured by its financial performance: a c-moat that was growing by leaps and bounds. The company's name was Facebook.

While Facebook didn't have much in terms of sales or profits, it attained what few Internet companies possessed: a sticky user base. In an ocean of online websites, Facebook had found a way to durably hold on to users. Once someone signed up, they tended to revisit the site over and over again, and with such strong user loyalty, it was only a matter of time before Facebook figured out how to be profitable.

The premise behind Facebook's site was simple. A person created an online personal profile and then linked their profile to the profiles of other people they knew. In this manner, a person could share information with other people that were invited to that person's community. This meant that rather than posting information publicly, a person could post pictures, life events, interesting articles, events, or anything else they cared about, to be shared only with the people they actually knew, such as friends and family.

The brilliance of the system was that, as more people joined, Facebook's services became more valuable to everyone else on it. Once a majority of a person's friends and family were using Facebook, the site became indispensible for keeping in contact with them.

During Facebook's early growth years, the company cleverly avoided capitalizing on users by refusing to bombard them with annoying advertisements. Importantly, this allowed for a faster growth rate until it could reach a critical mass of users where growth became self-sustaining. Once the company hit an inflection point where it was vastly larger than its competitors, in a virtuous cycle, people would sign up because most of their friends were using it, and as these people signed on, the site became even more compelling to others.

The Network Effect is the fourth moat builder, and it is the tool that Facebook used to achieve loyalty. A Network Effect is created when a business builds a system that uses its customers to improve the experiences of other customers. These systems can exist as both physical networks or intangible networks. Examples on the physical side are telephone lines and highways that link people together. As more people connect to these networks, the networks increase in value. On the intangible side, as more people use websites like Craigslist and Wikipedia, users increasingly benefit from the added contribution and sharing of information.

To build our own Network Effects, we want our customers to improve the experiences of our other customers. We want to ask, "How do we use customers to enhance customer satisfaction?"

A COAST-TO-COAST NETWORK EFFECT
Western Union Connects a Nation

Long before the Internet, in the 1850s, a small company named Western Union leveraged the power of Network Effects to dominate the burgeoning telegram industry. At the time, telegrams were a revolutionary new technology. Suddenly, messages could travel at near-instantaneous speeds to be delivered to far-off destinations. Messages were converted into Morse code and then transmitted as electrical signals along metal wires. The next fastest alternative was to deliver letters by horseback.

With this new technology, hundreds of companies began stringing up their own wires and offering messaging services. As the industry took shape, it became highly fragmented. Companies became highly territorial with each one's network built for private use, and they did not interconnect with one another.

For customers, this fragmentation created a big challenge. If anyone wanted to send a telegram across territories, a message could only travel to the edge of one network, where it had to be transcribed to paper, physically delivered to an operator at an adjacent network, and then sent again along its way. For telegrams traversing multiple territories, messages had to be physically handed from one network's operator to another, all the while incurring the fee of each carrier.[2]

It was only a matter of time before the Network Effect kicked in to consolidate the industry. By its nature, a larger company could more efficiently connect people while cutting out more middlemen. The main question was, "Which of the hundreds of competitors would be the last few to remain standing after the industry's consolidation?"

In 1861, Western Union decided to enter the arena by building a platform for gobbling up its rivals. The company constructed a new telegram line that stretched from Omaha, Nebraska, all the way across the Rocky Mountains to Sacramento, California. It was a monumental undertaking that marked the first time that a telegram line connected the Eastern United States to the West Coast.

When Western Union announced its ambitious project, it was met with great skepticism. Even President Lincoln chimed in with his doubts: "It will be next to impossible to get your poles and materials distributed on the plains, and as fast as you can complete the lines, the Indians will cut it down."[3]

Despite the apprehension, for 112 days, builders laid ten to twelve miles of line per day along jagged terrain with support from a steady stream of supply wagons. Within two days of the line's completion, the United States government stopped using the Pony Express for correspondence across the Rockies—which took roughly ten days to deliver a letter—and switched to Western Union's near-instant service.[4]

With monopolistic control over an arterial lane of communication, Western Union was poised to take over its rivals. The company began acquiring its neighboring networks and integrating them into its service. Over the next decade, Western Union absorbed more than five hundred competing networks into its system.[5]

As Western Union's territory expanded, a Network Effect kicked in. The larger the company grew, the more directly it could connect customers to one another. As rival networks became unable to compete against Western Union's scope, many sold out to the giant, further enhancing its dominance. Eventually, Western Union's market share would grow to account for 90 percent of all telegraphic communications in the United States.[6]

● ● ●

A century later, as telegrams became a thing of the past, Western Union continued employing Network Effects for its main business strategy.

In the 1980s, with demand for messaging services all but dried up—especially with the invention of the telephone and the Internet—Western Union began setting up its telegram network to serve a very different need: money transfer.

During this transition and in a series of unfortunate events, Western Union's management got sidetracked and fell under Wall Street's fad of using "highly leveraged balance sheets." Under the guise of maximizing shareholder returns, Wall Street investors pushed companies to borrow as much money as possible. The idea was that no dollar should sit idly on the sidelines when it could be used to generate even more profits. By borrowing as much money as possible, companies could use these proceeds to reward shareholders and invest in businesses that further increased earnings.

The idea to borrow as much money as possible was naïve. Nevertheless, Western Union—along with many other businesses—saddled its balance sheet with high amounts of debt. With little financial wiggle room for making mistakes or withstanding economic shocks, the company's balance sheet became fragile. In the early 1980s, when the economy tanked, this highly-leveraged, profit-maximizing scheme began to unravel.

Western Union had used its borrowed funds to purchase businesses that had little to do with strengthening its core c-moat. The company purchased a satellite communications business and an undersea cable business. These ventures were unrelated to money transfer and diverted management's attention. As such, when the economy fell into recession, Western Union's core business was not only weaker, but its earnings were lower, and it is debt stood at dangerously high levels. To stay afloat, the company was forced to borrow even more money to keep up with its interest payments.

By 1987, Western Union's situation fell into dire straits. To fund its operations, the company issued $500 million in junk bonds. In order to convince investors to buy the bonds, the yield was set at 16.5 percent. In 1989, as the company's trajectory continued downward, a special clause in the junk bonds reset interest rates to 19.25 percent. For $500 million in borrowings, Western Union was paying $96 million per year in interest.[7]

In 1991, Western Union finally declared bankruptcy, wiping out its shareholders and giving control to creditors. To shield Western Union's name from being dragged through the mud of the bankruptcy proceedings, the company was quickly renamed New Valley.[8]

During the reorganization, the cloud of debt that choked Western Union was lifted; the company's creditors became its new shareholders, and non-core assets were sold off to pay down debt. What remained was Western Union's venerable name along with its large network of agents.

Observing from the background, Charles Fote, the CEO of First Data, was keeping a close eye on the company. While Western Union's messaging services had dried up, Fote saw its money-transfer services as a potential shining star.

The way money-transfer service worked was that a person could send money to another person by simply depositing funds at a local agent location and then having those funds dispersible at a destination agent location; the service was fast, reliable, and easy. The alternative of mailing checks was slow, and setting up wire transfers between bank accounts was cumbersome and prohibitively expensive for smaller transactions.

Fote saw opportunity. If he could expand Western Union's agent base, it could become an increasingly valuable platform for moving money around, and a powerful Network Effect could develop.

In a hiccup to Fote's plans, his bid to buy Western Union's name and assets from bankruptcy proceedings failed. In 1994, a rival bidder named First Financial Management Corporation (FFMC) scooped Western Union out from under his grasp. But not to be outdone, Fote would still get his coveted prize. A year later, he orchestrated a merger between First Data and FFMC.[9]

With Western Union under Fote's control, from 1998 to 2003, the number of agent locations was tripled from 55,000 to 170,000—a tally larger than the combined numbers of McDonald's, Starbucks, and Wal-Mart locations.[10]

Western Union also expanded into less-developed countries that benefited from reliable money-transfer services. These countries often supplied immigrant or migrant-worker populations to well-developed countries. Workers needed a way to send money home to their families. In 2007, remittances from money-transfer services grew to account for 50 percent of Haiti's GDP, 20 percent of Jordan's GDP, and more than 15 percent of Jamaica's, Honduras's, and El Salvador's GDPs.[11]

For his insight into the value of expanding Western Union's Network Effect, Fote was rewarded handsomely. In five years, from 1998 to 2003, First Data's profitability tripled from $465 million to $1.23 billion.[12] Today, Western Union's services span more than two hundred countries with 500,000 agent locations and annually account for more than $85 billion in money transfers.[13] Network Effects can powerfully improve customer experiences and lead to enormous business success.

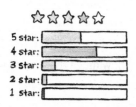

USER-GENERATED CONTENT
Network Effects of Shared Information

It is incredible to think that a million books can fit onto a single hard drive. While we might take this fact for granted, only thirty years ago, such a feat would have been difficult to envision. The economics of information are changing rapidly, and with it, new opportunities are popping up for developing Network Effects.

In particular, the Digital Age has not only made reproducing information cheaper, but the Internet has allowed a two-way information flow. Digital information is able to communicate simultaneously back and forth, and new systems of dialogues can be created.

The Zagat Survey, for example, was a popular local restaurant guide that used to be published once a year. Hard copies were sold in bookstores around the U.S. To compile its food reviews, Zagat polled thousands of people and aggregated the data into local editions. With changes in technology, today the Zagat guide exists mostly online. In embracing an online platform, Zagat has improved the speed and ability of restaurant-goers to help each other find better meals. (In 2011, Zagat was purchased by Google.[14])

Zagat represents one of the easiest methods for creating a Network Effect: using digital information to let customers share reviews with each other. Rotten Tomatoes and IMDb are also review-based sites that get people to share how much they enjoy various movies; Yelp and Google Maps get people to share their dining experiences; Amazon and Overstock get customers to share their thoughts on products.

Reviews provide people with the ability to make more informed decisions, which lead to better outcomes. Once a site has the most reviews, a strong Network Effect kicks in that draws in more people to its site, and it gains an edge in further growing its review database.

Beyond reviews, there are many other types of user-generated content that companies can tap. Résumés and CVs are shared on LinkedIn, pictures and events are shared on Facebook, and 140-character messages are shared on Twitter. Wikipedia is an online encyclopedia that invites people to write, edit, and update its entries. Any information that is shareable and useful can be used to create a Network Effect.

User-generated content can also originate indirectly from users. While reviews and résumés are direct forms of customer input, indirect inputs include things such as shopping habits, individual preferences, and behavioral patterns. Businesses can leverage this information to subtly improve customer experiences.

Pandora, for example, keeps records of how people rate songs when listening to its online radio stations. Users can rate a song thumbs-up or thumbs-down, or simply skip it. By tracking this information, Pandora is able to enhance the future listening experience of others. The more people who use Pandora, the better the company becomes at fine-tuning its music to fit peoples' specific tastes.

Google also tracks its customers and their behaviors to improve its search results. After a search results page is loaded, the company records which links are clicked. This allows Google to improve the ranking of its search results for future users. A user's location can also be paired with where the search was conducted. This improves Google's ability to supply localized answers as well.

As an example, the search term "Taj Mahal" might refer to a temple in India, a casino in Atlantic City, an American blues musician, or any number of different restaurants. By knowing where people are conducting their searches and which links are clicked, Google is able to re-rank its results based on what people are most likely looking for.[15]

In our own business, user-generated information is a valuable resource for improving our customer satisfaction. When we serve customers, is there any information that we can gather to help us bolster our offerings? We just need to ask, "What types of information do customers possess that can improve the experience of other customers?" After that, we just need to figure out a way to gather that information and develop a Network Effect from it.

STOCK EXCHANGES AND AUCTION HOUSES
Two-Sided Network Effects

Network Effects have so far been described as homogenous groups of people who create a benefit for others in the same group—moviegoers help moviegoers, music listeners help music listeners, and shoppers help shoppers. In some cases, two distinct customer groups can be paired together to mutually benefit each other. Each group will benefit from the other's presence, thus creating a two-sided Network Effect.

The most common type of two-sided Network Effects are brokers. These are middlemen who create platforms for facilitating high-quality matchmaking.

This can range from a newspaper classified section, where buyers are matched with sellers, to a farmers market, where produce growers are matched with urban shoppers. Advertising firms also act as matchmakers between ad space (i.e., targeted magazines, billboards, TV spots) and companies that benefit from the exposure.

The dynamic of two-sided Network Effects is that as the population of one group grows, the other group should benefit proportionally. In a farmers market, a greater number of produce stands means better selection for buyers. More selection means a better customer experience for buyers with more people wanting to visit the farmers market. In a positive cycle, each group's satisfaction feeds off the other group.

One of the most venerable two-sided Network Effects is the New York Stock Exchange (NYSE), the largest platform in the world for helping companies raise money from investors. While most of us know the NYSE as a place for buying and selling stocks, the exchange's main purpose is to link companies seeking financial resources with large pools of investor money. As the exchange becomes a better platform for trading stock, more companies will use it to raise capital and thus list their shares on it. As more companies list shares on the exchange, investors are also more likely to invest their funds into it. The NYSE is one of the most compelling investing platform for both businesses and investors.

Unsurprisingly, the oldest company to be listed on the NYSE also uses a two-sided Network Effect for its main strategy. The art auctioneer Sotheby's was founded in 1744, and for centuries it has dominated high-end art sales along with its rival Christie's. In 2013, the two auction houses held 55 percent of the global market share in fine art sales.[16]

In brokering high-end art transactions, Sotheby's has positioned itself as the best place for art sellers and art buyers. Knowing that sellers are looking for top dollar for their art, the company has learned that the best way to attain the high prices is by holding bidding wars between buyers. As such, to meet these needs, Sotheby's uses auctions to sell art and cultivates strong relationships with a Rolodex of wealthy buyers.

On the other side, Sotheby's knows that once it has sellers in its pockets, buyers must go through the auction house if they want to acquire unique pieces of fine art. As such, both sellers and buyers are compelled to use Sotheby's services.

Sotheby's also helps facilitate transactions between the two groups by vouching for the authenticity of works, managing shipping and handling, and sometimes even making collateralized loans on art pieces. The last of these supplies financial liquidity to the art market, thus making fine art a more appealing investment.

Visa and Mastercard are also successful two-sided matchmakers. Both were founded by a consortium of banks to standardize the platform for processing payments. Since then, the two companies have taken a life of their own by being spun off as independent entities. While neither company issues credit cards, they act as indispensible brokers between banks and retailers.

The beauty of these payment processors is that banks are now highly dependent on them to provide customers with a convenient way to buy goods. Retailers also need them to get customers to spend money at their stores. Both groups have a strong vested interest in being part of Visa's and MasterCard's network.

CREATING COMMUNITIES
Network Effects of Social Circles

If we took a poll and asked people, "What do you care about most in your life?" Near the top of the list would undoubtedly be "friends and family." For the great majority of us, satisfaction not only derives from the products and services of businesses but from the community of people around us. Importantly, we feel a sense of belonging to this community and gain satisfaction from it.

Businesses can develop Network Effects by fostering a sense of community within their customer base. Community interactions help customers to improve the experience of other customers. An apartment complex, for example, can host get-to-know-your-neighbor events that bring residents together, sports arenas can gather fans to cheer for a team in a unified cause, and churches and mosques can connect members to help each other get through difficult times. As people's bonds strengthen, these venues can become compelling places for people to gather.

Fostering a sense of community helps businesses enhance their retention rate. In my family's business, I was surprised to find that many of our customers didn't actually mind waiting in line. Our customers were a tightknit local community, and standing in line was a way for them to chat and catch up with each other. While people enjoyed socializing, we never abused this dynamic and we always kept the line moving. Our customers felt comfortable knowing that we were working as fast as we could to serve them and catching up with their neighbors was an added benefit.

Other examples of building communities involve gyms that encourage people to chat between workout sessions, bowling alleys that host league tournaments to get people to join in friendly competition, and neighborhood bars that host Taco Tuesday nights as a way to promote the gathering of friends. Community interactions can even take place online, such as on the user forums of Reddit or when groups of friends play video games together.

What is important is that when a business becomes a central place for hosting social interactions, the loyalty of its customers is enhanced.

CONSOLE WARS
The Game Theory of First-Mover Advantage

One attribute that Network Effects tend to possess is first-mover advantage. In game theory, "first-mover advantage" refers to a situation where the first player to take a turn holds an advantage over all subsequent players.

In tic-tac-toe, for example, the first player to go holds an enormous advantage over the second player. In fact, in this lopsided game, if the first player is worth their salt, the best outcome for the second player is to reach a stalemate. Here, the first-mover advantage is huge.[17]

First-mover advantage also crops up in how teams are chosen in middle and high school physical-education classes. Here, two team captains are appointed, and they take turns picking teammates from a pool of classmates. The first captain to choose not only gets the best player, but when there is an even number of players, gets to avoid the worst player.

Interestingly, Network Effects exhibit first-mover advantage traits as the first business to gain a head start can likely snowball its lead over rivals.

Because customer satisfaction scales with the size of the customer base, the company with the most customers can often provide the most satisfaction. If this margin of satisfaction grows wide enough during the early years of an industry's life cycle, then it becomes difficult for late competitors to catch up. Once a sizable lead is established, a company can often blow past its rivals in terms of providing satisfaction—hence Facebook's smart decision to focus on growth during its early years.

Late adopters of Network Effects will be in a tough spot. During the early years of an industry, there is still a chance for rivals to catch up by aggressively spending money to gain market share. However, once an industry grows larger in size, gaining market share becomes an increasingly costly venture. In mature markets, so much money will be required for gaining market share that a company will have to dip into negative profit margins to catch up. The natural combination of a growing market share and negative margins is extremely difficult to sustain. In other words, late adopters will have to spend enormous financial resources just to play catch up.

When creating Network Effects, it is thus important to be a first mover—or at least a very early adopter. Only after reaching a critical mass where growth is self-sustaining and the lead over competitors is immense, then should we start worrying about trying to shifting more tokens to the profit margin bucket.

● ● ●

In 1994, the fifth generation of video game console wars kicked off when Sony launched its PlayStation console. Nintendo followed eighteen months later by releasing the Nintendo 64 (N64) console.[18]

Each generation of console wars typically lasts six years. The contest is a fight between console manufacturers as they jockey to have their devices become the next dominant gaming platform. It is a race to see who can create a Network Effect that can blow past the others.

Console makers act as a broker of a two-sided Network Effect. They sit between game players and game developers. As game developers create more titles for a console, the console becomes more sought after by gamers. On the flip side, as more gamers purchase a particular console, game developers benefit from its larger audience. For each generation, one console usually emerges as the de facto winner, taking with it most of the industry's profits for years. The stakes are high.

During the fifth war, Sony's PlayStation took the crown as it trounced Nintendo by selling 102 million consoles compared to the latter's 32 million.[19]

In 2010, a research study conducted by Hongju Liu concluded that the biggest advantage that PlayStation held over the N64 was its release date.[20] Between the two competitors, the winner would have been determined by one of them having either a head start of 10 percent more game titles or one million more consoles. With this small but early lead, either Sony or Nintendo could have snowballed past the other to take the top spot.

For Nintendo, by the time its console hit the market, PlayStation had been sitting on store shelves nearly a year and a half. Not only did Sony have more game titles, but it held the important one-million-console lead.[21] While the N64 was popular and a fun gaming machine, it was too late for Nintendo to overtake Sony; both gamers and developers had already jumped aboard the PlayStation bandwagon.

● ● ●

In November 2001, the sixth generation of the console wars got under way and erupted into full-scale competition when Nintendo's Game-Cube and Microsoft's Xbox launched within a week of each other. For this sixth war, Sony had learned from its previous success. By the time that GameCube and Xbox hit the market, the PlayStation 2 (PS2) had been on shelves for almost a year. As the battle turned into a three-way contest, one analyst pointed out that for GameCube and Xbox, "[it] was already a race for second place."[22]

When GameCube and Xbox entered the market, they both offered superior value to the PS2. The GameCube was slightly more powerful than the PS2 but priced much cheaper at $199 compared to $299. On the other side, the Xbox was easily the most powerful of the three but priced at $299, the same as the PS2.

Despite the two consoles being better technological values, PS2's advantage was that it had already sold ten million units. By the end of 2001, PS2's library of games heralded 240 titles. In contrast, the Game-Cube carried 22 titles and Xbox had 30 titles.[23] If one million units or 10 percent more game titles was enough to snowball a lead in the previous generation, then the PS2 was on track to crush its rivals.

By the end of the sixth-generation video game console wars, the final sales tally was 21 million GameCube consoles, 24 million Xbox consoles, and more than 153 million PS2 consoles.[24] Sony tripled the combined sales of its two competitors. With its early grand theft of market share, Sony had easily hijacked the outcome of the war.

CHAPTER NINE

LOCATION (P)

The Location moat builder uses
physical position to increase the likelihood
that customers choose a business.

● ● ●

Chapter Overview: A good location strategy provides convenience to customers and territorial dominance to companies. Convenience not only includes the placement of businesses, but for retailers, their internal layouts as well. Locations can also create territorial dominance that discourages competitors from entering a market. In some cases, territorial behavior combined with timing elements can create powerful—albeit temporary—monopolies.

I n 2011, I had just moved to Seattle, and I decided to take a short drive from downtown to visit the neighborhood of Ballard. To my surprise, I discovered three different Brown Bear Car Washes along a two-mile stretch of 15th Avenue Northwest. I was perplexed by the sight, "In a city famed for its rain, did Seattle really need this many car washes? Was demand really that high?"

It turns out that Seattleites aren't prone to washing their vehicles more than residents of other cities. Instead, the multitude of locations was a way for Brown Bear to widen its c-moat in an otherwise fickle industry, and it did so by leveraging the unique features of the roadway.

The 15th Avenue corridor is considered a blessing and a curse for the retailers that line its sides. While the roadway is heavily trafficked, the stoplights are laid out in a manner that makes left turns very difficult; both left turns onto and off the street are a challenge. Adding to the struggle, the roadway becomes a drawbridge as one heads north and enters the Ballard neighborhood. As ships slowly pass beneath the bridge, traffic jams can stretch for over a mile.

Cleverly, Brown Bear has figured out how to use these traffic woes to its advantage. On each inbound lane to the bridge, the company has strategically placed a large car wash. A third, smaller car wash has been located on the outbound lane heading from the bridge to downtown.[1]

These three sites have given Brown Bear's customers a strong level of convenience along the busy street and eliminated the need to make left turns. When the bridge is drawn, rather than being stalled in traffic, drivers can easily stop in for a quick wash. There are even well-placed digital signs that alerts drivers when the drawbridge is raised to help them decide whether it is a good time to stop in. For commuters and errand runners, there is the added convenience of deciding whether to pull in for a wash on the initial leg of their trip or on the way back.

With its clever location strategy, Brown Bear has taken a challenging geography and used it to create a strong business.

● ● ●

The fifth tool in our arsenal is the Location moat builder. The old retailing advice goes, "Location, location, location." It is a simple fact that well-located businesses are more likely to be chosen by customers; a person's physical relationship to their surrounding will influence their decisions.

In general, there are two approaches to using the Location moat builder. The first is to increase a customer's desire to choose a business (i.e., by providing greater convenience), and the second is to eliminate the alternatives available to customers (i.e., by creating territorial dominance).

Brown Bear Car Wash showed us the former with its convenience. For the territorial side, the Ambassador Bridge toll road exemplifies how to use geography to limit the customer alternatives.

The Ambassador Bridge is undoubtedly the most important crossing between the United States and Canada. The bridge spans the border as it passes over the Detroit River and connects the cities of Detroit and Canada's Windsor.

The U.S.-Canada border itself is the longest in the world at 5,525 miles. The border starts its journey on the Atlantic Coast in Maine where it meanders westward towards New York until meeting the Great Lakes. Here, the border joins the lakes for two thousand miles, and upon reaching their end, slices due west with the precision of an X-Acto knife until meeting the Pacific Ocean. Along the Pacific coast, the border takes a brief pause before once again appearing where Alaska hugs the side of Canada as it stretches all the way to the Arctic Circle.

The political boundary of the border is immense. It is, however, where this boundary meets the unique features of the Great Lakes that give rise to the Ambassador Bridge's monopolistic stature.

With its five, large interconnected bodies of water, the Great Lakes are home to 21 percent of the world's fresh water. Their total surface area covers eighty thousand square miles, and the lakes are so massive that they are often referred to as America's Third Coast.

The Great Lakes create a large physical divide between the U.S. and Canada, but between two of the lakes, Erie and Huron, the Detroit River flows as it pinches the distance separating the two countries. On one side of the waterway sits the city of Detroit and on the other side Windsor; and at the river's narrowest crossing, the Ambassador Bridge spans the seven-thousand-foot gap.

The Ambassador Bridge is a four-lane toll road, and it has a smaller sister crossing, a two-lane tunnel that runs beneath the river.

While people might claim that the bridge is not a true monopoly due to its smaller underground sister, if toll prices were ever raised, travelers would have little choice but to pay up. In 2001, the Ambassador Bridge alone carried 7.8 million passenger vehicles. To bypass these two crossings, a traveler's closest alternative is sixty miles away, entailing a two-hour detour and significant fuel expenses.

It is hard to overestimate the importance of the Detoit-Windsor crossing. Over 23 percent of all merchandise traded between the United States and Canada passes between Detroit and Windsor, accounting for $79 billion of goods annually traversing this tiny choke point.[2]

As a business, perhaps the most amazing attribute of the Ambassador Bridge—other than its monopoly-like power—is that since 1979 it has been owned by a single individual, Manuel "Matty" Moroun.[3] He has reaped enormous profit from this investment.

In 2004, when a second bridge was proposed to be built and funded by the Canadian government, the plan was met with large opposition—mostly from Moroun. While another bridge was sorely needed, Moroun used various delay tactics to push back its approval until 2015 with a completion date scheduled for 2020.[4] In the meantime, Moroun knows that he can continue sitting back and collecting his tolls in confidence. With each vehicle passing, he knows that his customers are not going anywhere.

● ● ●

The Location moat builder is about using geography to increase the loyalty of customers through convenience and territorial dominance. In applying it, we want to ask, "How do we manage our physical locations to get customers to choose us more frequently?"

FROM NEIGHBORHOOD CORNER TO COUNTER CORNER

The Evolution of Convenience

The basic function of choosing a location is to provide customers with convenience. This means giving them easy access to our products and services.

See's Candies, for example, has done a great job at providing easy access to its candies. The company owns numerous retail outlets scattered across the country. To improve the odds that people stop in, the candy retailer often picks locations on the south side of streets. During hot summer months, the company has learned that pedestrians are more likely to walk on the shady side of streets. To take advantage of busy holiday seasons, See's Candies also temporarily expands its footprint through a large flux of kiosks placed in malls, shopping centers, and airports. In this way, See's Candies can grow its presence during its high-sale months without incurring year-round fixed costs. See's Candies also offers online shopping options as well as phone ordering through its direct mail catalogues. When customers are most likely to buy holiday candies, See's Candies is not far away.

7-Eleven is perhaps the greatest pioneer of location strategy. In 1927, the company invented the convenience store concept. During that summer, Jefferson Green, known as "Uncle Johnny," operated an ice station and began experimenting with stocking bread, eggs, and milk at his station. As the summer months faded, he noticed that sales of ice dropped off, but bread, eggs, and milk continued to sell strong.[5]

Sensing an opportunity, Uncle Johnny approached Joe Thompson, Jr., a young executive at Southland Ice, which owned the ice stations. They agreed that if Uncle Johnny supplied milk, bread, eggs, cigarettes, and a few canned goods and kept track of the sales, Thompson would distribute the items to his ice stations. They would afterward split the profit. The following year, Uncle Johnny handed Thompson a check for $1,000, and the convenience store was born.

In witnessing the popularity of the idea, Thompson continued to push his ice stations to dedicate more shelf space to general goods. Eventually, his stations evolved to be open-front drive-in stores that were open seven days a week from seven in the morning to seven at night.[6] With convenient locations and hours, they were a great fit for people's daily shopping habits. In 1945, station managers agreed to extend hours to eleven o'clock, and the company adopted the name 7-Eleven.[7]

Importantly, Thompson didn't just view himself as a seller of goods; he envisioned himself as a seller of convenience. His business mantra was, "What they want, when and where they want it."[8]

As 7-Eleven expanded upon its mission, the company opened its hundredth store in 1952, its thousandth in 1963, and by 1972, it had 4,455 locations.[9] The following year, the company expanded internationally into the U.K., Canada, Mexico, and Japan.

After five decades of rapid growth, 7-Eleven finally fell victim to its own success. In the 1980s, Thompson had long since stepped away, and 7-Eleven faced stiffer competition as gas stations entered the convenience business. With heightened competition, management made a few disastrous decisions that would lead the company on a path of bankruptcy.

Among these failures was a push to diversify into industries that had little to do with the company's c-moat. In 1983, 7-Eleven purchased the oil refinery Citgo, a business that the retailer had no experience running. Right as the deal was struck, the industry experienced one of its worst supply gluts. Seeing nothing but losses on the horizon, 7-Eleven sold Citgo three years later.[10]

Management also poured money into an expensive real estate development called Dallas Cityplace, a high-rise office complex. This project required $85 million a year in funding.[11] Major delays and a lack of demand led to only one of its two towers being built.

By 1986, these side projects had taken a toll on the company's finances. Consultants were brought in to restructure 7-Eleven's business. Their suggestion was to cut costs by laying off a large number of employees. As soon as their advice was implemented, the cohesion of the company dissolved and the morale of employees plummeted. A former company vice-president commented, "The company's forward momentum stopped . . . Discussion of who-will-get-it-next replaced brainstorming sessions . . . It was definitely the beginning of a malaise."[12]

With the business falling apart on all fronts, Joe Thompson's heirs provided the final straw to break the camel's back. In 1987, in an attempt to maintain control of the company, they announced a leveraged buyout of 7-Eleven. They funded their purchase by loading the company with $4 billion of debt.[13] Three months later, in what would become famously known as Black Monday, the stock market crashed 22 percent in a single day.

Facing a bad economy, a broken workforce, a fragmented collection of businesses, and the strains of a debt-laden balance sheet, 7-Eleven defaulted on its debts in 1990 and declared bankruptcy.

Ironically, bankruptcy would become a blessing in disguise. While 7-Eleven's old shareholders were wiped out, the new owners would bring the company back to its roots and set it on the right path again. The company's savior was none other than one of 7-Eleven's own franchisees.

As 7-Eleven was losing focus in the U.S., its popularity had exploded in Japan. Ito-Yokado was a major franchise operator in Japan and 7-Eleven Japan was the country's largest convenience store chain. Joining forces, the two purchased a 70 percent stake in 7-Eleven, giving them effective control over their parent company.[14]

Even though the convenience store concept originated in America, on the other side of the Pacific, the Japanese had been steadily refining it for years. As 7-Eleven's new owner, Ito-Yokado brought a test run of its operations to fifty-two 7-Eleven stores in and around Austin, Texas. The effects were remarkable. Sales increased 11.4 percent more than sales of comparable stores in Dallas.[15]

The difference was that the old 7-Eleven brought convenience to the neighborhood level, but the new Japanese 7-Eleven was bringing convenience down to the counter level.

With the Japanese system, each store was internally customized to fit the specific needs of its neighborhood and demographic. The new 7-Eleven went beyond convenient store locations to micro-managing the convenience of how goods were placed on store shelves. If children were prone to visit a particular store, candy would be placed on lower shelves that gave them easier access. If more single adults stopped in, more fresh prepared foods were offered. In California, a 7-Eleven located near a warehouse employing young adults dedicated an entire cooler just to energy drinks.

Under the new Japanese system, stores also installed advanced point-of-sale systems that provided real-time inventory tracking. While managing inventory became easier, the real purpose was to gain insight into customer behaviors. By combining past purchase history and forecasting, the system allows 7-Eleven store managers to predict the needs of their customers before they happen.

For example, 7-Eleven has learned that when temperatures drop below forty degrees, certain breakfast muffins will sell better than others. It knows that while cinnamon coffee is popular in SoCal, hazelnut coffee is preferred in the Pacific Northwest. The system even keeps tabs on weather patterns and suggest bringing umbrellas to the front of a store when rain is forecasted.[16]

In a typical store, five different customer demographics enter its doors during different times of the day. 7-Eleven has learned how to rotate its fresh foods to meet their varying preferences. David Podeschi, one of 7-Eleven's vice-presidents, has said, "We've gone from having no idea what we were selling to predicting what customers want even before they know it."[17]

Under its new ownership, 7-Eleven has experienced a phenomenal rebound in the United States. With an extreme focus not only on neighborhood convenience but internal store convenience, the company recorded its thirty-sixth consecutive quarter of same-store sales growth.[19] Amazingly, 7-Eleven's success—both past and present—stemmed from Joe Thompson's simple mantra: "What they want, when and where they want it."

Note: *The Location moat builder is technically a hybrid of the other moat building categories, and as such, its topics will overlap our other tools.*

"THERE CAN BE ONLY ONE"
Territorial Behavior and Choosing Battlegrounds

In the B-movie *The Highlander*, there is a famous quote that goes, "There can be only one." The story's plot revolves around a fabled group of outcasts who can only be killed by their own kind until one person remains standing. The movie is actually quite terrible. The quote, however, fits surprisingly well into our discussion of location strategy. In many instances, businesses can exhibit territorial behaviors to the point where "there can be only one."

When thinking about territorial behavior, it helps to picture a *radius of dominance* emanating around a business. Within this radius, customers will have a very high chance of choosing the business. This radius may extend out a few miles, a few blocks, or perhaps only as far as the doorstep. What is important is that within this area, it is not easy for competitors to encroach on a business's customers.

In New York, the dry cleaning business is highly territorial. Not only is the industry's basic function to provide convenience, but because driving is a hassle, many people walk to do their errands. As such, dry cleaners have a radius of dominance that extends outward for one or two blocks; after all, people will want to choose their closest cleaner.

For competitors, it also doesn't make sense to open a shop next door to existing dry cleaners as this creates the greatest territorial overlap and the fiercest competition. Three or four blocks out, however, the dominance of existing dry cleaners diminishes. This is why we often find dry cleaners spaced out, so that each will have a better chance of establishing its own territorial monopoly.

Another highly territorial industry is ready-mixed concrete, which involves trucks carrying drums of concrete to construction sites. Concrete itself is dirt cheap, but the transportation costs are high. The further away a construction site, the greater the fuel expenses. For longer distances, transporting concrete is cost-inefficient. In addition to fuel costs, concrete itself has a short life span. Once mixed, it must be used within two hours. From the moment it is loaded onto a truck, the clock starts ticking.

Because of the fuel costs and time-sensitive nature, contractors are usually better off choosing their nearest provider. This also helps contractors buffer against any potential delays. As such, ready-mixed concrete businesses tend to be highly-localized with a radius of dominance that extends for about a ninety minute drive out.

When gauging a radius of dominance, be aware that it can apply differently to different customer groups. A downtown diner, for example, might serve a weekday lunch crowd, weekday grab-and-go breakfast crowd, and weekend brunch crowd. Each group has its own mobility and time constraints. To better gauge a business's radius of dominance, think about how it might apply differently to each customer group.

● ● ●

Understanding the radius of dominance concept can also help us develop territorial dominance over customers. How do we pick multiple locations to saturate a given territory by overlapping multiple radiuses of dominance? In doing so, we are effectively trying to squeeze out the ability of competitors to enter the area and challenge us.

In previous chapters, we saw how Southwest Airlines disrupted the airline industry by flying nonstop routes between major cities. Its rivals faced steep price competition and eroding market share. Out of this turmoil, the strongest competitor to emerge was Continental Airlines—which in 2010 merged with United Airlines.

Interestingly, Continental's strategy ran opposite of Southwest's. While Southwest pushed into major metropolitan markets, Continental expanded its service into smaller rural towns and cities that were outside the reach of Southwest's larger Boeing 737 planes. Southwest had a radius of dominance around certain people who lived and traveled between major metropolitan areas, but it was nonexistent in these smaller cities. By employing smaller planes, like the fifty-seat Embraer jets and Bombardier CRJs, Continental dominated territories that Southwest couldn't touch.

Continental didn't just fly into smaller towns and cities, but it strategically chose airport locations that were roughly 100 miles apart from each other and could be connected to its major hubs. The company's largest hub, George Bush Intercontinental Airport in Houston, connected to thirty-one cities and towns across the Texas, Oklahoma, Arkansas, and Louisiana region. Through a pervasive territorial presence in the South Central United States, Continental built itself a strong c-moat.

● ● ●

During Wal-Mart's early growth years, Sam Walton also employed radius of dominance in developing a retailing strategy. The prevailing wisdom was to open stores in large, growing markets that provided the largest supply of customers.

Sam Walton wasn't as worried about the number of customers as much as he was about competition. Wal-Mart was still a tiny player back then and Walton knew that he would be crushed if it went head-to-head against the national giants of Sears, Kmart, and Ben Franklin.

Sam Walton specifically looked into building his stores in small towns with populations of twenty-five thousand people or fewer.[20] These markets were often overlooked by the large national retail giants, and when Wal-Mart entered, there would be little in the way of competition—the main rivals would be small mom-and-pop stores.

Just as important to his strategy was that the population of these small towns could only support one large box store. Once Wal-Mart was entrenched in these markets, rivals had a hard time justifying entering.

Using this expansion formula, Sam Walton dominated one small town after another until Wal-Mart reached a scale where it could compete squarely with the other national players.

By the time Wal-Mart was seen as a real threat, the other large national players were at a disadvantage. Wal-Mart had placed its stores in territories where competitors could not easily encroach; on the other hand, in the larger markets of the other retailing giants, Wal-Mart could easily add stores.

When choosing its locations, Sam Walton was smart in going where competition was the weakest and where major competitors would not follow. Today, Wal-Mart remains territorially dominant in the South. As cities and towns have grown larger, the company continues to add new retail stores to saturate these markets against potential competitors.

POCKETS OF TIME AND SPACE
Designing Temporary Monopolies

"Half of success is being at the right place at the right time." Can we take this advice one step further by creating a set of circumstances for putting our business "at the right place at the right time"?

The question is, "How do we pair location and timing to create stronger c-moats over people, even if only temporarily?" Are we able to develop pockets of space and time that exhibit monopolistic tendencies?

Movie theaters are a great example of capturing audiences. While people only stay on a theater's premises for a few hours at a time, during their visit, food and drink options are severely limited. As such, prices can be set much higher.

Cruise ships and amusement parks also exhibit this monopolistic trait. Once on their turf, customers cannot easily leave or re-enter. For the duration of a person's visit, these businesses will have a wide c-moat around them—high prices and all.

More recently, airports have become great spaces for developing temporary monopolies. After the rise of security standards due to 9/11, travelers are required to show up earlier for flights and plan for extra time getting through security. As such, people are spending more time lingering in airports. It is a perfect setup for retailers and restaurants. How often is there a captive audience of well-off individuals with lots of spare time and limited options?

In our own businesses, how do we create a strong radius of dominance and get people to stay within this territory for long periods of time? The better we can accomplish both of these tasks, the stronger our hold over customers.

CHAPTER TEN

BRANDING (P)

The Branding moat builder creates
mental associations with customers to increase
the likelihood that they choose a business.

● ● ●

Chapter Overview: Brands convey important messages that can sway the purchasing decisions of customers. Before these messages can be delivered effectively, however, brands must first create differentiation; only afterwards should meaning be attached to a brand. The message of a brand should be simple and contain a promise. Its power will depend on how highly it sits in customer minds and how strongly it resonates with customers. Storytelling and emotional connections are useful devices for helping brands associate better with people.

n 1982, seven people died when random bottles of Tylenol in Chicago-area drugstores were laced with cyanide poison. Within days, Tylenol's market share plummeted from 35 percent to 8 percent.[1]

Johnson & Johnson, the maker of Tylenol, faced a nightmare crisis as the public became fearful of its products. The act of presumably a single person had single-handedly brought the company to its knees.

During this dark time, James Burke, the CEO of Johnson & Johnson, took control of the delicate situation. To re-instill the public's confidence, Burke announced that, first and foremost, Johnson & Johnson was responsible to its customers and not to corporate profits. He then issued the largest product recall at the time, and within six days took all thirty-one million bottles of Tylenol off store shelves.[2]

Stores shelves sat empty of Tylenol's products for months. When Burke finally reintroduced Tylenol, he would do so in a first-of-its-kind triple-sealed, tamper-resistant packaging.[3] The cautious design ensured that no one could poison Tylenol's products again.

The recall and updated packaging were costly to implement, estimated at $150 million. Burke's actions, however, kept the brand from collapsing and instrumentally gave Tylenol a chance to regain consumer confidence and save its reputation.[4] Three months after the horrific poisonings, Tylenol's market share rebounded to 24 percent, and only eight months later, it recovered to pre-crisis levels.[5]

● ● ●

A company's image and reputation are vital to its success. The Branding moat builder shapes people's perceptions of a business by cultivating metal associations with it. The goal is to pass valuable information to shoppers that will influence their purchases.

Cultivating a brand will require great care. Brands are expensive to build but easy to tarnish. Warren Buffett said it best: "It takes twenty years to build a reputation and five minutes to ruin it. If you think about that you'll do things differently."[6] Trust is fragile and constantly needs to be nurtured.

When spreading the word about a brand, we will have to shout its message from the mountaintop. It will be a long, incremental process before the messages begin to stick. When facing bad publicity, however, remember the saying, "Nothing travels faster than bad news."

How do we develop an effective brand? The key is to forge strong mental associations between our brand and our customers. The big question is, "What types of mental associations should we create?"

Andrew Ehrenberg provided us with a vital clue. In his studies, he discovered that repeat loyalty was highly-correlated to market share. And of course this makes sense. As we strive to become number-one or number-two with our customers, we need to increase our rate of repeat loyalty.

A good branding strategy, therefore, not only sells people the first time, but it sells people over and over again. The priority of a brand's association is to create a lasting impression that keeps people returning.

This major reason for this is because brands are most effective at swaying repeat decisions if people have been exposed to it over and over again; brands are less effective on first time customers who have had only minimal exposure. The effort needed to sway a current customer is far less than the effort required to sway a new customer.

As such, the focus of the Brand moat builder is not on attaining new customers but on keeping existing customers. If we successfully accomplish this, then when new customers do try our business, we can get them to stick around.

When implementing the Brand moat builder, we want to ask, "What mental associations can we create with customers to increase their likelihood of choosing us?"

To clarify some common terms, a *brand* refers to how customers perceive a business, and this perception directly affects purchasing decisions. *Advertising* is how a business publicizes its offerings, and *marketing* is how a business sells its offerings. Advertising and marketing are subsets of our overall brand strategy.

HOW MUCH IS A NAME WORTH?
An Expensive Lesson in Branding

In 1961, Ray Kroc received a phone call in his Chicago office from Dick McDonald, one of the two founding brothers of the McDonald's fast food chain.[7]

Kroc was responsible for the restaurant chain's rapid expansion to 228 stores, with annual revenues of $37.8 million.[8] He supervised the franchisees, developed its supplier system, and redesigned the operational procedures that were key to the chain's efficiency.

The problem was that Kroc had clearly overstepped the bounds of his authority. He was acting like the company's CEO even though his official job title was National Licensing Agent.

For the most part, the McDonald brothers gave him the leeway to do whatever he wanted, but Kroc realized that they could pull the rug from out under him at any time. Kroc had poured his soul into McDonald's, and to protect his hard work, he needed to secure his future with the company. As such, he wanted to buy McDonald's from the two brothers.

"Are you there, Ray?" Dick McDonald's voice sounded over the phone. Infuriated, Kroc replied, "Didn't you hear the racket, that was the sound of me falling from the LaSalle-Wacker building to the pavement."[9] Dick McDonald was offering to sell the company to Kroc for $2.7 million. For Kroc, the offer was tantamount to highway robbery.

Even though McDonald's was rapidly growing, the vast majority of its profits flowed to its franchisees and not to its corporate headquarters. The parent company only owned a handful of stores, like the original San Bernardino drive-in, which profited $100,000 a year, but the head office earned a meager $77,000 a year. The $2.7 million price tag seemed exorbitant.[10]

Kroc relented and agreed to take the deal. As he drew up the papers, his frustration with the brothers would boil over into a deep vendetta. When the terms of the deal were brought up, Kroc was informed that the San Bernardino store was not included in the sale. According to Kroc's own estimation, the store alone was worth one-third the purchase price. For Kroc, it was the final straw in their relationship; the greed of the brothers had gone too far.

As painful as it was, Kroc purchased the company anyway. He later commented, "It was a lot of money to pay for a name . . . I suppose I could have called it 'McDougall's' and started over. But I was getting old—too old to fart around. I decided to take their deal anyway."[11] Importantly, Kroc finally owned his freedom and the McDonald's brand.

Within months of taking ownership, Kroc exacted his payback. He ordered the brothers to take down the McDonald's sign at the San Bernardino drive-in. He then erected a brand-new McDonald's less than a block away. The brothers had to rename their store to Big M.

The name change was devastating to Big M's sales. Even though Big M and McDonald's looked the same, ran the same operations, and even offered the exact same menu, people drove from all over to visit McDonald's, not Big M. In a few years, Big M's sales plummeted from $400,000 a year to $81,000.[12] In a turnaround attempt, the McDonald brothers sold the restaurant to a new operator, but it was to no avail. In 1970, Big M permanently shuttered its doors.

Kroc paid an enormous price for the McDonald's name, but he also learned a valuable lesson: brands can make or break a company. The irony was that the McDonald brothers fully realized the value of their brand when selling it to Kroc; as rivals, however, they then witnessed its ability to devastate the competition. Afterwards, Kroc would always stay vigilant in protecting the McDonald's name and its reputation.

THE ECONOMICS OF WATERED-DOWN MILK
Differentiation as a Prerequisite

The first step in developing a brand is to help customers differentiate our products and services from competitors. *Brand names* typically serve as this unique identifier because they are protected by law from being counterfeited, mimicked, or confused.

While unique differentiation does not make a company better per se, it will provide customers with a way to categorize useful information about our company's specific offerings.

In instances where marketplaces lack unique differentiation, deep economic challenges will crop up. When there is no reliable information for helping people distinguish between the quality of products, competing products will look similar, and in a sea of similar-looking choices, customers will gravitate towards the lowest-priced item.

The effect can be devastating for businesses and consumers. In the 1950s and 1960s, India's milk industry suffered a severe differentiation problem. At the time, milk was sold out of large, generic metal tins that were indistinguishable from one another. Vendors purchased milk from dairy farmers, stored it in these metal tins, and then brought the milk to the city to be sold. When vendors sold this milk in city markets, it was poured from these tins into containers supplied by customers.[13]

As the industry evolved, vendors discovered that they could fatten their profits by watering down their milk. Customers couldn't tell if the milk was adulterated by simply looking at it, and because milk was sold out of generic-looking tins, there was no way for customers to differentiate what they were buying.

With all milk choices looking similar, people defaulted to the cheapest option—after all, this was the safest bet for not getting ripped off.

As India's milk industry evolved, it became a race to the bottom. As poor-quality vendors undercut the prices of high-quality vendors, high-quality sellers became unable to compete with their cheaper-priced rivals and were forced to join in watering down their milk.

Interestingly, even as the price of milk dropped in India, its inferior quality led to a widespread decrease in consumption. In 1950, India's annual per-capita milk consumption was 139 grams; by 1970, it dropped to 105 grams—a 24 percent decline.[14]

In the 1970s, India's National Dairy Development Board (NDDB) was tasked with changing the market's status quo. The NDDB taught farmers and vendors how to test for milk quality by measuring fat content. The NDDB then improved the supply chain by scheduling more regular milk pickups in rural areas where the dairy farmers were located. And perhaps most significantly, the NDDB began selling their milk under branded names.

As customers learned to distinguish the difference between high-quality and low-quality milk products, the NDDB was able to purchase milk from farmers at 15 percent higher prices while still making a profit.[15] In addition, the NDDB's brand of ice cream became so popular and renowned for its top quality that it became a source of national pride.

The recovery of India's milk industry shows us the importance of differentiation as a fundamental prerequisite for informing people about products and services. When markets lack differentiation, both high-quality and low-quality products will look similar, and low prices will ultimately prevail. Under these settings, businesses will lack the basic incentives for creating higher-quality products.

KISS, A DIAMOND, AND A PROMISE
The Branding of Names

Differentiation begins with having a brand name. Once we have this unique identifier, we can begin to attach meaning to it. Since the ultimate goal is to increase the probability that customers continue to choose us in the future, a brand's effectiveness will depend on how strongly we can get customers to associate with it.

Perhaps the most overlooked principle in branding is KISS, or "Keep it simple, stupid." With a plethora of brands vying for people's attention, the one that sticks out the most will have the simplest and strongest message. When complexity enters the equation, people are quick to forget.

Some examples of strong associations are Southwest Airlines' reliable, no-frills, low-cost flying; BMW's sporty, luxury performance; and Volvo's safety focus. When we think about Apple, we have strong impressions of elegant designs that fit modern lifestyles. These brands carry simple messages; adding greater complexity would likely dilute their messages and our desire to choose them.

● ● ●

According to *Advertising Age* magazine, the highest-rated slogan of the twentieth century was, "A diamond is forever."[16] This advertising campaign was developed by De Beers and made it to the top of the list for both its scope and effectiveness.

(Note: De Beers is special in that it could advertise diamonds generically rather using a brand name because, at the time of the campaign, the company controlled 80 to 90 percent of the world's diamond supply.[17] We will take a closer look at this monopolistic feat in the next chapter.)

What makes De Beers's advertising campaign remarkable is that it sells a product that has virtually no industrial application. Other than a rarely needed cutting ability, diamonds have zero practical value. Demand is almost entirely driven by people's cultural desire to make a symbolic gesture.

Through a heavy bombardment of advertisements, De Beers has institutionalized diamonds as a necessary engagement gift. The slogan, "A diamond is forever," symbolizes people's aspiration to have long, lasting loves. When a person purchases a diamond ring for their fiancée, it is a sign of their dedication and commitment. Amazingly, De Beers has used advertisements to reshape our society's cultural norms.

As a statement to the ad campaign's effectiveness, in 1968, fewer than 5 percent of Japanese women received diamond engagement rings. By 1981, through heavy advertising, that number had risen to 60 percent.[18] De Beers has successfully reinforced a simple message: "If you want your love to be eternal, buy a diamond ring."

●　●　●

To the extent possible, we want our messages to be simple, but if necessary, complex messages can be attached to brands. Complex messages require far more resources to deliver. The principle of KISS still applies; the trick is to break complex messages down to their constituent parts and then treat each part as its own simple message.

American auto insurer GEICO has delivered a tough set of messages to its customers. GEICO's main business strategy is built around the Low Cost moat builder. By selling insurance policies over the phone and Internet, GEICO has skipped the expense of maintaining physical agent locations. This low-cost structure allows the company to pass greater savings to its customers through lower rates.

During the early stages of Internet commerce, GEICO faced an uphill battle of getting people to buy car insurance policies online. Making purchases over the Internet was still a new idea and convincing people to trust online transactions was not easy.

To be successful, GEICO had to deliver a complex set of messages: buying insurance online was going to be easy, the insurance purchased would be high-quality and trustworthy, and people could save money doing so. If any of these elements was missing, people had no great reason for buying online.

Addressing these potential barriers meant that GEICO needed to convince customers that it could deliver on every front. To achieve this, a multipronged ad campaign was developed that featured three distinct themes: GEICO's gecko mascot, customer testimonials, and the slogan, "So easy, a caveman can do it."[19]

The first of these advertisements featured a talking gecko with a British accent and a skittish personality. He presented an aura of sophistication and approachability. The commercial's biggest success was that it solidified the name GEICO by drawing associations to the word "gecko." GEICO stands for Government Employees Insurance Company, a name that hardly rolls off the tongue. GEICO's gecko made the name quite memorable.

Next in the lineup were the customer-testimonial commercials, which featured customers reading real letters that they sent in praising GEICO's outstanding service. To add a splash of humor, minor celebrities stood next to the readers by injecting their personal flair. In one commercial, a customer reads, "I love my car like I love my wife." Charo, from the game show *Hollywood Squares*, chimes in, "*Muy romantico!*"[20] Another commercial features singer Little Richard emphasizing a customer's letter by inserting his signature exclamation, "Mashed potatoes!" The testimonials were memorable and a strong endorsement of GEICO's high-quality customer care.

And the last of the ads became the most popular. These spots portrayed two cavemen feeling frustrated with living in a modern world. They struggled with being stereotyped. The ads were humorous, memorable, and proclaimed that GEICO could empathize with people's feelings and the small struggles that they encountered in daily life. Buying car insurance from GEICO was going to be easy; the voiceover at the end of the caveman commercials said it all: "GEICO. So easy, a caveman can do it."

At the end of all three ads, a final message unified the campaign's theme: "Fifteen minutes could save you 15 percent or more on car insurance." This message struck at the heart of GEICO's benefit and has been reinforced over and over again. The effect is that when a person wants to buy auto insurance, GEICO's message will likely pop into their head. And, of course, why not spend fifteen minutes for a chance to save 15 percent or more?

Running this three-pronged campaign has taken tremendous resources. To be effective, GEICO had to reiterate each message until it became clear. In 1995, GEICO spent $10 million on ads. In 2000, it spent $270 million, and by 2013, its ad budget reached an astonishing $1.18 billion.[21] For this money, GEICO has bought itself a prominent place in people's minds, and impressively altered the way people shop for auto insurance. The company has grown from 3.7 million vehicles insured in 1995 to 22 million vehicles insured in 2014.[22] Its market share has risen from 2.6 percent to 10.3 percent.[23] GEICO is now the second-largest auto insurance company in the U.S. and on pace to take the top spot as it steadily surpasses its rivals.

● ● ●

While the KISS principle is important to a message's potency, what should the actual message be?

The best messages will contain a promise. What is in it for customers if they choose a particular business or product? This promise should be authentic and be at the heart of a company's mission statement. It should also be tailored for each target audience.

Surprisingly, many businesses fail to deliver compelling promises in their branding. GoDaddy has produced highly memorable ad campaigns featuring attractive female NASCAR driver Danica Patrick. While these commercials cast a wide net and give GoDaddy broad name recognition, they fail to deliver a coherent promise. While many people may have heard of the GoDaddy brand, few know when or why they might choose the company.

In another botch, RadioShack purchased a thirty-second advertising spot during 2014's Super Bowl XLVIII. The estimated cost of this spot was $4 million.[24] The commercial featured famous characters from the '80s (Hulk Hogan, Alf, Teen Wolf, the California Raisins) entering a RadioShack and clearing out the store's entire inventory. The intended message to people was clear: the store had become outdated and needed to become more modern.

The ad was funny and entertaining, but the problem was that it didn't promise a benefit. Even if RadioShack became less stuck in the past, there was no compelling reason why anyone should visit a RadioShack store. While the retailer promised to do things differently, it didn't promise a real benefit to customers.

When developing our own brands, we need to provide compelling reasons for customers to choose us. Jimmy John's promises fast and fresh sub sandwiches, Virgin Airlines promises exceptional service and memorable experiences, and DeWalt promises tough, durable tools. Good brand will make clear promises and then deliver.

EYE PATCHES AND DRESS SHIRTS
The Branding of Narratives

It is said that a picture is worth a thousand words. For David Ogilvy, they were worth far more. At a glance, pictures could tell memorable and deeply compelling stories. In 1951, a print ad of a man wearing a dress shirt and sporting a $1.50 eye patch would catapult Ogilvy to advertising fame.[25]

Described as a flamboyant Englishman, Ogilvy was a relative latecomer to the advertising world. In his life, he always veered towards the road less taken. During World War II, Ogilvy worked for the British government, and after the war ended, he sought a more peaceful existence among the Amish in Lancaster, Pennsylvania. In a land without electricity, he leased a few acres and put down roots as a tobacco farmer. Ogilvy fondly recalled, "The years [I] spent in Lancaster Country were the richest of my life . . . but it became apparent that I could never earn my living as a farmer."[26]

At the age of thirty-seven, Ogilvy reversed course and headed to the Big Apple, where he decided to join the advertising industry. After contemplating a job application with Young & Rubicam, a rising firm in the advertising world, Ogilvy changed his mind. "I never thought that Y&R would hire me—I didn't think I had any credentials."[27]

Then in Ogilvy-esque fashion and against convention wisdom, with $6,000 in his pocket, no American advertising experience, and no clients, Ogilvy started his own agency.[28]

For a newcomer, the act was audacious. Ogilvy garnered a little support from his brother Francis, who was a managing director of the British ad firm Mather & Crowther and who helped him secure a $45,000 loan.[29] In 1948, Ogilvy opened shop under the moniker Ogilvy & Mather.

As the new face on the block, business was nothing short of underwhelming. Ogilvy & Mather was competing against three thousand other ad agencies that were trying to make a name for themselves. Fortunately, Ogilvy signed a partner who was well connected enough to land the firm a $3 million contract with Sun Oil—enough to keep the firm afloat.[30]

It would be a much smaller account that would define Ogilvy's career. In 1951, a small Maine shirt-maker named Hathaway approached Ogilvy with an advertising dilemma. The obscure dress-shirt producer wanted a print advertising campaign that could bring it into the national spotlight and challenge its largest competitor Arrow.

There was only one hitch. Ogilvy was given an advertising budget of $30,000 as opposed to the $2 million that Arrow was spending.[31] Despite being wary of such a small account with uncertain prospects, Ogilvy signed on anyway.

In the advertising industry, Ogilvy had become convinced that photographs were a more compelling medium than the typical drawn pictures of the day. During one of Hathaway's photo shoots, as Ogilvy walked to the studio, he chanced upon a drugstore and saw an eye patch in the window. He stopped in, bought the eye patch, and, upon showing up at the photo shoot, placed it on the male model's head. The man's image would become famously known as "the Hathaway Man," a well-dressed man donning an eye patch whose life was full of mystery and intrigue.

Photos depicted the Hathaway Man in a variety of curious settings. One moment, the well-dressed man would be driving a tractor; the next, he would be collecting butterflies; in another, he would be conducting the symphony at Carnegie Hall. Images of this mysterious man in intriguing situations created a backstory that captivated people's imagination and attention. The Hathaway Man thrust the obscure shirt maker into the limelight.

For his work, Ogilvy profited a mere $6,000.[32] The greater reward, however, was that the name Ogilvy became synonymous with the biggest, boldest ideas that advertising had to offer. Ogilvy himself became famous for his daring, effective ads.

Ogilvy's discovery was that brands weren't limited to describing products and services, but could also tell deeply compelling stories. People connected with stories on more personal levels than lists of product attributes, and they were far more memorable. Ogilvy didn't just sell people on products, he sold them on narratives.

Some of Ogilvy's later campaigns included Maxwell House Coffee's, "Good to the last drop," Rolls-Royce's, "At 60 miles an hour the loudest noise in this new Rolls-Royce comes from the electric clock," and American Express's, "Don't leave home without it."[33]

When it comes to branding, stories can be as compelling as the actual products and services. Customers identify more readily with stories because they empathize with them more than products.

How do we align our businesses to tell stories that will resonate with customer? And, just as importantly, how do we tell these stories in an authentic manner? What qualities do our customers admire and how do we portray these qualities using a narrative?

BOTTLING A LITTLE HAPPINESS
The Branding of Emotions

Coca-Cola is probably the most successful brand name in the world. For 157 years, Coca-Cola has shared in our culture and in our life's personal moments. It was there when we went to the movies, during our long road trips, and at our sports games. It has been served from restaurants to vending machines, from McDonald's to The Ritz-Carlton. Coca-Cola's presence has been ubiquitous.

Despite being a century and a half old, Coca-Cola's brand has remained surprisingly relevant. The brand has survived wars, fashion changes, depressions, and even vast technological advancements. In 2012, Coca-Cola still managed to take top title as the "world's most valuable brand."[34]

What is it about the Coca-Cola that makes it so special? How has its brand endured for so long?

In the early 2000s, researchers at the Baylor College of Medicine in Texas conducted a series of experiments to uncover Coca-Cola's secret.[35] In blind taste tests, subjects were given both Coca-Cola and Pepsi in unmarked cups. The subjects were asked which drink they preferred, and without knowing what was in each cup, respondents almost equally chose Coca-Cola and Pepsi.

During a second round of testing, subjects were again given two cups of soda. This time, they were told that one cup contained Coca-Cola, while the other may or may not be Coca-Cola. Unknown to tasters, both cups always contained Coca-Cola. When asked their preference, subjects overwhelmingly chose the cup labeled "Coca-Cola." When the same experiment was then conducted using Pepsi, the subjects only held a weak preference for the cup labeled "Pepsi" versus the unmarked cup. For some reason, people felt a stronger affinity for Coca-Cola's name.

Here is where the experiments got interesting. While subjects were performing their taste tests, they were also undergoing fMRI brain scans to map out their neural activity.

When drinking either soda, the subjects' ventromedial prefrontal cortexes, or pleasure centers, lit up. It was only when drinking soda labeled Coca-Cola that subjects also showed heightened brain activity in the hippocampus, dorsolateral prefrontal cortexes, and mid-sections of the brain—i.e., the areas responsible for short- and long-term memories. When drinking Coca-Cola as opposed to Pepsi, the brain activity in these memory centers was up to five times higher.

Coca-Cola achieved something remarkable As a carbonated beverage, Coca-Cola was not superior to Pepsi taste-wise, but when a drink was labeled "Coca-Cola," consumers' enjoyment of it was greatly enhanced by their past memories of it. People had strong mental associations to the Coca-Cola name, and it made them desire it more.

Coca-Cola's brand strategy is reflected in its core mission, "To offer a small pleasure that would make everyday living a little more enjoyable."[36] With every sip, Coca-Cola works to reinforce a small positive association in people. Over the years, these small positive associations have added up to creating strong preferences.

The company's past advertising slogans have included, "Delicious and refreshing," "Ice-cold sunshine," "Coca-Cola . . . makes good things taste better," "Have a Coke and a smile," and of course the timeless and nostalgic, "Always Coca-Cola."[37]

When building our own brands, each interaction between us and our customers—whether through advertising, person-to-person service, or even when fixing a mistake—is a chance for us to reinforce a positive image. We want to continually strengthen the idea that our business is the best place for customers and the best choice for their future purchases.

CHAPTER ELEVEN

SUPPLY (I)

The Supply moat builder reduces
the competitive intensity of an industry by limiting
the alternatives available to customers.

● ● ●

Chapter Overview: A simple way to increase the probability that
customers choose a business is to reduce their supply of alternatives.
The most basic method for achieving this is to form cartels and trusts
which limit competition; these groups attempt to create virtual
monopolies around customers. While highly effective, these arrange-
ments are often deemed illegal. A more condoned method of eliminating
competitors is through mergers and acquisitions—processes where two
competitors formally join forces by becoming a single entity. Here, two
businesses are able to eliminate each other as rivals and pare down
the playing field; the drawback, however, is that these processes are
difficult to implement and still subject to some regulatory scrutiny.

Perhaps surprisingly, governments play a large role in actively suppressing the competitive forces of some markets—though usually in a targeted manner and only for certain industries. The patent system, for example, grants innovators temporary monopolies as a reward for developing new inventions. Patents limit competition, but they do so to incentivize technological advancements. In addition, industries considered vital to our economy, such as electric utilities and banks, are more protected from competition than in typical markets. This reduced competition is often in exchange for higher regulation. Since these industries provide essential services to businesses and consumers, if they failed due to market forces, they would paralyze the entire economy.

The Supply moat builder is much like the Monopoly board game. When we play the game, we quickly learn that getting rid of the other players is highly profitable. If we can squeeze out rivals to gain control of a property color, rent will automatically double. If we can push opponents into bankruptcy, we will get to buy their properties and consolidate our power. Eliminating rivals is not only highly profitable; it is how the game is won.

Similar to the Monopoly board game, the Supply moat builder works to widen c-moats by eliminating the competition. When the *supply of alternatives* available to customers can be reduced, a business's chances of being chosen will increase. If all alternatives can be erased, the business will hold a monopoly.

There are two main avenues for reducing competition. The first is to work in conjunction with rivals to be less competitive. This takes the form of cartels, trusts, or trade groups that collude in raising prices; these organizations work to reduce the competitive intensity of an industry. The second is to pare down the number of competitors in a playing field. This involves activities such as mergers, acquisitions, and trying to bankrupt opponents through price wars.

Before applying the Supply moat builder, great caution is required. Many of its methods are considered anticompetitive and monopolistic and, as such, are deemed illegal. Before jumping into the fire with regulators, do your due diligence.

To implement the Supply moat builder, we want to ask, "How do we reduce the number of alternatives available to our customers? And if we can't reduce that number, how do we reduce the intensity of competition that is trying to take our customers away?"

INSIDE THE DIAMOND CARTEL
Price-Fixing Empires

Near the Smithfield market in the heart of London, a large fortress-like building sits quietly off the main street. It is easy for passersby to walk past the building without thinking twice about it. The six-story complex is made of stone and glass; its upper floors feature large, expansive windows that provide views of the city while the bottom two floors offer only narrow vertical slits for windows. A heavily-gated driveway guards the entrance. For those that see the building, it is imposing, but just bland enough to be easily forgotten.

Every five weeks like clockwork, a group of people secretly congregate behind this building's walls.[1] The members of this group, known as Sightholders, will each be handed a container roughly the size of a shoebox, and inside it, each Sightholder will find their allotment of precious uncut diamonds–the spoils of one of the world's longest running cartels.

The building's address is 17 Charterhouse Street and it is the world headquarters of De Beers. To the knowledgeable, this building is one of the most secure sites in all of Europe. At times, its vaults have housed a diamond supply worth $5 billion.[2] Importantly, during times of economic weakness, excess diamonds can be stored here rather than flood the marketplace.

To become a member of the De Beers family requires obeying a strict set of rules. Sightholders are not allowed to argue the quantity of diamonds they receive in a box. They cannot negotiate the price they pay for a box. And they are restricted from reselling any of its contents in uncut form. Like with the strictest father doling out allowances, disagreements are not tolerated.[3]

De Beers was originally founded by Cecil Rhodes in 1888. At the time, a new diamond deposit was discovered in South Africa, and in a shrewd move, rather than fighting the prospects of this new competitor, Rhodes decided that it would be better to gain control over it. He banded with other diamond producers to create De Beers Consolidated Mines as an entity to finance the purchase of all South African diamond mines.[4] In doing so, Rhodes also brought the majority of the world's diamond production under one roof, where volume and pricing could be centrally controlled.

This partnership served its members well until a misstep in 1902 threatened to unravel the cartel. De Beers concluded that a newly discovered mine in South Africa was "salted," or fraudulent. Sensing potential error, a man named Ernest Oppenheimer sent his brother to investigate the mine. Upon learning that the mine was indeed bona fide, Oppenheimer quickly secured the mining rights to it.

This oversight proved disastrous for the De Beers cartel. By 1907, Oppenheimer's mine was producing 1.9 million carats of diamonds, on par with the cartel's two-million-carat production.[5] The following year, in an attempt to maintain price control, De Beers had stockpiled eighteen months' worth of inventory.[6]

Oppenheimer was using his mine to drive a stake through the heart of De Beers. His ultimate intention, however, was not to destroy the cartel but to gain control over it. In 1910, Oppenheimer proclaimed, "Common sense tells us that the only way to increase the value of diamonds is to make them scarce, that is to reduce the production."[7]

In 1927, Oppenheimer finally got his wish. After a long and bitter struggle, De Beers capitulated and in a series of complex transactions, Oppenheimer folded his mines into the cartel while taking over as its leader.

For the next sixty years, De Beers would control 80 to 90 percent of the world's diamond production. During this period, the cartel systematically eliminated new competitors by bringing them under its umbrella. De Beers' practices were deemed so anti-competitive under United States law that De Beers' directors were prohibited from setting foot on American soil out of fear of immediate arrest.[8]

It was not until the 1990s that De Beers' grip over the industry finally began to loosen. The collapse of the Soviet Union in 1991 dissolved the cartel's contract to sell Russia's diamonds through De Beers.[9] Russia held vast diamond deposits in the far, frozen reaches of Siberia. The loss of this contract was a blow to the cartel's influence.

Then in 1996, Australia's Argyle mine also broke membership from the cartel. In 1994, the Argyle mine ranked as the world's most productive by volume, and it single-handedly accounted for one-third of the world's diamond production. While production has since tapered off, the mine's decision further eroded De Beers's market share.

And more recently, new diamond deposits have been discovered in Canada, pushing the country to become the world's third-largest diamond-producer. These factors, among others, have caused De Beers's market share of diamond production to slip from a peak of 80 to 90 percent to 65 percent.[10]

De Beers is an impressive story of collusion on a global scale. Unfortunately, De Beer's history has not been without its unsavory moments. To operate its African mines at low cost, De Beers supported Apartheid in South Africa, which indentured people to work under brutal, slave-like conditions. The humanitarian abuses associated with De Beers have caused deep suffering for the people of South Africa and many Africans in general.[11]

While cartels and trusts are now widely disdained as inhibitors of competitive markets, they have historically given rise to enormous wealth. Other famous cartels and trusts include John Rockefeller's Standard Oil, Andrew Carnegie's U.S. Steel, and the Organization of Petroleum Exporting Countries (OPEC)—which stands outside of U.S.

jurisdiction. Within the United States, trusts and cartels have been deemed illegal by Congress with the Sherman Antitrust Act in the 1890s and the Clayton Antitrust Act in 1914.

ELIMINATING RIVALS THE OLD-FASHIONED WAY
The Theory of Mergers and Acquisitions

Cartels and trusts are illegal for an obvious reason; their memberships exist for the sole purpose of controlling prices. When it comes to mergers and acquisitions, however, the picture becomes a bit murkier. While mergers and acquisitions tend to create entities that wield greater market share and pricing power, they can also sometimes benefit customers.

Mergers and acquisitions are essentially two flavors of the same activity: the formal joining of two companies. The difference is that while *mergers* combine two similarly sized businesses, *acquisitions* involve a larger business taking over a smaller business.

When engaging in either practice, companies are trying to widen their c-moats. The potential benefits are from better *Economy of Scale, High Satisfaction* for customers, and a reduced *Supply* of competitors.

These benefits, however, are not a slam dunk for businesses. When mergers and acquisitions are poorly implemented, they can backfire to destroy value for both shareholders and customers.

The biggest wild card is what happens to the Operation moat builders (i.e., Low Cost and High Satisfaction) during the integration process. Combining two organizations is a tricky process, and when performed improperly, dysfunctions can occur in the operations that result in major losses in productivity. These losses can more than wipe out any gains created by the Economy of Scale and Supply moat builders.

● ● ●

When it comes to mergers, the truth is that most fail to create value for their owners. A 1999 KPMG report discovered that "83 percent of mergers were unsuccessful in producing any business benefit as regards shareholder value." Only 17 percent of these combined entities created greater value, 30 percent produced no discernable difference, and 53 percent went on to destroy shareholder value.[12]

With such a high failure rate, the question becomes, "Why are companies so willing to merge?"

The big carrot, of course, is the potential to raise prices. In a study called "The Effect of Mergers on Consumer Prices: Evidence from Five Selected Case Studies," researchers Orley Ashenfelter and Daniel Hosken analyzed the effect of five mergers on consumer prices at retail stores.[13]

These mergers took place in the categories of liquor, motor oil, feminine protection, pancake syrup, and cereal.

The following table lists the market share of the *pre-merged companies* and their *post-merged combined size*.

TABLE 11.1 The Five Consumer Product Mergers of Ashenfelter and Hosken's Study

INDUSTRY	COMPANY 1 MARKET SHARE	COMPANY 2 MARKET SHARE	POST-MERGER MARKET SHARE
Liquor	21%	22%	43%
Motor Oil	29%	9%	38%
Feminine Protection	25%	19%	44%
Pancake Syrup	19%	15%	34%
Cereal	28%	4%	32%

Within three months, consumer prices in the first four product groups—liquor, motor oil, feminine protection, and pancake syrup—increased on average 3 to 7 percent. In the last product category, cereal, there was no discernible difference in price.

It turned out that tremendous wealth was created by these mergers; a 3 to 7 percent price rise is massive for a company's bottom line. (For more information on this, refer to chapter 3's section on "Snowballing Small Changes: A Billion Little Reasons to Raise Prices.")

To move the price needle, mergers need to have a meaningful impact on an industry's market share. A 20 percent company merging with another 20 percent company creates a 40 percent entity that can reshape the alternatives available to customers. On the other hand, a 20 percent company combining with a 1 percent company will probably not significantly alter the dynamics of an industry—hence what occurred with cereal. When market share impact is minimal, customer alternatives and prices will be affected less.

With such an enormous carrot for raising prices, what are the downsides to mergers? To phrase this question differently, how do most mergers manage to wipe out the gains of a price increase and the benefits of Economy of Scale?

The answer has two parts. The first has already been mentioned: mergers are notoriously difficult to implement. From an operational standpoint, they can temporarily—and in a worst case scenario, permanently—debilitate a company's organizational structure.

Common sense tells us that combining two similarly sized entities with different cultures, different procedures, and different methods of serving customers will be turbulent at best. During the integration process, if neither entity holds a strong upper hand in changing the other, a stalemate can occur that paralyzes the organization and thus hampers productivity.

Often this challenge is compounded by the touted benefit of *cost synergy*. This is a fancy way of describing EoS's ability to lower costs by eliminating redundancies associated with overlapping business functions—or in layman's terms, layoffs.

While eliminating redundancies does in fact lower costs, how it gets implemented can cause adverse effects that spill negatively into a business's Operations. Specifically, during the layoff process, if workers are left in the dark or fear job losses, then this instability will distract them from serving customers. If you personally felt that you might lose your job in the next few months, how focused would you be on serving customers?

Therefore, to conduct successful mergers, cost synergy must be enacted in a way that minimizes harm to a workforce's ability to serve customers. The smoother this integration and the less distracted the workforce, the greater the rewards.

The second answer as to why mergers fail is that there is a structural flaw in how the CEOs of large corporations get paid. Pay packages often incentivize CEOs to conduct mergers regardless of the outcome on shareholders. This is because these pay packages stipulate that CEOs will receive accelerated vesting of stock options and restricted stock units when a company gets merged. In other words, when a merger is triggered, performance-based compensation that should be paid out over many years can suddenly be paid in one large upfront sum and without a CEO needing to hit performance targets.

This misaligned incentive gives CEOs the ability to earn massive paychecks even if their dealings have poor results for their companies and are bad for their shareholders.

● ● ●

In general, acquisitions are a safer way to approach to market-share consolidation than mergers. Acquisitions benefit from the EoS and Supply moat builders but with less downside risk from disruptions in Operations. This means a higher chance of success.

The alignment of interests is also far better for stakeholders. CEOs of the acquiring businesses tend to stay at the helm, so there is no financial incentive to make bad deals. Shareholders are able to avoid a bet-the-farm approach that is often associated with large deals. And workers can feel more comfortable about their job security, which means that they can stay focused on the most important task at hand: staying the best at serving customers.

Since a major goal behind acquisitions is to reduce the supply of customer alternatives, the question becomes, "Does it really matter whether a business snaps up 10 percent more market share in a single large gulp or 10 percent more market share though many small sips?" From a customer's perspective, both have the same effect of narrowing the alternatives. Multiple acquisitions can be as effective as large mergers.

● ● ●

One realization is that financial war chests and partnerships can be useful for paring down the ecosystem of future rivals. When businesses are able to invest in or partner with smaller competitors early on, it gives them a greater hand in shaping future rivalry.

In 2007, Google lost in its attempt to buy a stake in Facebook. The rising popularity of the social media website presented a new competitor that could effectively challenge Google's presence in online advertising. Google had no control over this new entrant and Facebook was actively denying Google access to its closed system of information.

How could Google continue to stay dominant in the fast-evolving tech world if it had no influence over its potential competitors?

To avoid a repeat of this mistake, the following year, Google put together plans to start a venture capital fund. This fund would invest in start-ups that might not otherwise be interested in a buyout. Google was already active in acquisitions—between 2007 and 2012, the company acquired 165 companies at a cost of $20.8 billion[14]—but this venture capital fund gave Google an even stronger hand in shaping the technology industry.

To seed the fund, Google committed $100 million a year, which has since increased to $300 million per year.[15] By 2014, the fund had invested in 282 companies, with a portfolio value reaching $1.6 billion.[16] Some of its early investments include ride-sharing Uber, online retailer Jet, and home device company Nest, which Google acquired in 2014.

While Google's venture capital fund designates that it does not invest on Google's behalf or share information with Google, without a doubt, it provides Google a stronger foothold with its potential competitors. The company not only provides financing to these start-ups, but offers access to its array of products and expertise. By forging such close ties, when the time comes and the next Facebook shows up, Google hopes it will not be left out in the cold again.

● ● ●

When analyzing mergers and acquisitions, we need to think about two aspects of how customers will be affected. First off, will the deal impact the landscape of choices available to customers—both currently and in the future? And second, will the combined company be able to maintain its operational effectiveness in serving customers?

If the option of mergers and acquisitions is unavailable, as an alternative, can we take minority stakes in our competitors or develop partnerships with them?

PUMPING OUT PATENTS
Reducing the Supply of Competitors

The patent system is an effective method for reducing the number of competitors. To incentivize innovation, the United States Patent and Trademark Office grants patent protection to inventions for roughly fourteen to twenty years. This gives inventors a temporary monopoly as they can prevent competitors from copying their new products.

The pharmaceutical industry is one of the biggest benefactors of this system. The trade group Pharmaceutical Research and Manufacturers of America (PhRMA) estimates that it takes ten to fifteen years to develop a new drug at an average cost of $1.2 billion.[17] Vast sums are spent on testing, research, and safety trials. At any stage of a drug's development, it can fail to pass the current round of testing and be shut down; there is no guarantee that any invested money will pay off.

To subsidize the enormous expense and possibility for a zero payout, the government sweetens the deal by allowing pharmaceutical companies to patent their drug discoveries. As such, when pharmaceuticals gain FDA approval on a drug, they can reap massive windfalls from their monopoly. This is intended to make up for any losses associated with drugs that don't make it to market.

The payout of a blockbuster drug can be staggering. From 2002 to

2011, Pfizer's drug Lipitor accounted for more than $110 billion in sales.[18] In November 2011, when the drug's patent protection was lifted and generics were allowed to enter the market, Lipitor's sales plunged 59 percent, from $9.6 billion in 2011 to $3.9 billion in 2012.[19] As Warren Buffett would say, "Competition is the destroyer of profits."

● ● ●

So, how do we use patent protection to pare down the field of competitors? In 1964, Robert Taylor was working out of his garage developing innovative bath products. He formulated more than a hundred different items that he then sold to department stores.[20]

Even though many of Taylor's products were popular, he discovered that he had trouble maintaining a foothold in stores. As soon as he created a successful item, giants like Procter & Gamble or Lever Brothers copied his creations. These larger players then used their position to squeeze him out of the market.

In one instance, during the 1970s, Taylor developed a popular fruit shampoo that became a fast rising hit. Soon afterwards, Clairol, a division of Procter & Gamble, followed suit by launching a similar line called Herbal Essences. Taylor's shampoos were knocked off store shelves.

Not wanting the same thing to happen, in 1980, Taylor developed a liquid hand soap that used a new type of pump as a dispenser. The product was called Softsoap. This time, Taylor had a game plan. The design of the pump was owned by two patent holders. To ensure that the pump became exclusive to Softsoap, and to prevent competitors from copying his product, Taylor made a purchase order to buy one hundred million pumps.[21]

It was a massive gamble, but it paid off. With such a large purchase order, Taylor essentially wiped out the supply of pumps for years and gave Softsoap time to establish itself before competitors could close in. During Soft Soap's first six months of sales, Taylor sold twenty-five million units, and by the end of the second year, he successfully reached the one-hundred-million-unit mark.

With patents, it is important to think about how they can limit supply and keep competitors out of a market. Which patents are necessary for serving customers, and are we able to register patents that limit the supply of alternatives?

● ● ●

In recent years, the technology industry has witnessed a vast consolidation of patents that has whittled down certain segments to a handful of powerful players.

The most evident consolidation has been in mobile operating systems—the software that runs cell phones. Today, two giants control this industry: Apple and Google (with Microsoft in distant third). According to IDC, in the second quarter of 2015, Apple's iOS and Google's Android together ran 96 percent of all cell phones shipped.[22]

Consolidation of market share between these two players began in earnest in 2011 when Apple threw the first stone by suing Samsung for using Google's Android software. Apple claimed that Samsung was infringing on its patents.

To shore up its legal defense, Google began purchasing patents related to mobile devices and software. With a strong patent portfolio of its own, Google and Samsung countersued Apple. In an escalating battle, lawsuits were thrown back and forth. Apple, which already held a significant number of patents, began to amass an even larger portfolio by banding with others to buy Nortel's patents for $4.5 billion in 2011.[23] In response, in 2012, Google paid $12.5 billion to purchase Motorola for its patent portfolio.[24] (A few years later, Google sold Motorola without its patent portfolio for a mere $2.9 billion.)

Finally, in May 2014, Apple and Google ended their patent dispute with both sides agreeing to settle in a stalemate, and each company dropped its lawsuits against the other.[25] Interestingly, while neither side was declared the victor, both companies came out winners. Combined, the two companies secured almost all the essential patents required for creating a competitive mobile operating system. During their patent war, Apple and Google went from having 74 percent market share to 96 percent market share while wiping out any possibility for a potential competitor to emerge in the future.

UTILITIES, BANKS, AND RAILROADS
The Logic behind Government-Regulated Industries

For some industries, governments will provide lower competition in exchange for higher regulation. This typically occurs in sectors that are vital to the functioning of an economy—such as electric utilities, banks, and railroads.

In these industries, the free market does a poor job of preventing systemic failures. Imagine if our utilities, our banks, and our railroads went bankrupt in large numbers. How difficult would it be to run an economy with no electricity, no ability to borrow money, and no means to move goods? All business operations would come to a grinding halt.

Industries that provide these essential services also wield monopolistic pricing traits. If they increase their price, we have little choice but to pay up. As such, they can easily price-gouge our economy in a way that siphons off the vast majority of its profits. Governments regulate these industries to protect people and businesses from such monopolistic abuses and to prevent mass failures that could tank our economy.

● ● ●

In 1998, California's electric grid operator began a bold experiment to deregulate the state's electricity market. Pressured by advocates of free-market economics, the state began loosening the rules governing utility companies. The assumption was that a freer market would be more competitive and drive down prices.

Prior to the rule changes, electric utilities sold their energy under regulated price schemes. Under the new deregulated model, they could sell their energy on the open spot market, a system where electricity was bought and sold using current market prices. By mid-1999, California lifted its price caps, and the free market took over.[26]

Within a year, in May of 2000, California's energy grid operator declared a state of emergency as wholesale electricity prices tripled. The following month, California experienced its worst blackout since World War II.[27] For months, rolling blackouts plagued the state. By December 2000, wholesale prices reached $1,400 per megawatt-hour compared to only $30 per megawatt-hour a year earlier.[28]

Amazingly, California was experiencing an energy shortage during a time when the state had ample generating capacity. California's utilities could generate 54 gigawatts of electricity while the state was only consuming 26 gigawatts.[29]

It turned out that under a deregulated market, the doors were not only opened to competition but to market manipulation. Companies like Enron learned that electricity was an essential service wherein people had no alternative, and shortages could lead to exponential spikes in price. People needed electricity regardless of its price.

If the supply of electricity could be dwindled below demand, energy traders could make vast profits. Under the guise of "trading innovation," Enron discovered various ways to push prices higher. These trading schemes carried names like Ricochet, Death Star, and Fat Boy—the last being an allusion to the two nuclear bombs dropped in World War II.[30]

Ricochet involved selling California's electricity out of state to create a shortage while selling the same amount back to the state at a higher rate. Death Star created an illusion that electricity grid would be overloaded and Enron would receive a payment for relieving the congestion. Fat Boy entailed overscheduling electricity production and then selling the excess back to the state at a profit.

Deregulation was a disaster for California. The problem was that the rules no longer prevented participants from denying a vital resource as a way to raise prices. With weak controls, industry players were able to gouge California's customers for billion of dollars while taking the economy hostage.

It turns out that free markets are dangerous when industries hold monopolistic power; regulations need to exist to ensure healthy competition in a manner that helps rather than harms customers.

• • •

In the late 1990s, the deregulation of the banking industry led to a similarly disastrous fate. Only, this time, it took two decades for events to play out and it plunged the world into its deepest economic decline since the Great Depression.

It began in 1999 with the repeal of the Glass-Steagall Act. Originally passed by Congress in 1933, the act prevented financial institutions from gambling away people's life savings. One of the main tenets of the act was to separate the three major types of financial institutions: banks, insurance companies, and brokerage firms. In particular, this ensured that banks could not take on excessive risk that might jeopardize customers' deposits.

During the Great Depression in 1920s, risky bets by banks led to a collapse of the financial system. Banks loaned money to people for speculative investments such as buying stock. When the stock market crashed, the value of these investments evaporated and banks incurred massive losses. Soon, banks became unable to pay back their depositors. As people feared the loss of their life savings, bank runs became prevalent with people trying to withdraw their money.

As banks failed, the big challenge was not just their bankruptcy but the systemic seizure of the financial system. With losses piling up, banks could no longer loan out money. Suddenly businesses found themselves unable to borrow the money they needed for purchases or supporting their day-to-day activities. Businesses began to fail in large numbers, and the economy fell into a tailspin.

During the Great Depression, the unemployment rate skyrocketed from 5 percent to 25 percent and the stock market plunged 90 percent.

By 1999, memories of the Great Depression had largely faded. Under heavy lobbying by banks, Congress repealed the Glass-Steagall Act. Banks claimed that they no longer needed the antiquated rules that protected the industry; they touted their ability to self-regulate against bad behavior.

As the laws were relaxed, banks once again began putting their money in higher-risk investments. Bank loans, which used to be boring but safe, were no longer profitable enough to satisfy the desires of bankers. As such, banks developed "innovative" financial products that provided much higher rates of return. Among these were derivatives and naked credit default swaps (CDSs).

Derivatives were financial products built upon other financial products. This could be something like the interest portion of a loan, which could then be sold separate from the principle. *Naked* CDSs were insurance policies that paid out when a company defaulted on its loans. With naked CDSs, banks didn't need to own the original underlying loan to purchase the insurance policy. In essence, naked CDSs were pure gambles on whether companies would default on debts. The value of these risky bets became so huge that they ran many orders of magnitude larger than the debt itself.

Under this guise of "financial innovation," banks attained the higher profits they were seeking—though in return for much higher risk. Under lax accounting rules and given the underfunding of regulatory agencies, banks could book their profits on paper while their true risks were hidden from the ledger. In creating vast fictitious riches, bank CEOs and workers rewarded themselves with huge bonuses.

In 2008, the housing bubble burst. Many of the derivatives responsible for the banking industry's profits were based on housing loans. When these derivatives lost value, the paper riches of banks disappeared. What would have been reasonable losses if banks owned simple loans became massive losses with derivative products. Investor Warren Buffett would describe derivatives as "financial weapons of mass destruction."[31]

In addition to mounting losses, banks had stretched their balance sheets thin in an effort to make the most money possibly. Many of the largest banks had reached leverage ratios of 30 to 1—which implied they were using $30 of someone else's money for each $1 of their own.[32] In other words, if the assets of a bank dropped in value by 3.4 percent, it would be enough to wipe out its equity and send it into bankruptcy. As an example, by the end of 2007, Bear Stearns had $11 billion of equity to support $395 billion of assets, and the company held derivatives worth a notional value of $13.4 trillion.[33] It didn't take much to push the bank over the edge.

By the end of 2008, nearly all of the equity of the U.S. banking system had been wiped out. In a replay of the Great Depression, banks lost their ability to make loans, businesses became squeezed for cash, and within 18 months, the unemployment rate jumped from 5 percent to 10 percent. In a deepening spiral, the banking system seized up and pushed many businesses into bankruptcy, leading to even greater losses for banks.

To prevent a total economic collapse, the U.S. government was forced to step in with the biggest bank bailout since the Great Depression. Fortunately, these actions curtailed the collapse of the banking system and halted the unemployment rate from rising further. These measures provided time for the economy to recover while the government recapitalized the banking system.

Banks were essentially given free passes on their massive losses. To recapitalize banks, the government orchestrated an enormous transfer of wealth from the federal government directly to bank coffers. This was done through a clever system of providing banks with cheap loans that the government then re-borrowed at a higher rate.

Today, bankers continue to lobby for removing the rules that protect customers and businesses from their risky behavior. The challenge is that bank executives know they can become rich during good times while leaving the government and taxpayers on the hook during bad times.

With deregulation, bankers are able to push up their short-term profits while awarding themselves huge paychecks. When things go south, the bankers will already be rich and their institutions will be safe in knowing that they are too important to fail.

As entrepreneurs and consumers, we are forced by the government to open up bank accounts and to put our money in federally approved banking institutions. As such, we should require these institutions be regulated from being able to gamble away our money. When banks lose our money, we will end up paying for the losses one way or another, either as banking customers or as taxpayers.

CHAPTER TWELVE

DISTRIBUTION (I)

The Distribution moat builder creates
pathways to customers that
rivals cannot access.

● ● ●

Chapter Overview: In situations where the number of rivals can't be reduced, the next best option is to make it more difficult for rivals to reach customers. The Distribution moat builder is about creating distribution platforms to customers that can effectively squeeze out competitors. This is accomplished by embedding anchor points (i.e., direct links of distribution) with customers; these anchor points must also prevent competitors from being able to piggyback on them. As anchor points become more embedded with customers, it will be more difficult for competitors to take them away. Multiple anchor points can be used to build ecosystems of products around customers.

O n a fateful February day in 2010, Louie Sulcer, a resident of Woodstock, Georgia, and a seventy-one-year-old grandfather, downloaded Johnny Cash's song, "Guess Things Happen that Way," onto his iPod Nano. After listening to a thirty-second preview of the song, he purchased it on iTunes. Unknown to Sulcer at the time, he was setting an incredible milestone by downloading the ten billionth song off of the Apple's iTunes store.[1]

Only nine years earlier, Steve Jobs, the CEO of Apple, walked on stage to announce the iPod. While standing on an empty stage, he teased the audience about whether they wanted to see the next generation device that would change the world. He then pulled from his shirt pocket a tiny portable music player.

The iPod was an amazing music player. It not only held more songs than rival devices but it was beautifully designed. Other digital players had the capacity to store up to two hundred songs, but the iPod could carry over a thousand. Other players had clunky interfaces while the iPod was crafted with elegant simplicity; every song and setting on the device was reachable within three clicks.[2] To achieve this feat, Apple developed an innovative touch wheel that scrolled while also dually functioning as a set of buttons.

When the iPod hit shelves, it became an instant hit. During the first week, it sold 110,000 units. Within a few months, Apple's market share in digital music players soared from zero to 51 percent.[3]

The success of the iPod was impressive, but what made it remarkable was how it set the stage for the future success of the iPod 2, iPod Mini, iPod Shuffle, iPod Nano, iPod Touch, iPhone, and iPad. Creating one blockbuster hit was an amazing achievement, but developing a string of consecutive hits has been nothing short of phenomenal.

History has shown that it is difficult to maintain momentum on the back of a blockbuster product. In 2004, Motorola introduced the Razr mobile phone, the world's thinnest flip phone. The Razr shattered industry records by selling 130 million units in four years—a world record for a clamshell device—and brought Motorola's market share in mobile handsets from 13.5 percent to 19 percent.[4] In 2006, when the company introduced the Razr2, the new phone was met with far less enthusiasm and Motorola's momentum dissipated. From 2006 to 2007, Motorola's market share fell from 22 percent to 11 percent.[5]

Nintendo faced a similar challenge with its Wii console. In 2006, the Wii launched to such fierce demand that its consoles were being resold on eBay for $450 versus its retail price of $250.[6] With its immense popularity, the Wii sold 5.8 million units in fiscal 2007, 18 million units in fiscal 2008, and 26 million units in fiscal 2009.[7] For Nintendo's next-generation console, the Wii U, the company only managed sales of 7.2 million units during its first two years.[8]

In a world of high-flying successes followed by earth-shattering plummets, how did Apple defy the odds to achieve blockbuster after blockbuster? From 2003 to 2010, Apple maintained more than 70 percent market share in digital music players—a number that does not include the subsequent successes of the iPhone or iPad.[9]

It started in 2000, when Jobs began working on a new vision for Apple. At the time, Apple was still considered a computer manufacturer, but Jobs had greater ambitions for the company. At the core of his thinking was a realization that the world was moving beyond owning physical goods to also owning digital goods. In the years ahead, information would be bought and sold much like groceries or clothes. Rather than taking place physically at a store, however, this new marketplace would exist digitally. If Apple could become the storage locker from which people managed their ownership of digital goods, people would be attached to its hardware.[10]

As Jobs developed a strategy around this idea, he realized that music was the perfect entry point into people's digital lives. Music files were relatively small pieces of digital information and people were used to owning their music collection.

In January 2001, Jobs unveiled the first piece of a two-part strategy to capture the digital music market. For the first piece, he released the iTunes software, a program that managed MP3 collections and from which music could be purchased legally. iTunes solved the rampant problem of illegal music downloads. File-sharing of music had become the norm in part because there weren't many viable alternatives. Apple's iTunes gave people legal access to digital music while maintaining copyright protection for music labels.

The second piece of the strategy arrived seven months later with the launch of the iPod. Jobs introduced the portable music device as the purest music-listening experience. In adhering to a simplicity of design, complex functions such as managing playlists and buying songs were offloaded to the iTunes computer software. In a seamless marriage, iTunes helped people organize the music on their iPod.

With both pieces set, Apple was ready to capture the digital music market. The iPod became a hit and it got people invested in using iTunes to manage their music library, but thereafter, it was iTunes that kept people attached to buying future iPods. Once a person got hooked on managing their playlists on iTunes, it was only natural for them to keep buying iPods rather than switch to a competitor's product. Impressively, Jobs found a way to use digital goods as a way to keep people loyal to Apple's hardware.

After the success of the iPod, Apple strengthened its digital locker strategy. Its digital hub grew to include movies, books, games, and applications, as well as picture and document storage. To accommodate these various media types, Apple evolved a lineup of products to support them: the iPod Touch, iPhone, and iPad.

In 2010, Sulcer helped Apple surpass the ten-billion-song milestone. In 2011, Apple reached its ten billionth application download.[11] And in April 2014, Apple boasted having eight hundred million active credit card accounts on its iTunes store.[12]

With a strong presence in managing people's digital goods, Apple has been able to keep its users extremely loyal. In February 2015, Apple reached a stock market value of $710 billion, the largest valuation in the world and more than twice the size of the world's second largest company.[13]

● ● ●

The Distribution moat builder is the last tool in our arsenal. While the Supply moat builder reduced the *supply of alternatives* to customers, the Distribution moat builder seeks to limit *competitor access* to customers by building dedicated pathways to them. In other words, in situations where you can't get rid of your competitors, the next best thing is to hinder their ability to reach your customers.

For Steve Jobs, the iPod was a blockbuster hit, but it was the anchor point of iTunes (and later, also the App store) that kept consumers loyal to its hardware. iTunes was the anchor point that prevented rivals from taking Apple's customers away.

To apply the Distribution moat builder, we ask, "How do we build anchor points with customers for distributing our products and services, and then how do we use these anchor points to squeeze out competitors?"

TROJAN HORSES IN CUSTOMER LIVES
Distributing Anchor Points

In the 1800s, Gillette's razor-and-blade strategy increased the loyalty of its customers by developing an anchor point with them. After a person purchased a Gillette razor, competitors found it far more difficult to get that person to switch to a different product. The razor acted as a strong distribution platform for keeping people buying Gillette's products (i.e., replacement blades).

If we deconstruct Gillette's strategy, it turns out that there are three attributes necessary for forming a distribution pathway: (1) there must be an anchor point with customers, (2) the anchor must create the switching cost for customers, and (3) the anchor point needs to be exclusive to a business or at least have very limited access by rivals.

For Gillette, razors were the anchor point. The switching cost was that once a person owned a Gillette razor, it became harder for them to justify purchasing a competitor's product, especially when the expense of buying replacement blades was lower than a competitor's razor. And to limit access to this anchor point, Gillette razors were proprietarily designed and could only use Gillette's replacement blades.

Generally speaking, the switching cost of a distribution pathway does not need to be high to be effective, it just needs to be enough to sway a person's decision so that they stay the course. Each time Gillette's customers faced a choice between buying a replacement blade or a whole new shaving device, Gillette just needed for it to be a little easier to continue buying replacement blades than switch to something new.

Today, printer manufacturers adopt a similar strategy. The companies have learned that the bulk of their profits do not come from selling printers but from selling consumables, such as ink and toner.

When selling a printer, a manufacturer is competing against many other manufacturers. When selling consumables, however, a manufacturer is only challenging a few third-party re-inkers.

Once a consumer owns a particular printer, they are essentially tied to its proprietary ink and toner. Switching printers involves wasting money and the time spent on the current one—a practice that most people try to avoid. It is cheaper to continue buying consumables for the current printer than to buy a new printer—even if consumables are a little pricey.

The strategy of printer manufacturers is therefore to use cutthroat pricing to grab printer market share, knowing that once this anchor point is established, they can profit down the road.

Coca-Cola has also developed a distribution platform. If Coca-Cola were to only sell its beverages through grocery stores, the company would be fighting for every inch of shelf space and be largely at the mercy of retailers. To reduce its reliance on these stores, the company has created exclusive paths to reach its customers that are also inaccessible to competitors.

In the U.S., these anchor points take the form of hundreds of thousands of soda fountain machines and more than 6.9 million vending machines.[14] With these anchor points, Coca-Cola and its bottlers have created dedicated sales channels for their products. To promote exclusivity with soda fountains at dining establishments, contracts often stipulate higher-volume discounts, thus incentivizing restaurants to only carry one supplier's products (i.e., Coca-Cola products). Vending machines are also contracted to be exclusive for a given territory with a promise of profit sharing, such as at universities and theme parks.[15]

Another interesting place where anchor points are found is with bank ATMs. Have you ever wondered why ATM fees are so high? If you aren't an account holder, why do banks charge you $3 for even a small withdraw that costs them practically nothing?

The reason is that banks have learned that ATMs are powerful distribution gateways—like vending machines—that provide anchor points of convenience. ATMs offer convenience to a bank's customers, but by charging hefty fees for non-customers, a bank is able to exclude other banks from that convenience.

Surprisingly, the real purpose of the high fee is not to make more money off transactions, but to increase the switching cost of a bank's current customers. The higher the ATM fees, the less likely customers will defect.

THE POINT OF THE GAME
Reward Programs as Anchor Points

So how do we create anchor points with customers? A cheap and easy way is through reward programs. When giving out reward points, we are meeting all three criteria of a distribution pathway. There is an anchor point because customers own the reward points, there is a switching cost because customers will lose the value of points if they quit shopping with us, and the anchor point is exclusive because no other company can issue or redeem our points.

Reward systems come in all shapes and sizes. One of the simplest— and most successful—was Subway's loyalty stamp card. With every six-inch sub purchased, a customer received a stamp. When eight stamps were collected, the card entitled the bearer to a free sub.[16] When customers decided what to eat for lunch, this reward program made it easier for people to default to Subway; after all, it put them one step closer to a free sandwich.

Panda Express also at one time offered a loyalty program but with a more progressive set of rewards. The Asian fast food chain gave out cards and issued a stamp for every two-item entrée purchased. When customers reached four stamps on a card, they were rewarded with a drink; at eight stamps, they received an egg roll; and at twelve stamps, they earned a free two-item entrée. By doling out prizes progressively, the more often people ate at Panda Express, the bigger the reward.[17]

For years, the island-country of Taiwan struggled to get small businesses to pay sales tax. Mom-and-pop stores largely operated with cash, and with rampant underreporting, the government found it difficult to enforce its tax laws.

In a brilliant move, the government decided to standardize retail sales receipts. Each receipt was given a unique identifying number, and every two months, receipt numbers were entered automatically into a national lottery for cash prizes.

Because customers wanted a chance to win these prizes, small businesses were pressured to issue receipts, and thus log their sales. While the net effect of paying taxes was to raise prices for both businesses and customers, people did not want to give up something by not getting a receipt. The lesson is that reward programs can be effective tools at raising pricing power.

For our own business, we must remember that for reward programs to be effective, customers must attach compelling values to these points, such as the ability to earn prizes or attain a higher status. The goal is to increase a customer's switching costs. The rewards must to be enticing enough to change future purchasing behavior.

As reward points are accumulated, customers will also become more heavily invested in a business and less willing to let these points go to waste. As such, when designing reward systems, it is often helpful to incentivize customers to work towards larger prizes, which keeps them more deeply embedded. When prizes do get redeemed, customers should always carry a residual balance of points rather than being able to use them all. This small leftover value will help keep customers coming back just a little more often.

• • •

Some reward programs have grown so powerful that they have become their own business. In May 1981, American Airlines introduced AAdvantage, a first-of-its-kind frequent-flyer program that would transform the airline industry.[18] The setup was simple. The more a person flew more, the more mileage points they accrued, which earned them seat upgrades or future flights. In an industry where lowest price prevailed, this program greatly enhanced customer loyalty.

Other airlines quickly followed suit by creating their own frequent-flyer programs. Airlines then began to notice a trend: the redemption rate for mileage points was far below the rate at which they were being issued; people were collecting points faster than they were spending them. For the year 1985, the airline industry awarded ninety-four billion points and only fifty-seven billion points were redeemed.[19]

Witnessing this trend, airlines decided to take things one step further by selling their mileage points to other businesses. Companies like credit card issuers found it useful to piggyback off these loyalty programs.

Airlines charged other businesses about 2¢ per mileage point.[20]

A round-trip ticket was typically worth about $300 to $400 and could be exchanged for about 25,000 points, which equated to 1.2¢ to 1.6¢ per point. Not only did airlines make money selling points, but with a low redemption rate, they could extend the payment out for years.

Impressively, for the year 2005, the airline industry issued 2.7 trillion points out of which 894 billion were used—a one-third redemption. During this time, the backlog of outstanding points has grown to 14 trillion points, enough to purchase 560 million round-trip flights with an estimated value of $168 billion.[21] Reward points have not only transformed the dynamics of the airline industry from a commodity to a loyalty-based business, but it has led to innovations in how to sell that loyalty.

In 2011, Southwest Airlines decided to update its own frequent-flyer program to base its reward points on the cost of ticket rather than miles flown.[22] The more money a person paid for a ticket, the more points a person would get per dollar spent. Cleverly, Southwest has taken advantage of the fact that business flyers often make ticket purchases while it is the business that actually picks up the tab. By allocating rewards based on ticket price, Southwest incentivizes business travelers to purchase its more expensive fares even though the flights are the same.

WELLS FARGO'S GOLDEN NEST
Ecosystems of Anchor Points

When it comes to diversification, there are two opposing schools of thought. The first is the classic, "Don't place all your eggs in one basket," a wise choice for spreading out risk and reducing the susceptibility to one-time disasters. The second runs completely opposite: "Place all your eggs in one basket and then watch that basket carefully." By concentrating risk in one place, eggs can be managed with greater oversight, and thus better decisions can be made for protecting them.

What does this have to do with distribution pathways? It turns out that one method for increasing the switching cost of customers is to be more central in people's lives. When people own an iPhone, an iPad, and a MacBook, it becomes harder to get them to switch out of Apple's ecosystem. When people own a cordless DeWalt drill, a cordless DeWalt saw, and a cordless DeWalt impact driver that all use interchangeable batteries, it is likely that they will stick to buying DeWalt's tools. Ecosystems of products deepen customer loyalty. In other words, the more eggs that people put in one company's basket, the more attached they become to it.

On April 9, 2009, during one of the bleakest moments of the Great Recession, Wells Fargo shocked the financial industry by announcing record quarterly earnings. As soon as the news hit the wires, the stocks of all the major U.S. banks shot up by 13 to 35 percent.[23] The news was astonishing, especially during the middle of a banking collapse and deeply contracting economy.

Wells Fargo largely bucked the bad behaviors that plagued its rivals. The bank avoided most of the risky bets that were built on the subprime lending bubble. For the most part, the company stuck to its guns and made plain vanilla mortgage loans. These mortgages made sense for both the bank and its customers.

After the crisis, Goldman Sachs paid a rather offhand compliment to Wells Fargo. Goldman Sachs was sued by the U.S. Securities and Exchange Commission for a record $550 million for bundling the riskiest subprime mortgages, selling these mortgages to investors, and then privately betting against the mortgages. During the trial, it came out that hedge fund manager John Paulson sent an e-mail to Goldman Sachs suggesting that it would be better not to include Wells Fargo's mortgages, because Wells Fargo was "generally perceived as one of the higher-quality subprime loan originators."[24] For Goldman Sachs, Wells Fargo's loans were *too* creditworthy.

The quality of Wells Fargo's loans was not due to random chance; it was staked in a strategy that took root in 1986 when Richard Kovacevich became chairman and director of the bank. At the time, the bank's name was Norwest Bank and it was a small regional outfit with 238 branches spanning seven states. In 1993, Kovacevich took over as CEO, and over the next five years, he embarked on a shopping spree to gobble up seventy-seven other banks, most of them much smaller. By 1998, Norwest's footprint expanded to 3,830 offices covering sixteen states.[25]

It was at this point that Kovacevich merged Norwest with Wells Fargo, taking the Wells Fargo name with it. With a little humor, Kovacevich acknowledged, "Norwest sounds like a mispronounced airline that gives bad service . . . That was not a hard decision."[26]

Both before and after the merger, Kovacevich's strategy remained the same. In an interview, he succinctly laid out his plan: "The average consumer has fifteen financial relationships. If you can get only four of those, you are profitable. If you get eight or nine or ten, you are really profitable."[27] Kovacevich wanted to sell each customer on having more Wells Fargo products.

Over the years, Wells Fargo has executed on this ambition. The company has gone from having 3.5 products per household in 1999 to 6.26 products per household in 2011.[28] During this period, the industry average has consistently remained at 2.2 products per household.[29]

FIGURE 12.1 Wells Fargo's Loyalty Measure

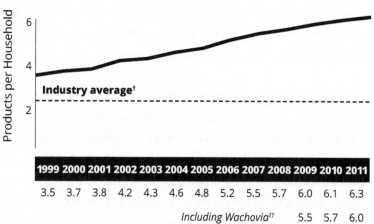

	1999	2000	2001	2002	2003	2004	2005	2006	2007	2008	2009	2010	2011
	3.5	3.7	3.8	4.2	4.3	4.6	4.8	5.2	5.5	5.7	6.0	6.1	6.3
Including Wachovia[tt]											5.5	5.7	6.0

[t]From 2001 to 2011, the industry averaged 2.2 products per household. [tt] In 2009, Wells Fargo merged with Wachovia. The first row represents comparable year-over-year figures.

There were many benefits to having multiple financial relationships with customers. Firstly, since Wells Fargo was a retail bank, it made sense from an EoS perspective to sell more products to drive greater revenue per square foot. This savings could be passed onto customers.

Secondly, as customers used more Wells Fargo products, the bank could paint better pictures of a people's financial profiles. This helped with loan decisions. If a person wanted a home loan but only had a credit card account, there was not a lot of information to go by. If a person applied for a home loan but already had a checking account, savings account, retirement account, and car loan, Wells Fargo could have a clear picture of their creditworthiness.

And last—but perhaps most importantly—when a person held numerous Wells Fargo products, the customer's financial life became intertwined with the bank's. When a customer's finances became concentrated with the bank, they were less likely to engage in shenanigans; and likewise, since each customer was so valuable revenue-wise to Wells Fargo, the bank strived to maintain the greatest possible service and to avoid harming this relationship. There was no incentive to nickel-and-dime customers or to sell them beyond their means.

The strength of this mutual relationship showed during the Great Recession. In 2008, Wells Fargo was able to contact ninety-four out of every hundred customers who fell behind two or more mortgage payments. Out of those contacted, the bank helped half avoid foreclosure with new repayment plans, refinancing, short sales, extensions, reduced interest rates, no charges on principal, or other means.[30] Because Wells Fargo was close to its customers, it was able to work alongside them to solve the problem.

By contrast, banks with weaker relationships to their customers were likely to foreclose on mortgages in sweeping manners, which forced many people out of their homes. Just as often, customers with weak ties to a bank were also more inclined to simply walk away, leaving a bank with large losses.

By 2013, Wells Fargo had largely recovered from the housing bubble of the Great Recession. With its strong customer base still intact, the bank posted a return of 1.55 percent on assets, whereas JPMorgan Chase returned 0.69 percent, Citibank 0.73 percent, and Bank of America 0.53 percent.[31] In the same year, Wells Fargo reach a rank of world's largest bank by stock market value.

David Pottruck, the CEO of Charles Schwab, commented on Richard Kovacevich, saying, "He's probably the best executive in the business."[32] Wells Fargo laid out a simple strategy for its success and delivered on it. The company's 2008 annual report summed it up, "All we do is try to create the best customer experience and then keep count: How many financial products do our customers have with us, and how can we earn all their business?"[33]

When thinking about multiple anchor points, we want to ask, "How do we get our customers to place more of their eggs into our business, and then how do we work to keep them there?" The more essential that we become in their lives, the greater the loyalty and more we can both benefit.

PART III

THE ORIGIN OF PROFITS

———————— ◆ ————————

"The purpose of models is not to fit the data but to sharpen the questions."

SAMUEL KARLIN

THE LAST PIECE
OF THE PUZZLE

O ur quest is almost complete. Nearly all the pieces of the puzzle are in place for answering the question, "What is the origin of profits?" The last remaining piece is for CMF to take into account the variable of *market size*.

As a quick review, so far we have established that c-*moats* are the intrinsic probability that customers choose a business. As c-moats widen, businesses benefit from greater *market share* and/or higher *profit margins*. *Price* is the mechanism for allocating between these two outcomes. The *eight moat builders* are the fundamental tools for driving wider c-moats and increasing the intrinsic probability that customers choose our businesses.

All of these elements were captured in the *Customer Moat Formula* as presented at the end of chapter 4 and again below.

FIGURE 13.1 Customer Moat Formula
(Taken from Chapter 4)

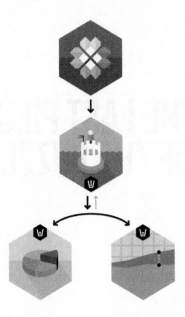

To complete our understanding of business strategy, all that is left is a bit of reverse-engineering. Afterwards, the CMF will explain the origin of profits: it will tell us how the eight actions of the moat builders drive intrinsic loyalty, and it will show us how this intrinsic loyalty goes on to affect our bottom-line profits.

To begin, accounting provides us a method for calculating profits with the equation *profit = revenue x profit margin*. The variable of revenue can also be broken down into *revenue = market size x market share*. Thus we arrive at the formula: *profit = (market size x market share) x profit margin*.

The CMF has already explained two of these variables: market share and profit margin. The last remaining piece is *market size*.

RIDING OUT ECONOMIC TURBULENCES
Buffering Fluctuations in Market Size

Market size is the total demand for products and services based on how a business has defined its markets. (For help on defining a market, please refer to chapter 2.) In dollar terms, market size is the amount of money spent by a customer demographic on serving a particular need.

While market share and profit margin can be controlled through price and c-moat adjustments, market sizes tend to fluctuate outside our control. We are often at the mercy of macro events such as wars, disasters, epidemics, recessions, and weather patterns—all of which powerfully affect people's spending.

In the long run (measured in decades), market sizes should fluctuate around a steady average; after all, the proportion of a society's wealth spent on serving a particular *need* should not shift dramatically over the years.

We can simply reflect that, a hundred years ago, people spent a significant portion of their income horse and buggy rides. Today, people still spend money on transportation, but instead, our society has switched to automobiles and airplanes. While the specific products and services have changed, the basic need for transportation has not.

In the short run (measured in fewer than ten years), we can expect major spikes and dips in market size. These swings can sometimes be violent. For example, oil usage plunged during the Great Recession, sending oil prices down 70 percent in a matter of months. The SARS epidemic in Asia boosted the price and sales of medical face masks for over a year.[1] And Hurricane Sandy led to a boom in construction which buffeted the building supply industry for months.[2]

When experiencing sharp spikes in economic growth, we must realize that there are likely corresponding declines down the road. Likewise, when economic pullbacks occur, there will be an eventual bounce back. Businesses need to be prepared to handle these market fluctuations.

Economically speaking, the rule of thumb is that as populations grow and average incomes increase, market sizes will also grow in relation. Negative population growth, however, will pose a far more challenging situation.

In normal growing markets, if we happen to witness our market size shrinking with no end in sight, the most likely failure was forgetting to define our market around a customer need. The camera film and newspaper industries, for example, are often seen as industries in decline, but the real case is that their customers are being better served by newer technologies, such as digital cameras and websites. The basic need for capturing memories and good journalism has not disappeared; it is just that the customer preference for their delivery methods have changed. Sometimes, to maintain a lead in serving a customer need, we will have to reinvent ourselves.

Since market-size fluctuations lie mostly outside our control, we should work to insulate ourselves from its swings and potential ravages. When macro events work against a business for too long or in a string of bad luck, it can be a difficult situation to cope with. As such, we want to insulate ourselves from these fluctuations so that they do not create an Achilles heel to our businesses.

Fortunately, what keeps businesses afloat is simply money. To ride out economic storms, we just need enough resources to keep us from drowning. Luckily, money is the one thing that keeps businesses solvent and it is easily stored.

Cash buffers not only help shelter businesses from economic downturns but essentially insure us against catastrophes—even those of our own making. The larger the cash buffer, the less sinkable the enterprise.

One of the most pronounced boom-and-bust periods of the U.S. economy occurred in the early 1980s during Wall Street's fad of leveraged buyouts. Private equity groups "unlocked value" by purchasing publicly traded companies, taking them private, and then loading them with debt. The proceeds of this debt were used to pay dividends to owners and buy back shares. Afterwards, the private equity groups sold these debt-laden companies back to public investors.

When the economy eventually slowed—as was inevitable—the market sizes of many industries temporarily shrank. With heavy debt loads and depleted cash buffers, many of these companies did not have the funds to weather the downturn. The outcome was a cash crunch that led to a mass of bankruptcies.

Even after this episode, many on Wall Street still view holding cash as an inefficient use of resources. They consider rainy-day funds as counter to the idea of maximizing short-term profits. This shortsightedness, however, undervalues the vast importance of cash during economic crises. In downturns, cash keeps businesses solvent and its gives businesses the ability to be opportunistic. Remember, when the world is falling apart, cash is king.

THE ART AND CRAFT OF MEASURING
Three Methods for Estimating C-Moat Width

Before reaching the end of our journey, it is helpful to cover a few basic methods for measuring c-moats. How do we know if our c-moats are getting wider or narrower?

Ideally, we would be able to measure the width of a c-moat to pinpoint accuracy. We could say, "Customers are intrinsically choosing our business 27.8 percent of the time." Unfortunately, we don't live in such a precise world; the good news is that estimations can be more than adequate for driving good decision making.

A good rule of thumb—and one which statisticians will tell you—is that estimations are sufficient 99 percent of the time. For us, the accuracy of a measurement only needs to be good enough to drive quality decision-making; anything beyond is unnecessary.

The most important information to gather is whether our c-moats are getting wider or narrower, and in what capacity. It doesn't matter whether a c-moat's intrinsic loyalty (i.e., probability) currently stands at 15.1 or 25.4 percent. What does matter is that we are doing a better job today than we were yesterday. Are we making headway against our competitors or are we losing ground? There is wisdom in the saying, "Where I am is not as important as where I am going."

There are three basic methods for estimating c-moat width. Each is listed along with its pros and cons.

Method 1: Measure the same-store sales growth and compare it to changes in market size. Are we growing faster or slower than the overall market? This statistic is very useful and easy to track. Its big limitation is that it does not take into account market-share changes related to price adjustments by either us or our competitors.

Method 2: Measure the number and percentage of our sales coming from repeat customers. This method involves logging individual shopping patterns, which can sometimes be expensive but is almost always worthwhile. Reward programs can also be a great resource for gathering this information. The limitation of this method is that it also fails to take into account price adjustments in the marketplace.

Method 3: Take a poll of customers and their top shopping choices. Because c-moats represent the *intrinsic probability* that customers choose us, this probability can be measured in a hypothetical scenario where all businesses have shifted all their tokens to the market-share bucket—thus, stripping out price effects and setting prices to cost. We can design questionnaires to ask customers how they would choose between different products when these products are priced at cost. This polling method is useful because it measures our underlying customer loyalty and lets us know if we are becoming more competitive. The limitation is that it does not take into account the pricing actions of our competitors or the price sensitivity of customers.

Whichever method (or methods) we decide to use, the most important thing is to stick with it and be consistent. Measurements should indicate how well our business is doing, and they should tell us if we are making headway or ceding ground. At the end of the day, they should point us in the right direction and show which activities we are doing right, which activities we are doing wrong, and what we can do to improve.

CUSTOMER MOAT FORMULA
(PART 3 OF 3)

Arriving at the Origin of Profits

The Customer Moat Formula is now a complete framework for explaining the origin of profits. All we have to do is merge the CMF (from chapter 4) with the profit equation: *market size x market share x profit margin = profit*.

The transformation is shown in the two figures below.

FIGURE 13.2 Customer Moat Formula
(From Chapter 4)

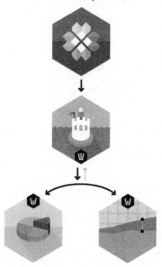

FIGURE 13.3 *Final Version of* Customer Moat Formula
(Adding "Market Size" and "Profit")

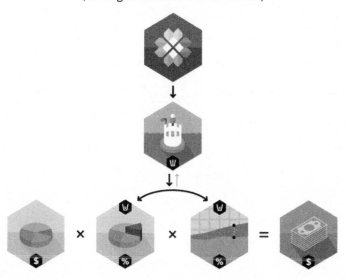

The CMF presents a unified model for explaining how our actions affect our profits. With it, we can trace the origin of profits for businesses and we have eight tools for increasing the intrinsic loyalty of customers as a method for growing our profits.

At the top of figure 13.3, we have the eight moat builders that are the actionable tools for creating our c-moats. Below that, we have the c-moat which we can convert to market share and/or profit margin based on our pricing (i.e., the token-bucket method). And lastly, we have the elements of market size, market share, and profit margin, which determine our profit.

So, what comes next? Where one journey ends, another begins. Federico Fellini said it best, "There is no end. There is no beginning. There is only the infinite passion of life." The CMF provides us with tools and game plans for developing highly-durable, actionable, and profitable strategies; the rest is up to you and that is where the real fun begins.

AFTERWORD

As this book is being sent to the printers, my parents are preparing for their retirement. It is an event that was unimaginable to us only eight years ago. I am proud of their hard work, their perseverance, and their deep desire to help customers lead better lives.

Knowledge is a living entity that must be nurtured for it to evolve. My hope is that this book adds to our greater conversation of economics, business strategy, and how these systems shape our lives.

One frontier that could use further research is the Operations moat builders. This book barely scratches the surface of this topic. It is the question of, "How do groups of people achieve far more than the sum of their individual parts? How do we structure the resources of workers, processes, and physical assets to drive greater achievement?" This is the one of the great experiments (and fun) of running a business. I look forward to the many discoveries that lie ahead in this field.

As for my own journey, other topics are near and dear to my heart—in particular, the issues of childhood education and income inequality. Economics and business represent our systems of production, but if a society is not better off for this production, then the rules that govern them need to be reconsidered. While we must accept that the world we live in is governed by economic laws, we must also accept that we have the power to shape and regulate how these laws affect us. I can think of no greater civic duty than helping our communities become more responsible stewards of this amazing world that we all inhabit.

ACKNOWLEDGMENTS

I owe a special thanks to many people. To my mom and dad, thanks for your support. Your encouragement of this project has been unconditional. This book would not be the same without you.

I am deeply thankful to an amazing team of people that helped put this book together: Karen Yin for her talented editing skills; Stasia Burrington for her amazing illustrations; Dana Kublin for her cover, graphics, and layout design; and Greg Orlov for the author photo.

I am also deeply indebted to the invaluable input of Steven Ho and Ellen Sung. Their role as devil's advocate has helped me work through many tough topics and narrative challenges. I owe Edwin Barnett thanks for his early guidance in setting up the story elements of the book, and Kevin Chen and Allie Kilgore for their copyediting skills.

And, last but not least, thanks to the following for their helpful suggestions over the years: Helen Kim, Katherine Skwarczek, Moses Bloom, Zarina Zainul, Samson Kim, and Michelle Lin.

ENDNOTES

Preface

1 The eight definitions of "competitive advantage" can be found in Rumelt et al. (2003).

2 Dictionary definition of "competitive advantage" is from Cambridge Dictionaries Online, dictionary.cambridge.org.

One

1 Yenne (2010); Padfield (2010); HubPages, http://hubpages.com/hub/Alexander-the-Great-Spanks-the-City-of-Tyre; and About.com, http://militaryhistory.about.com/od/battleswarsto1000/p/Wars-Of-Alexander-The-Great-Siege-Of-Tyre.htm.

2 Walton's quote is famous but can be found in Bergdahl and Walton (2010).

3 *Blue MauMau*, http://www.bluemaumau.org/6057/ten_largest_restaurant_franchisors_systemwide_sales.

4 Robinson et al. (2007).

5 An in-depth look at McDonald's advertising can be found in Brownell and Horgen (2004); the figure is on p. 102.

6 Schlosser (2001, p. 41).

7 Ehrenberg (2006, pp. 8–9). A more technical look into his work can be found at Ehrenberg (1972).

8 *Small Business*, April 2003, pp. 44–49.

9 *Fortune International (Europe)*, June 27, 2005, pp. 30–32.

10 *Small Business*, April 2003, pp. 44–49.

11 Ibid.

12 Ibid.

13 *Advertising Age*, January 27, 2003, pp. 3–5.

14 Strombom et al. (2002).

15 Pick (2005, p. 25).

16 Warren Buffett's lecture to MBA students at the University of Notre Dame as recorded in Buffett (1991).

17 Warren Buffett often quoted his mentor Benjamin Graham as documented in Berkshire Hathaway Inc. (2009).

18 Buffett (1998) and Miles (2003, p. 258).

19 Price rise is extrapolated from 1972 numbers as given in Buffett (1998) and 2008 price data from Yelp, http://www.yelp.com/biz/sees-candies-alameda. Cost rise is based on the U.S. Bureau of Labor Statistics' inflation calculator at http://data.bls.gov.

20 Buffett (1998).

21 Berkshire Hathaway Inc. (2008).

Two

1   Berra and Kaplan (2010, p. 39).

2   Amazon.com Inc. (2000).

3   Starbucks Corp. (2013) and Starbucks, http://www.starbucks.com/about-us/company-information/mission-statement.

4   Google Inc. (2005).

5   Kirby and Stewart (2007).

6   About Money, http://retailindustry.about.com/od/retailbestpractices/ig/Company-Mission-Statements/Radio-Shack-Mission-Statement.htm.

7   *Forbes*, http://www.forbes.com/sites/antoinegara/2015/02/05/radioshack-cuts-the-cord-after-90-years-files-for-bankruptcy/.

8   Welch and Byrne (2003, pp. 105–154).

9   Ibid., p. 106.

10 Ibid., p. 145.

11 Ibid., p. 142.

12 The story of specialization as an evolutionary force can be found in Weiner (1994). Specialization only scratches the surface in terms of how competitive forces drive change.

13 Ibid., p. 60.

14 *Businessweek*, April 21, 2003, p. 74.

15 Kaveel (2013).

16 *Christian Science Monitor*, http://www.csmonitor.com/Business/2009/0915/organic-s-crunch-once-high-flying-firms-face-three-big-threats-to-growth.

17 Huck (1995, pp. 72–78).

18 Ibid., p. 175.

19 *Harvard Business Review*, http://hbr.org/2013/08/the-innovation-mindset-in-acti-3.

Three

1   Amazon.com Inc. (2015).

2   CNN Money, http://money.cnn.com/2012/08/20/technology/apple-most-valuable-company; and Apple Inc. (2013).

3   Berkshire Hathaway Inc. (1992).

4   *New York Times*, http://www.nytimes.com/2011/10/25/technology/netflix-lost-800000-members-with-price-rise-and-split-plan.html.

5   USA Today, http://usatoday30.usatoday.com/tech/news/2011-07-13-netflix-customers-angry_n.htm.

6   *Wall Street Journal*, http://buy.wsj.com/shopandbuy/order/subscribe.jsp.

Four

1   Disney Parks & Travel, http://disneyland.disney.go.com/tickets.

2   The Pentium was a long-running processor that debuted in 1993 and has contributed billions of dollars of Intel's revenue, if not tens of billions. Intel Corp. (2001).

3   *Wall Street Journal*, http://blogs.wsj.com/digits/2011/06/21/google-notches-one-billion-unique-visitors-per-month/.

4   Internet World Stats, http://internetworldstats.com.

5   Search Engine Land, http://searchengineland.com/googles-search-market-share-67-percent-pc-83-percent-mobile-203937.

6   "Google Container Data Center Tour," http://www.youtube.com/watch?v=zRwPSFpLX8I.

7   For an in-depth account of the 20 percent rule, check out Schmidt et al. (2014, pp. 225–231).

8   For an interesting look into how Instant Search came about, refer to "Google Instant Launch Event," http://www.youtube.com/watch?v=i0eMHRxlJ2c.

9   The addition of "google" to the dictionary can be found at CNET, http://www.cnet.com/news/google-joins-xerox-as-a-verb.

10   Isaacson (2011, p. 98). Steve Jobs attributed the quote to Picasso.

Five

1   The original quote, "A penny saved is two pence cleared," can be found in Franklin (2007, p. 5).

2   *Washington Post*, http://www.washingtonpost.com/wp-dyn/content/article/2007/03/28/AR2007032802185.html.

3   *New York Times* (*Late Edition–East Coast*), March 19, 1985, p. D1, and February 2, 1990, p. D1.

4   Murphy (December 2000).

5   West (1998, 42:00–46:00).

6   West (1998, 45:23).

7   Murphy (December 2000).

8   Mayo et al. (2006, p. 114).

9   *New York Times* (*Late Edition–East Coast*), March 20, 1985, p. D1.

10   *New York Times* (*Late Edition–East Coast*), March 19, 1985, p. A1.

11   *Fortune*, April 5, 1993.

12   *New York Times* (*Late Edition–East Coast*), August 1, 1995, p. A1.

13   The return of a $10,000 investment in 1958 was $17,000,000 during the sale to Disney, according to West (1998, 56:30). Original shareholders like Murphy earned five to six times the return, according to West (1998, 59:00).

14   Ohno (1988, p. 74).

15   Reingold (1999, p. 48).

16   Ibid., p. 46.

17   Ibid., pp. 42–43.

18   Ibid., p. 43.

19   Ibid., p. 45.

20   MIT Sloan Management Review, http://sloanreview.mit.edu/article/what-really-happened-to-toyota.

21   Washington Post, http://www.washingtonpost.com/wp-dyn/content/article/2009/01/21/AR2009012101216.html.

22   Fortune, October 30, 2006, pp. 126–132.

23   Ibid.

24   This Beautiful Frugal Life, http://www.beautifulfrugallife.com/costco-home-mailer-coupon-matchups-october-30-november-23/#more-22542 and personal experiences.

25   Cascio (2006, p. 32).

26   Ibid., p. 31.

27   Chu (2008).

28   Businessweek, October 20, 2008, pp. 58–60.

29   Consumer Reports, August 2010, p. 9.

30   Supermarket News, October 12, 2009, p. 8.

31   Supermarket News, June 1, 2009, p. 8.

32   Lee (1995).

33   Boguslaski et al. (2004).

34   Freiberg and Freiberg (1996).

35   Smith and Flanagan (2006).

36   Boguslaski et al. (2004).

37   A first turnaround was born out of necessity. Southwest had four planes, but one was sold because the company needed cash. To maintain the flight schedule with only three planes, the "ten-minute turn" was born. Freiberg and Freiberg (1996, p. 34).

38   Boguslaski et al. (2004).

39   Washington Post, http://www.washingtonpost.com/archive/business/2004/02/13/southwest-to-undercut-competition-in-philadelphia/9b710fba-b9ef-4c6c-9e50-5af0848282a5.

40   New York Times (Late Edition–East Coast), May 10, 2004, p. C1.

41   eTurboNews, http://www.eturbonews.com/18249/fares-expected-drop-20-30-southwest-starts-newark-flights.

Six

1   Cobb (2008).

2   Starbucks Corp. (2008).

3   "Coffee Jitters" is from Brandweek, November 10, 2008, pp. 22–26; "Starbucks: Decline of an Empire" is from Market Leader, fall 2008, pp. 41–43.

4   Travel Agent, January 21, 2008, p. 10.

5   Training, May 2008, p. 10.

6	*Advertising Age*, March 3, 2008, p. 1.

7	JCK, July 2006, p. 163, "Success Stories" side bar.

8	*Businessweek*, October 24, 2005, p. 16.

9	*Advertising Age*, March 3, 2008, p. 1.

10	Starbucks Corp. (2012).

11	Starbucks Corp. (2009).

12	Dwyer (2012).

13	*New York Daily News*, http://www.nydailynews.com/news/national/hear-comcast-employee-customer-difficult-time-asked-cancel-service-article-1.1867728.

14	Love (1986, p. 121).

15	Ibid.

16	Ibid., p. 122.

17	The 5 percent figure comes from Love (1986, p. 121), and modern numbers are 2012 potato-crop usage according to Agricultural Marketing Resource Center, http://www.agmrc.org/commodities__products/vegetables/potato-profile/.

18	Love (1986, p. 126).

19	According to Robbins et al. (2014), McDonald's sells 9 million servings of fries per day, which translates to 3.2 billion servings per year.

20	Marcus et al. (1999, pp. 133–135).

21	Ibid., p. 142.

22	Ibid.

23	*Business 2.0*, http://money.cnn.com/magazines/business2/business2_archive/2005/01/01/8250213.

24	Vasilash (2003).

25	*Car and Driver*, http://www.caranddriver.com/reviews/2004-toyota-sienna-first-drive-review.

26	Vasilash (2003).

27	*Car and Driver*, http://www.caranddriver.com/reviews/2004-toyota-sienna-first-drive-review.

28	Vasilash (2003).

29	Ibid.

30	*Forbes*, February 17, 2003, p. 56; and *Automotive News*, February 24, 2003, p. 26.

31	*Forbes*, February 17, 2003, p. 56; and Wielgat (2003).

32	Toyota Motor Sales data via PR Newswire, http://www.prnewswire.com/news-releases/toyota-announces-best-sales-year-in-its-46-year-history-breaks-sales-record-for-eighth-year-in-a-row-58704747.html; and Toyota Motor Sales data via PR Newswire, http://www.prnewswire.com/news-releases/toyota-reports-2005-and-december-sales-53130127.html.

33	*Forbes*, September 12, 1994, p. 162.

34	*Complex*, http://www.complex.com/pop-culture/2012/11/halo-4-secrets-easter-eggs/double-rainbow.

35	Hayward (2001, p. 8).

Seven

1   Smith and Skinner (1999, pp. 109–110).

2   Ibid.

3   Ibid.

4   Stern and Deimler (2012, pp. 12–13).

5   Stern and Deimler (2012, pp. 31–34), "Rule of Three and Four" by Bruce Henderson.

6   This story is largely taken from Kiechel III (2010, pp. 39–45) and does a good job explaining the fault of market-share strategies.

7   Ibid., pp. 42–43.

8   Kiechel III (2010, p. 42) and *Vcalc.net*, http://www.vcalc.net/ti-hist.htm.

9   Kiechel III (2010, p. 43).

10   Ibid., p. 44.

11   *Boston Globe*, June 26, 1994, p. 29.

12   Henderson (1989).

13   Kazanjian and Joyner (2004, pp. 21–22).

14   *Wall Street Journal*, September 16, 2004, p. C1.

15   *Wall Street Journal*, January 19, 2005, p. A1.

16   Taken from personal observations and off-the-record conversations with suppliers.

17   Tsang (2000, p. 14).

18   Ibid., pp. 13–15.

19   Heller (2000, p. 7).

20   Swedin and Ferro (2007, p. 95).

21   Ferguson and Morris (2002, p. 141).

Eight

1   *Fortune International (Europe)*, May 26, 2008, p. 19.

2   For information on the fragmentation of the industry, please refer to Harding and Oswald (1986).

3   Bagley (2014, p. 247).

4   *Finding Dulcinea*, http://www.findingdulcinea.com/news/on-this-day/September-October-08/On-this-Day--First-Transcontinental-Telegraph-Ends-Run-of-Pony-Express.html.

5   Skrabec Jr. (2012, p. 47).

6   Reprinted from *El Defensor Chieftain*, http://www.aoc.nrao.edu/~pharden/hobby/History/WESTERN_UNION.pdf.

7   *New York Times*, http://www.nytimes.com/1989/11/29/business/market-place-added-troubles-at-western-union.html.

8   *International Directory of Company Histories*, http://www.encyclopedia.com/doc/1G2-2842100109.html.

9   *New York Times*, http://www.nytimes.com/1995/06/14/business/first-data-to-acquire-archrival-in-a-6.6-billion-deal.html.

10   *Business 2.0*, October 2004, pp. 66–69.

11   Vargas-Lundius et al. (2008).

12   First Data Corporation (1999, 2004).

13   Western Union, http://corporate.westernunion.com/Corporate_Fact_Sheet.html.

14   TechCrunch, http://techcrunch.com/2011/09/08/google-acquires-zagat-to-flesh-out-local-ratings.

15   *Google Official Blog*, http://googleblog.blogspot.com/2010/10/more-transparency-and-control-over.html.

16   *Bloomberg View*, http://www.bloombergview.com/articles/2014-12-03/how-sothebys-and-christies-went-wrong.

17   The war-game dynamics of tic-tac-toe can be found at *Stephen Ostermiller's Blog*, http://blog.ostermiller.org/tic-tac-toe-strategy.

18   Liu (2010) and *Time*, http://time.com/3613610/sony-playstation. Liu describes the PlayStation as the third-generation console after Atari; it is widely accepted that Atari represents the second generation of consoles.

19   Fox (2013, p. 359).

20   Liu (2010).

21   Ibid.

22   The Free Library, http://www.thefreelibrary.com/Strategy+Analytics%3A+Games+Console+Sales+to+Hit+41.9M+Units+in+2002%3B...-a092909163.

23   *Brandweek*, January 7, 2002, p. 12.

24   Fox (2013, pp. 359–360).

Nine

1   The third Brown Bear location was relatively small and closed a few years after author moved to Seattle. It did not seem to materially affect Brown Bear's strategy.

2   Canada-U.S.-Ontario-Michigan Border Transportation Partnership (2002). The passenger vehicle count for Ambassador Bridge is listed on p. 18, and $79.7 billion worth of goods traverse between Detroit and Windsor out of a total of $346.6 billion traded in goods between the U.S. and Canada.

3   *Businessweek*, May 7, 2012, pp. 70–76.

4   Ibid. and *Land Line*, http://www.landlinemag.com/Story.aspx?StoryID=27523.

5   *Convenience Store News*, July 13, 2009, pp. AN21–32.

6   Ibid.

7   Pederson (2000, pp. 414–419)

8   *Chain Store Age*, December 2003, pp. 32–34, interview with 7-Eleven CEO Jim Keyes.

9   *Convenience Store News*, July 13, 2009, pp. AN21–AN32.

10   *Business 2.0*, January–February 2005, pp. 92–100.

11   Kotabe (1995).

12   Ibid.

13   Pederson (2000, pp. 414–419)

14   Ibid.

15   Kotabe (1995).

16   *Business 2.0*, January–February 2005, pp. 92–100.

17   Ibid.

18   Ibid.

19   *Convenience Store News*, December 19, 2005, pp. 34–44.

20   Ortega (1998, p. 57).

Ten

1   Shrivastava et al. (1988).

2   *Time International (Canada Edition)*, October 6, 2008, p. 23.

3   Shrivastava et al. (1988).

4   Ibid.

5   Riggs (2000, p. 1058) and Shrivastava (1988).

6   Lowenstein (1995, p. 111).

7   This story is largely taken from Love (1986, pp. 188–189).

8   Ibid.

9   Ibid.

10   Ibid.

11   Ibid., p. 195.

12   Ibid., p. 201.

13   The milk problems described in Pakistan were the same ones facing India. Klitgaard (1991, p. 30).

14   Ibid., p. 52.

15   Ibid., p. 54.

16   Bergenstock and Maskulka (2001).

17   *Fortune*, February 19, 2001, pp. 186–206.

18   McDonough and Egolf (2002), "De Beers Consolidated Mines, Inc."

19   *Television Week*, March 12, 2007, p. 10.

20   *Adweek*, September 4, 2006, p. 24.

21   The 1995 and 2000 numbers are from *Adweek*, October 24, 2005, pp. 32–33; the 2013 number is from *Insurance Journal*, http://www.insurancejournal.com/news/national/2014/07/03/333757.htm.

22   Berkshire Hathaway, Inc. (1996). GEICO's history can be found at GEICO, http://www.geico.com/about/corporate/history.

23   *Wall Street Journal*, http://www.wsj.com/articles/SB949350126329222999; and *Value Walk*, http://www.valuewalk.com/2014/05/berkshire-hathaway-earnings-preview-a-look-at-geico/.

24   *Advertising Age*, http://adage.com/article/special-report-super-bowl/super-bowl-ad-chart-buying-super-bowl-2014/244024.

25   Gross (1996, p. 165).

26   Ibid., pp. 159–163.

27 Ibid.

28 Ibid.

29 Ibid., p. 164.

30 *Business Strategy Review*, spring 2006, pp. 76–78, "Business Heroes: David Ogilvy."

31 Gross (1996, p. 165).

32 Ogilvy (2004, pp. 145–146).

33 Ibid., pp. 167–168, and Roman (2009, p. 136).

34 *Bloomberg*, http://www.bloomberg.com/news/articles/2012-10-03/coca-cola-retains-title-as-world-s-most-valuable-brand-table-.

35 McClure et al. (2004).

36 Taken from an interview with Robert Woodruff, who was president of Coca-Cola for six decades, found at *Food Engineering & Ingredients*, May 2001, pp. 39–41.

37 Coca-Cola, http://www.coca-colacompany.com/stories/coke-lore-slogans.

Eleven

1   *Fortune*, February 19, 2001, pp. 186–206.

2   Ibid.

3   Ibid.

4   Ibid.

5   Farrell-Robert (2007), chapter 4.

6   Ibid.

7   Zoellner (2007, p. 130).

8   Farrell-Robert (2007), chapter 9.

9   *Fortune*, February 19, 2001, pp. 186–206.

10 Ibid.

11 A deeper look into De Beers and apartheid can be found in chapter 1 of Farrell-Robert (2007).

12 Kelly et al. (1999).

13 Ashenfelter and Hosken (2008).

14 Google Inc. (2008–2013).

15 *TechWorld*, http://www.techworld.com/startups/q-with-eze-vidra-from-google-ventures-europe-3624259.

16 *VentureBeat*, http://venturebeat.com/2014/12/15/for-google-ventures-2014-yielded-16-exits-and-a-strong-focus-on-life-sciences-and-health-tech.

17 PhRMA (2013).

18 Pfizer Inc. (2005, 2008, 2011, 2013).

19 Pfizer Inc. (2013).

20 *New York Times*, September 11, 2013, p. B19.

21 Ibid.

22 IDC, http://www.idc.com/prodserv/smartphone-os-market-share.jsp.

23   Somaya et al. (2011).

24   *eWeek*, September 5, 2011, p. 12.

25   *Time*, http://time.com/103640/apple-google-patent-truce.

26   U.S. Energy Information Administration, http://www.eia.gov/electricity/policies/legislation/california/subsequentevents.html.

27   First rolling blackouts since World War II. U.S. *News & World Report*, January 29, 2001, p. 26.

28   *Economist*, December 23, 2000, pp. 30–31, "Unplugged."

29   The installed generation capacity is taken from Leveque (2007, p. 58), and the average hourly demand is for electricity usage in December 2000, according to California ISO, found in Joskow (2001).

30   *Austin Chronicle*, http://www.austinchronicle.com/news/2002-05-17/86618.

31   Schroeder (2009, p. 604).

32   Kalemli-Ozcan et al. (2011).

33   Information can be found in the case study of Bear Stearns by Ryback (n.d.).

Twelve

1   *Rolling Stones*, http://www.rollingstone.com/music/news/itunes-prize-winner-to-steve-jobs-yeah-right-who-is-this-really-20100225.

2   Isaacson (2011, p. 388).

3   *Bloomberg*, http://www.bloomberg.com/bw/stories/2003-07-01/how-apple-spells-future-i-p-o-d.

4   *Businessweek*, December 5, 2005, p. 44.

5   USA *Today*, http://usatoday30.usatoday.com/tech/wireless/phones/2007-10-24-motorola-future_N.htm.

6   USA *Today*, http://usatoday30.usatoday.com/tech/gaming/2006-12-13-wii-ps3-last-call_x.htm.

7   Nintendo Co. Ltd. (2007–2009).

8   *NintendoLinked*, http://www.nintendolinked.com/nintendo-reveals-q2-financial-results-wii-u-sales-7-2-million-3ds-45-4-million.

9   *Stratechery*, http://stratechery.com/2010/apple-innovators-dilemma.

10   Isaacson (2011, pp. 378–393). Steve Jobs wanted to connect devices that could share digital information.

11   Apple Press Info, http://www.apple.com/pr/library/2011/01/22Apples-App-Store-Downloads-Top-10-Billion.html.

12   *Business Insider*, http://www.businessinsider.com/apples-astronomical-800-million-itunes-accounts-could-give-it-a-huge-advantage-in-payments-2014-4.

13   *Bloomberg*, http://www.bloomberg.com/news/articles/2015-02-10/apple-closes-at-record-market-value-of-more-than-700-billion.

14   Coca-Cola, http://www.coca-colacompany.com/stories/16-things-you-didnt-know-about-vending-machines-in-japan-and-around-the-world#TCCC.

15   Examples are *New York Times*, http://www.nytimes.com/1998/05/08/business/
      pepsico-sues-coca-cola-on-distribution.html; and *The Lantern*, http://thelantern.
      com/2013/12/refreshing-restricting-ohio-states-32m-deal-coca-cola-brings-
      questions-transparency-costs-vs-benefits. A quick Internet search will bring up
      a list of Coca-Cola's many exclusive vendor contracts.

16   From author's experiences living in Chicago.

17   Ibid.

18   *Executive*, February 1993, pp. 60–72.

19   Economist Books Staff (2006, p. 223).

20   *Consumer Reports*, July 1998, p. 45.

21   Economist Books Staff (2006, p 223). With fourteen trillion points divided by
      twenty-five thousand points per ticket, multiplied at a value of $300, we arrive
      at $168 billion.

22   Budget Travel, http://www.budgettravel.com/blog/
      southwest-waters-down-its-rapid-rewards-program,11611.

23   *Bloomberg*, http://www.bloomberg.com/bw/stories/2009-04-09/sizing-up-wells-
      fargos-surprisebusinessweek-business-news-stock-market-and-financial-advice.

24   *Businessweek*, January 31, 2011, pp. 43–44.

25   *Forbes*, August 16, 2004, pp. 91–100.

26   Interview of Dick Kovacevich found in *SF Gate*, http://www.sfgate.com/business/
      ontherecord/article/On-the-Record-Dick-Kovacevich-2600294.php.

27   Ibid.

28   Wells Fargo & Company (2000–2012).

29   *Businessweek*, November 24, 2003, p. 96; and Bancography (2011).

30   Wells Fargo & Company (2009).

31   Shaffer et al. (2010).

32   *Money*, September 2003, pp. 49–50.

33   Wells Fargo & Company (2009).

Thirteen

1   *USA Today*, http://usatoday30.usatoday.com/money/industries/retail/
      2003-04-02-sars_x.htm.

2   *DailyFinance*, http://www.dailyfinance.com/2013/02/26/
      home-depot-earnings-hurricane-sandy.

REFERENCES

Amazon.com Inc. 1999 *Annual Report*. 2000.

———. 2014 *Annual Report*. 2015.

Apple Inc. 2012 *Annual Report*. 2013.

Ashenfelter, Orley, and Daniel Hosken. "The Effect of Mergers on Consumer Prices: Evidence from Five Selected Case Studies." *National Bureau of Economic Research (Working Paper Series)*, 2008.

Bagley, Will. *South Pass: Gateway to a Continent*. Norman, OK: University of Oklahoma Press, 2014.

Bancography. "From Transaction to Interaction: A New Mission for Sales Management." *Bancology* 40 (September 2011): 4.

Bergdahl, Michael, and Rob Walton. *The 10 Rules of Sam Walton: Success Secrets for Remarkable Results*. Hoboken, NJ: John Wiley & Sons, 2010.

Bergenstock, Donna, and James Maskulka. "The De Beers Story: Are Diamonds Forever?" *Business Horizons* 44, no. 3 (2001): 37.

Berkshire Hathaway Inc. 1991 *Annual Report*. 1992.

———. 1995 *Annual Report*. 1996.

———. 2007 *Annual Report*. 2008.

———. 2008 *Annual Report*. 2009.

Berra, Yogi, and Dave Kaplan. *What Time Is It? You Mean Now? Advice for Life from the Zennest Master of Them All*. New York: Simon & Schuster, 2010.

Boguslaski, Charles, Harumi Ito, and Darin Lee. "Entry Patterns in the Southwest Airlines Route System." *Review of Industrial Organization* 25 (2004): 317–50.

Brownell, K., and K. B. Horgen. *Food Fight: The Inside Story of the Food Industry, America's Obesity Crisis, and What We Can Do about It*. Chicago: McGraw-Hill Education, 2004.

Buffett, Warren. "Three lectures on business at University of Notre Dame." Transcribed and edited by Whitney Tilson, Spring 1991.

———. "Video & Notes: Warren Buffett Speaks with Florida University." University of Florida School of Business, Gainesville, October 15, 1998. https://hurricanecapital. wordpress.com/2015/02/01video-notes-warren-buffett-speaks-with-florida-university/.

Canada-U.S.-Ontario-Michigan Border Transportation Partnership. *Planning/Need and Feasibility Study*. Ontario: URS, 2002.

Cascio, Wayne F. "Decency Means More than 'Always Low Prices': A Comparison of Costco to Wal-Mart's Sam's Club." *Academy of Management Perspectives* (August 2006): 26–37.

Chu, Jeff. "Thinking Outside the Big Box." *Fast Company* (November 2008): 128–32.

Cobb, Chris. "Wake Up and Smell the Publicity: A Look at Starbucks' Brand Revitalization." *Public Relations Tactics* 15, no. 6 (2008): 18.

Dwyer, Judith. *Communication for Business and the Professions: Strategies and Skills*. Frenchs Forest: Pearson Australia, 2012.

Economist Books Staff. *Business Miscellany*. London: Profile Books, 2006.

Ehrenberg, Andrew. "My Research in Marketing: How It Happened," 2006. http://www1.lsbu.ac.uk/bus-ehrenberg/documents/EhrenbergBibliography/HowItHappened.pdf.

———. *Repeat-Buying: Theory and Applications*. Amsterdam: North-Holland, 1972.

Farrell-Robert, Janine. *Glitter and Greed: The Secret World of the Diamond Cartel*. Newburyport, MA: Red Wheel/Weiser, 2007.

Ferguson, Charles H., and Charles R. Morris. *Computer Wars: The Post-IBM World*. Washington, DC: Beard Books, 2002.

First Data Corporation. *1998 Annual Report*. 1999.

———. *2003 Annual Report*. 2004.

Fox, Matt. *The Video Games Guide: 1,000+ Arcade, Console and Computer Games, 1962–2012*. 2nd ed. Jefferson, NC: McFarland, 2013.

Franklin, Benjamin. *Poor Richard's Almanack*. New York: Skyhorse, 2007.

Freiberg, Kevin, and Jackie Freiberg. *Nuts! Southwest Airlines' Crazy Recipe for Business and Personal Success*. New York: Broadway Books, 1996.

Google Inc. *2004 Annual Report*. 2005.

———. *2007 Annual Report*. 2008.

———. *2008 Annual Report*. 2009.

———. *2009 Annual Report*. 2010.

———. *2010 Annual Report*. 2011.

———. *2011 Annual Report*. 2012.

———. *2012 Annual Report*. 2013.

Gross, Daniel. *Forbes Greatest Business Stories of All Time*. New York: John Wiley & Sons, 1996.

Harding, Robert, and Alison Oswald. *Guide to the Western Union Telegraph Company Records*. Washington, DC: National Museum of American History, 1986.

Hayward, George. "When 10 Cents Is Worth More than a Dime." *Industry Safety & Hygiene News* 35, no. 5 (2001): 8a.

Heller, Robert. *Bill Gates*. Business Masterminds Series. New York: Dorling Kindersley, 2000.

Henderson, Bruce. "The Origin of Strategy." *Harvard Business Review* (November–December 1989): 139–44.

Huck, Virginia. *Brand of the Tartan: The 3M Story*. New York: Appleton-Century-Crofts, 1995.

Intel Corp. *2000 Annual Report*. 2001.

Isaacson, Walter. *Steve Jobs*. New York: Simon & Schuster, 2011.

Joskow, Paul L. "California's Electricity Crisis." *Oxford Review of Economic Policy* 17, no. 3 (2001): 365–88.

Kalemli-Ozcan, Sebnem, Bent Sorensen, and Sevcan Yesiltas. "Leverage across Firms, Banks, and Countries." *National Bureau of Economic Research (Working Paper Series)*, 2011.

Kaveel, Alina. "Oligopoly in Cereal Industry," 2013. http://www.academia.edu/5297462/Oligopoly_in_Cereal_Industry.

Kazanjian, Kirk, and Amy Joyner. *Making Dough: The 12 Secret Ingredients of Krispy Kreme's Sweet Success*. Hoboken, NJ: John Wiley & Sons, 2004.

Kelly, John, Colin Cook, and Don Spitzer. "Unlocking Shareholder Value: The Keys to Success." *Mergers and Acquisitions: A Global Research Report*, 1999.

Kiechel III, Walter. *The Lords of Strategy: The Secret Intellectual History of the New Corporate World*. Boston: Harvard Business Press, 2010.

Kirby, Julia, and Thomas A. Stewart. "The Institutional Yes." *Harvard Business Review* 85, no. 10 (2007): 74–82.

Klitgaard, Robert. *Adjusting to Reality: Beyond "State versus Market" in Economic Development*. San Francisco: ICS Press, 1991.

Kotabe, Masaaki. "The Return of 7-Eleven . . . from Japan: The Vanguard Program." *Columbia Journal of World Business* 30, no. 4 (1995): 70–81.

Lee, Bill. "Southwest Airlines' Herb Kelleher: Unorthodoxy at Work." *Management Review*, January 1995.

Leveque, Francois, ed. *Competitive Electricity Markets and Sustainability*. Cheltenham, UK: Edward Elgar, 2007.

Liu, Hongju. "Dynamics of Pricing in the Video Game Console Market: Skimming or Penetration?" *Journal of Marketing Research* 47, no. 3 (2010): 428–43.

Love, John F. *McDonald's: Behind the Arches*. Toronto: Bantam Books, 1986.

Lowenstein, Roger. *Buffett: The Making of an American Capitalist*. New York: Doubleday, 1995.

Marcus, Bernie, Arthur Blank, and Bob Andelman. *Built from Scratch: How a Couple of Regular Guys Grew The Home Depot from Nothing to $30 Billion*. New York: Random House, 1999.

Mayo, Anthony J., Nitin Nohria, and Laura G. Singleton. *Paths to Power: How Insiders and Outsiders Shaped American Business Leadership*. Boston: Harvard Business School Publishing, 2006.

McClure, Samuel M., Jian Li, Damon Tomlin, Kim S. Cypert, Latané M. Montague, and P. Read Montague. "Neural Correlates of Behavioral Preferences for Culturally Familiar Drinks." *Neuron* 44, no. 2 (2004): 379–87.

McDonough, John, and Karen Egolf. *The Advertising Age Encyclopedia of Advertising*. Chicago: Fitzroy Dearborn, 2002.

Miles, Robert P. *The Warren Buffett CEO: Secrets from the Berkshire Hathaway Managers*. New York: John Wiley & Sons, 2003.

Murphy, Thomas. Interview by Amy Blitz. Harvard Business School, December 2000. http://www.hbs.edu/entrepreneurs/pdf/tommurphy.pdf.

Nintendo Co. Ltd. *2007 Annual Report*. 2007.

———. *2008 Annual Report*. 2008.

———. *2009 Annual Report*. 2009.

Ogilvy, David. *Confessions of an Advertising Man*. London: Southbank, 2004.

Ohno, Taiichi. *Toyota Production System: Beyond Large-Scale Production*. Cambridge: Productivity Press, 1988.

Ortega, Bob. *In Sam We Trust: The Untold Story of Sam Walton and How Wal-Mart Is Devouring America*. New York: Random House, 1998.

Padfield, David. "Destruction of Tyre," 2010. http://www.padfield.com/acrobat/history/tyre.pdf.

Pederson, Jay. *International Directory of Company Histories Vol. 32*. Detroit: St. James Press, 2000.

Pfizer Inc. *2004 Annual Report*. 2005.

———. *2007 Annual Report*. 2008.

———. *2010 Annual Report*. 2011.

———. *2012 Annual Report*. 2013.

PhRMA. *2013 Profile: Biopharmaceutical Research Industry*. Washington, DC: Pharmaceutical Research and Manufacturers of America, 2013.

Pick, Margaret Moos. *See's Famous Old Time Candies: A Sweet Story*. San Francisco: Chronicle Books, 2005.

Reingold, Edwin. *Toyota: People, Ideas and the Challenge of the New*. London: Penguin Books, 1999.

Riggs, Thomas, ed. *Encyclopedia of Major Marketing Campaigns*. Vol. 1. Detroit: Gale, 2000.

Robbins, Stephen P., Rolf Bergman, Ian Stagg, and Mary Coulter. *Management*. 7th ed. Melbourne: Pearson Australia, 2014.

Robinson, Thomas N., Dina L. G. Borzekowski, Donna M. Matheson, and Helena C. Kraemer. "Effects of Fast Food Branding on Young Children's Taste Preferences." *Archives of Pediatrics and Adolescent Medicine* 161 (2007): 792–97.

Roman, Kenneth. *The King of Madison Avenue: David Ogilvy and the Making of Modern Advertising*. New York: Palgrave Macmillan, 2009.

Rumelt, Richard P, Harry Kunin, and Elsa Kunin. "What in the World Is Competitive Advantage?" *The Anderson School at University of California* (Working Paper), 2003, 1–5.

Ryback, William. *Case Study on Bear Stearns*. Toronto Leadership Centre, [n.d.].

Schlosser, Eric. *Fast Food Nation: The Dark Side of the All-American Meal*. Boston: Houghton Mifflin Harcourt, 2001.

Schmidt, Eric, Jonathan Rosenberg, and Alan Eagle. *How Google Works*. New York: Grand Central, 2014.

Schroeder, Alice. *The Snowball: Warren Buffett and the Business of Life*. New York: Bantam Books, 2009.

Shaffer, Blake, Jordan Carr, Ryan Baue, Curtis Durr, and Maria Krejci. *Wells Fargo & Co.* Krause Fund Research, 2010.

Shrivastava, Paul, Ian I. Mitroff, Danny Miller, and Anil Miglani. "Understanding Industrial Crises." *Journal of Management Studies* 25, no. 4 (1988): 285–303.

Skrabec Jr., Quentin R. *The 100 Most Significant Events in American Business: An Encyclopedia*. Santa Barbara, CA: Greenwood, 2012.

Smith, Adam, and Andrew Skinner. *The Wealth of Nations*. 3 vols. Harmondsworth, Middlesex: Penguin Books, 1999.

Smith, Jaynie L., and William G. Flanagan. *Creating Competitive Advantage: Give Customers a Reason to Choose You over Your Competitors*. New York: Crown, 2006.

Somaya, Deepak, David Teece, and Simon Wakeman. "Innovation in Multi-Invention Contexts: Mapping Solutions to Technological and Intellectual Property Complexity." *California Management Review* 53, no. 4 (2011): 47–79.

Starbucks Corp. 2008 *Annual Report*. 2008.

———. 2009 *Annual Report*. 2009.

————. 2012 Annual Report. 2012.

Stern, Carl W., and Michael S. Deimler, eds. *The Boston Consulting Group on Strategy: Classic Concepts and New Perspectives.* 2nd ed. Hoboken, NJ: John Wiley & Sons, 2012.

Strombom, Bruce A., Thomas Buchmueller, and Paul J. Feldstein. "Switching Costs, Price Sensitivity and Health Plan Choice." *Journal of Health Economics* 21, no. 1 (January 2002): 89–116.

Swedin, Eric G., and David L. Ferro. *Computers: The Life Story of a Technology.* Baltimore: Johns Hopkins University Press, 2007.

Tsang, Cheryl. *Microsoft First Generation: The Success Secrets of the Visionaries Who Launched a Technology Empire.* New York: John Wiley & Sons, 2000.

Vargas-Lundius, Rosemary, Marcela Villarreal, Guillaume Lanly, and Martha Osorio. *International Migration, Remittances and Rural Development.* Rome, Italy: International Fund for Agricultural Development, 2008.

Vasilash, Gary S. "Considering Sienna: 53,000 Miles in the Making." *Automotive Design & Production* 115, no. 3 (2003): 34.

Weiner, Jonathan. *The Beak of the Finch.* New York: Vintage Books, 1994.

Welch, Jack, and John A. Byrne. *Jack: Straight from the Gut.* New York: Grand Central, 2003.

Wells Fargo & Company. *1999 Annual Report.* 2000.

————. *2000 Annual Report.* 2001.

————. *2001 Annual Report.* 2002.

————. *2002 Annual Report.* 2003.

————. *2003 Annual Report.* 2004.

————. *2004 Annual Report.* 2005.

————. *2005 Annual Report.* 2006.

————. *2006 Annual Report.* 2007.

————. *2007 Annual Report.* 2008.

————. *2008 Annual Report.* 2009.

————. *2009 Annual Report.* 2010.

————. *2010 Annual Report.* 2011.

————. *2011 Annual Report.* 2012.

West, Don. *Thomas Murphy Interview.* Video. New York: Broadcasting & Cable, October 22, 1998. http://www.emmytvlegends.org/interviews/people/thomas-murphy#.

Wielgat, Andrea. "Vantastic Voyage." *Automotive Industries* 183, no. 3 (2003): 26–31.

Yenne, Bill. *Alexander the Great: Lessons from History's Undefeated General.* World Generals Series. New York: St. Martin's Press, 2010.

Zoellner, Tom. *The Heartless Stone: A Journey through the World of Diamonds, Deceit, and Desire.* New York: St. Martin's Press, 2007.

CPSIA information can be obtained at www.ICGtesting.com
Printed in the USA
BVOW08s2328220916

462888BV00003B/6/P